BUDDHIST STUDIES

PAPERS OF THE 12TH WORLD SANSKRIT CONFERENCE
Vol. 8

Buddhist Studies

Edited by

RICHARD GOMBRICH
CRISTINA SCHERRER-SCHAUB

MOTILAL BANARSIDASS PUBLISHERS
PRIVATE LIMITED • DELHI

PAPERS OF THE 12TH WORLD SANSKRIT CONFERENCE HELD IN HELSINKI, FINLAND, 13-18 JULY 2003
VOL. 8

General editors:
PETTERI KOSKIKALLIO & ASKO PARPOLA

*First Edition : Delhi, **2008***

ISBN: 978-81-208-3248-0

MOTILAL BANARSIDASS
41 U.A. Bungalow Road, Jawahar Nagar, Delhi 110 007
8 Mahalaxmi Chamber, 22 Bhulabhai Desai Road, Mumbai 400 026
203 Royapettah High Road, Mylapore, Chennai 600 004
236, 9th Main III Block, Jayanagar, Bangalore 560 011
Sanas Plaza, 1302 Baji Rao Road, Pune 411 002
8 Camac Street, Kolkata 700 017
Ashok Rajpath, Patna 800 004
Chowk, Varanasi 221 001

PRINTED IN INDIA
BY JAINENDRA PRAKASH JAIN AT SHRI JAINENDRA PRESS,
A-45 NARAINA, PHASE-I, NEW DELHI 110 028
AND PUBLISHED BY NARENDRA PRAKASH JAIN FOR
MOTILAL BANARSIDASS PUBLISHERS PRIVATE LIMITED,
BUNGALOW ROAD, DELHI 110 007

PREFACE

The impressive growth of Buddhist Studies in recent years is the result of several factors. Important collections of manuscripts have been found, and monuments unearthed, in nearly all parts of Asia where Buddhism existed; political and social events bringing East and West together have increased interest in both scholarly research and Buddhist religious practices. The spread of Buddhism outside its birthplace, Madhyadeśa, first in India and soon throughout Asia, prompted its followers constantly to invent new discursive strategies and to adjust the rules to local customs and administrations. This explains the dynamism and openness of Buddhist doctrine (*dharma*) and the complex casuistry of the corpus of Buddhist institutional rules (*vinaya*).

Centred upon the study of *avadāna* fragments, in the collection of "British Library Kharoṣṭhī Manuscripts" (ca. 1st century AD), the article by Jason Neelis illustrates in an exemplary way how and why Buddhist literature adapted to a new and specific context. While this material forms part of the "unique (literary) sources for the history of Buddhism in northwestern India", attesting to local toponyms, onomastics and titulature, it also sheds important light on how early Buddhist texts were transmitted and redacted. It thus contributes to a better understanding of some puzzling questions raised by the existence of various later recensions.

From this point of view, Jason Neelis's allusion to the use of the literary device of "abbreviated prose outlines" immediately leads the reader to Ilona Manevskaia's and Peter C. Verhagen's interest in compositional techniques and manuals of exegesis in Indo-Tibetan Buddhist tradition. The study of hermeneutical and exegetical principles plays an important role in Buddhist Studies in establishing the validity of tradition, and seems a natural development of the early binary analysis based on *yukti* and *āgama*. By the 5th century AD Vasubandhu composes a systematic exegeical treatise, the *Vyākhyāyukti*, based upon the ancillary disciplines (grammar, lexicography, logic and the art of debate) common to Buddhist and Brahmanic scholars of the time. Vasubandhu illustrates the application of these techniques with well known passages drawn from the scripture, among them the paradigmatic type of scholastic reasoning (*yukti*), i.e. the *pratītya-samutpāda* (Verhagen, pp. 241-243). Ilona Manevskaia introduces material on the idea of "compositional techniques" (*tantrayukti*) common to Brahmanic and Buddhist sources, taking the cases of Vātsyāyana Pakṣilasvāmin's *Nyāyabhāṣya*, a treatise almost contemporaneous with the *Vyākhyāyukti*, and of the 7th-century *Yuktidīpikā* lists of the compositional techniques used in *śāstra*, the eleven *tantraguṇas*. This shows how Indian scholars became increasingly intertwined, a fact well attested in the impressive corpus of philosophical treatises of the time.

This theme is further developed by Marek Mejor in his original study of the *Abhidharmakośa*'s use in Brahmanic and Jaina sources. The topics of the debate are related to philosophy; they range from dispute about the cause of the variety of the world (*lokavaicitrya/jagadvaicitrya*), polemics against Vasubandhu's refutation of the existence of the *ātman,* and Akalaṅkadeva's criticism of Dignāga's definition of *pratyakṣa* to ontological/sociological questions, such as Siddhasenasūri Gaṇi's criticism of Vasubandhu's notion of "murder" (*prāṇāpāta*).

In the wake of mutual resonance between Brahmanic and Buddhist tradition, P. Szczurek, while considering Ježić's theory of textual stratification in the *Bhagavadgītā*, compares ideas in *Bhagavadgītā* 2 with parallel ideas attributed to early Buddhism. He thus revives a subject which was discussed by Etienne Lamotte, whose work has been re-edited with a foreword by Professor Minoru Hara.

An interesting aspect of the interrelation between Buddhist institutions and social context is evidenced in Giulio Agostini's inquiry into the debate concerning the precepts to be taken by a layperson (*upāsaka*). Agostini's careful reading and dating of the Pāli Nikāya, Chinese Āgama, commentaries, historiographical and scholastic treatises concludes that the debate concerning *upāsaka* status "can be understood if we distinguish *upāsaka* – who acted as intermediaries between monks and the surrounding society – from ordinary laypersons". As Giulio Agostini clearly and interestingly states, "Monks needed *upāsaka* who enjoyed the respect of all people. The formal acceptance of the five precepts helped satisfy this need. Where 'ideal' *upāsaka* were hard to find and local custom was not demanding, monks could afford *upāsaka* who did not take all precepts."

Equally rich in diversity is the practice related to the "rule against gold and silver" discussed in the *Vinaya* of various schools, a topic that has been treated by several authors, and which Bhikkhunī Juo-Hsüeh revisits. Particularly meaningful, with respect to Agostini's conclusion, is the institution of the role of "legitimiser" (*kappiya-kāraka*) to serve as an intermediary between the monk and society in transactions where the direct intervention of the monk could infringe a precept. Bhikkhunī Juo-Hsüeh notes that the *Bhikkhunī Vibhaṅga* is less strict in the matter of handling "gold and silver". In her opinion, nuns "accepted or in most cases begged for funds in the name of the Saṅgha, of a group of nuns or even an individual nun". The author suggests that, at the time of the *Bhikkhunī Vibhaṅga* redaction, these were "ordinary practices and presumably would not be unique to nuns", and that "some *Vibhaṅga* for monks contain very limited information, but the corresponding *Vibhaṅgas* for nuns make up for the deficiency." Be that as it may, various aspects of the role and impact of women in Indian Buddhism – one of them is here portrayed by Sundari

Siddhartha following the story of the Sundarī of the *Therīgāthā* – are, in recent times, becoming increasingly evident.

This volume would not have appeared without the support of the Finnish Cultural Foundation and the generous and illuminating assistance of Petteri Koskikallio, to whom we express our sincere gratitude.

RICHARD GOMBRICH
CRISTINA SCHERRER-SCHAUB

CONTENTS

CONTRIBUTORS

GIULIO AGOSTINI
Via IV Novembre, 16
I-24043 Caravaggio (BG)
ITALY
e-mail: agostini_giulio@yahoo.com

JUO-HSÜEH SHIH
11 Jialun, Dawang Village
Taimali Township
Taitung 963
TAIWAN
e-mail: roche.shih@msa.hinet.net

ILONA MANEVSKAIA
pr. Morisa Toreza, d. 33, kv. 209
194223 Saint Petersburg
RUSSIA
e-mail: imanevskaia@yahoo.com

MAREK MEJOR
Sniegockiej 5/8
00-430 Warsaw
POLAND
e-mail: mejor@interia.pl

JASON NEELIS
Department of Religion
130 Anderson Hall
P. O. Box 117410
University of Florida
Gainesville, FL 32611-7410
U.S.A.
e-mail: jneelis@religion.ufl.edu

SUNDARI SIDDHARTHA
7, Sriram Colony
Theosophical Society
Chennai 600020
INDIA
e-mail: mahagouri@yahoo.com

PRZEMYSŁAW SZCZUREK
University of Wroclaw
Institute of Classical Philology and Ancient Culture
ul. Szewska 49
50-139 Wroclaw
POLAND
e-mail: szczurek@uni.wroc.pl

P. C. VERHAGEN
Kern Institute
Leiden University
P.O. Box 9515
NL-2300 RA Leiden
THE NETHERLANDS
e-mail: p.c.verhagen@let.leidenuniv.nl

Partial *Upāsakas*

GIULIO AGOSTINI

Little scholarly interest has been paid to an ancient Buddhist controversy: how many precepts, if any, must *upāsaka*s (lay brothers) take? The deepest research on this topic remains that of Louis de La Vallée Poussin, Étienne Lamotte, and Hirakawa Akira[1]. They presented many sources, but neglected others that are very important. In particular, they did not consider all available versions of the *Mahānāmasūtra*, the *locus classicus* for the controversy, they did not look for evidence in post-canonical Theravāda sources, they did not try to provide a model for the chronological development of the controversy, and they did not pose the question why the issue was important at all. My purpose here is to fill these gaps, as far as possible, on the basis of old and new evidence.

A definition may be necessary to start with: partial (Pāli *aparipūri*, Skt. *aparipūrṇa*) *upāsaka*s and *upāsikā*s are those lay brothers

---

[1] Already Minayeff (1894: 164-165), on the basis of the *Abhidharmakośa*, pointed out that *upāsaka*s were not obliged to take all precepts. Most important are La Vallée Poussin 1925 and, closely related, Lamotte 1955 (not superseded by the chapter in Lamotte 1960: 11-25; see also Lamotte 1958, I: 73-82, especially 76-77). In spite of their importance, these learned articles are hardly mentioned in later publications, usually devoted to larger topics. See, e.g., Lopez 2001: 167-168; Freiberger 2000: 206; Harvey 2000: 83; Gethin 1998: 101-106; Ahir 1996; Hirakawa 1990: 61-62 (but see Hirakawa 1995, mentioned below); Lamotte 1984: 53a, 54a; Warder 1980: 191; Bareau 1966: 66; Schlingloff 1962-63, II 13; etc. Hirakawa 1995 is extremely useful, but on many points cannot be trusted (see Agostini 2002: v-viii and below, *passim*).

and sisters who do not take – or take less than – five precepts, and yet ask to be accepted as *upāsaka*s and *upāsikā*s.

EVIDENCE IN THE ĀGAMAS/NIKĀYAS

In the *Paṭhamasaraṇānisakkasutta* and in the contiguous *Dutiya-saraṇānisakkasutta*[2] the *upāsaka* Saraṇāni dies, and the Buddha states that he is a saint, a *sotāpanna*. People are astonished, as they know that his morality was not complete (*aparipūrakāri*) and that he drank liquor.[3] They are indignant.[4] The Buddha explains: "He who for a long time, as an *upāsaka*, has gone for refuge to the Buddha, the Dharma, and the Saṃgha, how could he be reborn in an inferior existence?"[5] No precepts are here mentioned, and the problem for the people is not that an *upāsaka* drinks liquor, but that he should be recognized as a saint. The pious redactors solved this problem: at the end of both *sutta*s Saraṇāni, on the verge of death, takes all the precepts and dies.[6] Albeit late, his compliance with full

---

[2] SN 5.375-377 and 378-380 (*Chattha Sangayana* 3.326-328 and 328-331). Both are in the *Sotāpattisaṃyutta*. The first has two Chinese versions in two translations of the *Saṃyuktāgama*: T.99 II 239c21-240b11 and T.100 II 434b12-c22. Since the proper name Saraṇāni also means 'refuges', we might see a pun: he is the typical *upāsaka* who stops at the refuges. According to some manu-scripts, however, the name is Sarakāni (see the apparatus in the PTS edition). His name in the two Chinese versions is 百手 (Śatapāṇi?) and 蟲手 (...-pāṇi?) re-spectively.

[3] *sikkhādubbalyam āpādi majjapānaṃ apāyī ti* (SN 5.375); *sikkhāya apari-pūrakārī ahosī ti* (SN V 378); 犯戒飲酒, "he broke the precepts, he drank liquor" (T.99 II 239c26); 毀犯禁戒。飲彼酒漿(same translation; T.100 II 434b17).

[4] *ujjhāyanti* (SN 5.375)...*ettha dāni ko na sotāpanno bhavissati* (SN 5.375, 378, where *etthadāniko* is printed).

[5] *yo so Mahānāma dīgharattam upāsako buddhaṃ saraṇaṃ gato dhammaṃ saraṇaṃ gato saṅghaṃ saraṇaṃ gato kathaṃ vinipātaṃ gaccheyya* (SN 5.375).

[6] *maraṇakāle sikkhaṃ samādiyī ti...maraṇakāle sikkhāya paripūrī ahosī ti* (SN 5. 377, 380). Cf. the Chinese versions: "Saraṇāni, when he was on the verge of death, took the pure precepts, abandoned drinking liquor, and then died", 百手釋氏臨命終時。受持淨戒。捨離飲酒。然後命終 (T.99 II 240b8-9); "he did not commit offences of nature [i.e. murder, theft, adultery, false speech]. He committed offences of disobedience [i.e. drinking wine]. On the verge of death, he repented what he had done; because of his repentance, his morality was ful-

morality is needed to support the recent news of his sainthood, but is not needed to support the old news that he was an *upāsaka*.

In the *Gavesīsutta*[7] the *upāsaka* Gavesī was the teacher and leader of five hundred *upāsakas*[8]. None of them had taken the precepts, and therefore they were "incomplete" (*aparipūri*) *upāsakas*[9]. Later, Gavesī decided to take the five precepts. He marked his new status with a formal declaration: "Oh long-lived one, from today onwards, take me as a complete practitioner of the precepts"[10]. His disciples soon did the same, and eventually they all became monks and saints.

According to this text, the distinction between partial and full *upāsaka*s is not merely based on the personal ability to fulfill all

---

filled, and he obtained [the fruit of] stream-enterer", 不犯性重。犯於遮戒。臨命終時。悔責所作。以悔責故。戒得完具。得須陀洹 (T.100 II 434c18-20). The Pāli commentary (SN-a III 288; *Chattha Sangayana* 3.318) glosses *sikkhāya* as *tīsu sikkhāsu*, suggesting that just before dying Saraṇāni reached perfection in the trainings in higher morality (*adhisīla*), higher meditation (*adhisamādhi*), and higher wisdom (*adhipaññā*). The commentary thus tries to avoid the obvious meaning of the *sutta*: *sikkhā*, here opposed to the three refuges, means the five precepts.

[7] *Upāsakavagga*, AN III 214-218 (*Chattha Sangayana* 2.188-192). La Vallée Poussin already noticed this text (La Vallée Poussin 1923-31, III: 74, end of note from the preceding page). I do not know of any Chinese version, and no parallel text is registered in Akanuma 1929.

[8] *Gavesinā kho Ānanda upāsakena pañcamattāni upāsakasatāni paṭidesitāni samādapitāni* (AN 3.215; *Chattha Sangayana* 2.189). The commentary explains: *paṭidesitānī ti upāsakabhāvaṃ paṭidesitāni. samādapitānī ti saraṇesu patiṭṭhāpitānī ti attho* (AN-a 3.306; *Chattha Sangayana* 3.63). On these lay fraternities see Warder 1980: 199 and Chakravarti 1987: 84. The latter says that these "disciples may have then become followers of the Buddha through their own *gahapati*, which suggests that the *gahapatis* played an important role in the extension of popular support to Buddhism." This is perhaps confirmed by the *Gavesīsutta* as the *upāsaka* Gavesī even initiates his fellow *upāsakas*, but I do not know if he is their *gahapati* (landlord, employer).

[9] *sīlesu aparipūrakārī...sīlesu aparipūrakāriṇo* (AN 3.215; *Chattha Sangayana* 2.189). The commentarial gloss is important as it explicitly says that they had not taken the precepts: *sīlesu aparipūrakārī ti pañcasu sīlesu asamattakārī* (AN-a 3.306; *Chattha Sangayana* 3.64).

[10] *ajjatagge maṃ āyasmanto sīlesu paripūrakāriṃ dharethā ti* (AN 3.215; *Chattha Sangayana* 2.189).

obligations deriving from a single *upāsaka* status, but is based on the recognition of different *upāsaka* statuses: some *upāsaka*s formally take precepts, and others don't.

With the *Gavesīsutta* agrees a passage from the *Ekottarāgama*. The Buddha is asked: "As for the *dharma* of a man of pure faith, he should take/keep how many precepts? By breaking how many precepts is he not an *upāsaka*?"[11], 夫清信士之法應持幾戒。犯幾戒非優婆塞. The Buddha in his answer mentions the standard *upāsaka* ordination, with its five precepts, but immediately adds that[12]:

> 若持一戒。餘封四戒。若受二戒。餘封三戒。若受三戒。餘封二戒。若受四戒。餘封一戒。若受五戒。當具足持之.
>
> If he takes one precept, he excludes the other four, if he takes two precepts, he excludes the other three, if he takes three precepts, he excludes the other two, if he takes four precepts, he excludes the remaining one, if he takes five precepts, he should completely (*paripūrṇa*?) observe them.

Finally, in the *Mahānāmasūtra* Mahānāman asks the Buddha, "To what extent (*kiyatā*) is one an *upāsaka*?" In other words: what are the minimum requirements for *upāsaka* status? Since this text will take most of our attention in the following discussion, it is worthwhile to quote the shortest available version of the six extant[13]:

> 如是我聞。一時佛在迦毘羅衛國尼拘陀林。時釋摩男往詣佛所。頂禮佛足。在一面坐。而白佛言。
> 世尊。云何名爲優婆塞義。唯願如來。爲我敷演。佛告釋摩男。在家白衣。**歸依**三寶。以是義故名優婆塞汝即其人。
> 1. 時釋摩男。復白佛言。世尊。云何名優婆塞**信**。佛告釋摩男。於如來所。深生信心。安住信中。終不爲彼沙門婆羅門若天若魔。若梵若人。不信所壞。是名優婆塞信。

---

[11] T.125 II 649c12-13.

[12] T.125 II 650a3-6. Cf. T.125 II 649c20-24. Hirakawa (1995: 21b-c), referring to this whole passage, states that this "recognition of a partial acceptance of the precepts assumes that one is qualified as an *upāsaka* just by accepting the three refuges". Still, I believe that according to this passage *upāsaka*s must at least take the precept not to kill living beings.

[13] *Saṃyuktāgama*, T.100 II 431b5-23.

2. 時釋摩男。復白佛言。云何優婆塞戒。佛告釋摩男。不殺不盜。不婬不欺。及不飲酒等。是名優婆塞戒。
3. 又問。云何施具足。佛告釋摩男。優婆塞法。應捨慳貪。一切眾生。皆悉爲彼貪嫉所覆。以是義故。應離慳貪及嫉妒意。生放捨心。躬自施與。無有疲厭。是名施具足。
4. 又問。云何智慧具足。佛告釋摩男。優婆塞。如實知苦。如實知苦集。如實知苦滅。如實知苦滅道。知此四諦。決定明了。是名慧具足。
佛說是已。諸比丘聞佛所說。歡喜奉行

Thus have I heard. At one time, the Buddha was staying in Kapilavastu, in the Nigrodha grove. Then Mahānāman the Śākya with his head revered the Buddha's feet, sat at one side, and said to the Buddha: "Honored in the World, in what sense is one called *upāsaka*? Please, may the Tathāgata extensively explain it to me." The Buddha said to Mahānāman the Śākya: "A white-clad householder **goes for refuge** to the Three Jewels. In this sense is one called *upāsaka*. You are such a person."

1. Then Mahānāman the Śākya again said to the Buddha: "Honored in the World, what is called the **faith** (*śraddhā*) of an *upāsaka*?" The Buddha said to Mahānāman the Śākya: "One produces a deep thought of faith toward the Tathāgata and is established in faith. He never lacks faith or is evil towards *śramaṇas*, *brāhmaṇas*, or gods (*deva*), or demons (*māra*), or *brahmā* [gods]. This is called the faith of an *upāsaka*."

2. Then Mahānāman the Śākya again said to the Buddha: "What is the **morality** (*śīla*) of an *upāsaka*?" The Buddha said to Mahānāman the Śākya: "Not to kill, not to steal, not to seduce, not to lie, and not to drink liquor, etc. This is called the morality of an *upāsaka*."

3. He also asked: "How is one possessed of **liberality** (*tyāga*)?" The Buddha said to Mahānāman the Śākya: "It is a rule (*dharma*) for an *upāsaka* that he should abandon stinginess. Towards all living beings, without exception, stinginess and envy are destroyed by him. Therefore, he should abandon any thoughts of stinginess and envy, and he should produce thoughts of liberality and personally donate, tirelessly. This is called 'possessed of liberality'."

4. He also asked: "How is one possessed of **wisdom** (*prajñā*)?" The Buddha said to Mahānāman the Śākya: "An *upāsaka* knows suffering according to reality, knows the collection [classical wrong translation for *samudaya*, "arising"] of suffering according to reality, knows the extinction of suffering according to reality, and knows the path to the extinction of suffering according to reality. He knows these four truths. He understands [them] with certainty. This is called 'possessed of wisdom'."

After the Buddha had said this, the monks, hearing the Buddha's words, rejoiced and practised accordingly.

All versions of the *Mahānāmasūtra* agree on this much: the formal requirement for *upāsaka* status is taking the refuges. This status entails some effort in cultivating four or five well-known virtues: 1. faith (*śraddhā*), 2. morality (*śīla*), 3. learning (*śruta*, sometimes, as here, missing)[14], 4. generosity (*tyāga*), and 5. wisdom (*prajñā*). One Chinese version applies the term **paripūri* to *upāsakas* who successfully practise these virtues, but nothing allows us to assume that it envisions a formal distinction between full and partial *upāsakas*[15], which is the distinction found in the *Gavesīsutta* and in the *Ekottarāgama*.

The *Mahānāmasūtra* underwent considerable editorial activity, resulting in at least six versions belonging to two recensions (see below). A comparison might shed some light on what words or paragraphs the monks were interested in modifying and on what point the definition of *upāsaka* was still unsettled.

The sequence *śraddhā-śīla-śruta-tyāga-prajñā*, used to structure the *Mahānāmasūtra*, is a traditional one. Its items should always occur in this order, whether in a compound or in separate phrases or paragraphs[16]. However, if we compare all versions of the *Mahānāmasūtra*, the order is not always the same.

---

[14] In a *sutta* of the *Aṅguttaranikāya*, too, *suta* is missing (AN 2.66 ff; *Chattha Sangayana* 1.377 ff).

[15] In this version, Mahānāman asks two questions (T.99 II 237a2-20). Taking the refuges answers the first one, which is about the definition of *upāsaka*. Practising the other virtues answers the second one, which is about the definition of a complete *upāsaka*.

[16] Among the many possible examples: *yassa kassaci, Mahānāma, dīgharattaṃ* ***saddhā****paribhāvitaṃ cittaṃ* ***sīla****paribhāvitaṃ cittaṃ* ***suta****paribhāvitaṃ cittaṃ* ***cāga****paribhāvitaṃ cittaṃ* ***paññā****paribhāvitaṃ cittaṃ, tassa* ... (SN V 369; *Chattha Sangayana* 3.322). For this type of sequence see Allon 1997: 249, where our sequence is also mentioned (Allon 1997: 214, n. 36). This and other related types of sequences "aid composition by acting as an organizational principle" and "can also be considered to have a mnemonic function" (Allon 1997: 252).

TABLE 1:
***Mahānāmasūtra* – Three short versions compared**

	Saṃyuktāgama T.99	Saṃyuktāgama T.100	Saṃyuttanikāya
Paragraph order	*śaraṇa*	*śaraṇa*	*śaraṇa*
	śraddhā	*śraddhā*	***śīla***
	śīla	*śīla*	***śraddhā***
	śruta	*tyāga*	*tyāga*
	tyāga	*prajñā*	*prajñā*
	prajnā		

In Table 1, I compare the paragraph order of three *Mahanāma-sūtras*[17], representing what I call the short recension. Each column represents one version; each row represents one paragraph, marked by a keyword. The Pāli version, in the third column, does not respect the common order of the five virtues: *śīla* is promoted, as it comes close to the *śaraṇa* paragraph, while *śraddhā* is demoted, as it is separated from that same paragraph.

TABLE 2:
***Mahānāmasūtra* – Three long versions compared**

	Saṃyuktāgama T.99	Aṅguttaranikāya	Dharmaskandha
1	*śaraṇa*	*śaraṇa*	*śaraṇa*
2	What about an *upāsaka* who has fulfilled everything?		

[17] T.99 II 236b12-c10 (Sarvāstivādin according to Mayeda 1985: 99). T.100 II 431b5-23 (completely translated above). SN 5.394-395 (*Chattha Sangayana* 3.344-345; it is part of the *Sotāpattivagga*, and therefore it should describe a superior type of *upāsaka*).

3	***śraddhā***	***śīla***	***śīla***
4	***śīla***		
5	***śruta***		
6	remembers the *dharma*		
7	investigates the meaning		
8	practises according to *dharma* and *anudharma*		
9	How does an *upāsaka* comfort himself, but not others?	How is an *upāsaka* on the road to his own good and not to the good of others?	An *upāsaka* abstains from killing etc. for his own good, and encourages others to do the same for their own good.
10	***śīla*: is established in the precepts**	***śraddhā***	***śraddhā***
11	***śīla*: keeps pure morality**	***śīla***	***śīla***
12	***tyāga***	***tyāga***	***tyāga***
13	visits monks	visits monks	visits monks
14	listens to the *dharma*	listens to the *dharma*	listens to the *dharma*
15	remembers the *dharma*	remembers the *dharma*	remembers the *dharma*
16	investigates the meaning	investigates the meaning	investigates the meaning
17	practises according to *dharma* and *anudharma*	practises according to *dharma* and *anudharma*	practises according to *dharma* and *anudharma*
18	Possessed of how many *dharma*s does an *upāsaka* cause his own good and the good of others? ...	How is an *upāsaka* on the road to his own good and to the good of others? ...	... Ten Courses of Good Action, ...

In Table 2, I compare the paragraph order of three other *Mahānāmasūtras*[18], representing what I call the long recension. The version from the *Dharmaskandha* (third column) actually belongs to the later (roughly speaking) *abhidharma* period, but it clearly inherits most of its traits from an unknown Sarvāstivādin āgamic version, and therefore I include it in this context. In the *Saṃyuktāgama* (first column), part of the old structure is retained: the paragraphs on *śraddhā*, *śīla*, and *śruta* occur in the correct order (rows 3, 4, and 5). But in the *Aṅguttaranikāya* (second column) and in the *Dharmaskandha* (third column) only a paragraph on *śīla* occurs (row 3). Further down in the paragraph order, the old sequence *śraddhā-śīla-tyāga* (rows 10,11,12) is retained in the *Aṅguttaranikāya* and in the *Dharmaskandha*, whereas in the *Saṃyuktāgama* *śraddhā* has vanished to make room for one more paragraph on *śīla*[19].

These comparisons show the same trend. The *Mahānāmasūtra* started as a simple text that juxtaposed two sections that also occur elsewhere in Buddhist literature: one on the refuges, and one on the four or five virtues.[20] The second section underwent various modifications as among the five virtues recommended to *upāsakas*, morality (*śīla*) was often singled out as the most important one, so

---

[18] *Saṃyuktāgama*, T.99 II 236c29-237b20; *Aṅguttaranikāya* IV 220-222 (*Chattha Sangayana* 3.55-57; the immediately following *Jīvakasutta* reads exactly the same, except that the *nidāna* is in Rājagaha, in the Jīvakambavana, and instead of Mahānāman we find Jīvako Komārabhacco. Both *sutta*s are part of the *Gahapativagga*); *Dharmaskandha*, Sanskrit text in Dietz 1984: 73-80.

[19] There are two paragraphs on *śīla*, not one long paragraph: "The Buddha said to Mahānāma: [1.] if an *upāsaka* can establish himself in the precepts, [but] is not able to cause others to establish themselves in the right precepts, [2.] on his own keeps the pure precepts, [but] is not able to cause others to keep the precepts completely", 佛告摩訶男。若優婆塞能自立戒。不能令他立於正戒。自持淨戒。不能令他持戒具足 (T.99 II 237a21-23).

[20] For example, there is a text addressed to an *upāsaka* (Anāthapiṇḍika) and based only on the second section (AN 2.66-67; *Chattha Sangayana* 1.377-378): the Buddha teaches that a noble disciple (*ariyasāvaka*) fulfills the requirements of *saddhā*, *sīla*, *cāga*, *paññā*, in this order. The *sutta* is not about the definition of *upāsaka*, which term does not even occur, and the refuges are not listed.

much so that it made a pair with the refuges. The old structure –one section on the refuges followed by another one on the five virtues – yielded to a new one: one section on the refuges and the precepts followed by another one based on an open list of virtues. Still, all āgamic versions of the *Mahānāmasūtra* are ambiguous enough to leave room for interpretation: is there an *upāsaka* who is not expected to observe the precepts?

EVIDENCE IN THE *VINAYAS*

In the Pāli *Vinaya* one finds the definition of lay sisters: *upāsikā nāma buddhaṃ saraṇaṃ gatā dhammaṃ saraṇaṃ gatā saṃghaṃ saraṇaṃ gatā*[21]. The precepts are not mentioned, but this does not mean that such an *upāsikā* would not be expected to observe them. The same definition occurs in the parallel passages of most other *Vinayas*: Mahīśāsaka (T.1421 XXII 23a4-5)[22], Mahāsāṃghika (T.1425 XXII 290c13-15), Sarvāstivādin (T.1435 XXIII 28c13-14), Mūlasarvāstivādin (T.1442 XXIII 710c6-7: "she has produced deeply respectful thoughts toward the Buddha, the Dharma, and the

[21] *Vinaya* 3.189 (*Chattha Sangayana* 287). The commentary does not add anything.

[22] Hirakawa (1995: 20b-21a) maintains that the Mahīśāsakas required *upāsakas* to take both the refuges and the five precepts. His evidence is the following passage from the Mahīśāsaka *Vinaya*: "[Yaśas' father,] having seen the *dharma* and obtained the fruit [of the path], took the three refuges and next the five precepts." This is [meant by the statement:] of *upāsakas*, among men, Yaśas' father was the first one to take the three refuges and the five precepts, 見法得果已。受三自歸次受五戒。是爲諸優婆塞於人中耶舍父最初受三歸五戒 (T.1421 XXII 105b26-28; Hirakawa also refers to contiguous passages where other laypersons take both the refuges and precepts). I assume that, since in many parallel passages of other *Vinayas* the precepts are not mentioned, Hirakawa sees this Mahīśāsaka passage as prescriptive: all *upāsakas* should take the five precepts. It might be so, but this passage might also merely envision an ideal *upāsaka*. Indeed, at this point of the narration in the same *Vinaya*, the Buddha has already converted other laypersons who have only taken refuge in the Buddha and the Dharma, the Saṃgha being yet to be established; they have not (explicitly) taken the precepts. In one case at least the laywoman so converted is called *upāsikā* (T.1421 XXII 103b27).

Saṃgha, and has obtained an unbreakable faith"). In the Dharmaguptaka *Vinaya* (T.1428 XXII 601b11-12) the five precepts are mentioned, which suggests that according to this school all *upāsaka*s had to take all precepts. This interpretation is supported by a statement found in the *Vinayamātṛkā* (possibly a Dharmaguptaka text; see below) and by the fact that, as far as I can tell, in the *Dīrghāgama* (most probably a Dharmaguptaka text) laypersons who convert to Buddhism never stop at the refuges, but always recite the formulas of the precepts[23]. By contrast, in the Pāli canon the precepts often are not mentioned.

In a different section of the Mahāsāṃghika *Vinaya* one finds a remarkably explicit statement[24]:

> 優婆塞者三歸一分行少分行多分行滿分行隨順行。此法是名優婆塞。
>
> An *upāsaka* accepts the three refuges, and then progressively follows a single precept, some precepts, most precepts, and all the precepts. [A person who follows] this *dharma* is called an *upāsaka*.

EVIDENCE IN CANONICAL ABHIDHARMA

The *upāsaka* section of the *Śāriputrābhidharmaśāstra*[25] does not explicitly mention the *Mahānāmasūtra*, but is clearly based on it. After the section on the refuges[26], we read the following statements[27]:

---

[23] Hirakawa (1995: 20b), too, was of the opinion that the Dharmaguptakas required *upāsaka*s to take the five precepts. His evidence is a single *sūtra* from the *Dīrghāgama* where a layperson takes the refuges and the precepts, precepts not being mentioned in the parallel Pāli passage. He also wrote that the Dharmaguptaka *Vinaya* takes the same position, but in the note (Hirakawa 1995: 20b and n. 31) he actually referred to the Pāli *Dīghanikāya*.

[24] T.1425 XXII 306a19-20. Translation according to Hirakawa (1995: 21a). He thought that this passage even makes room for *upāsaka*s who only take the refuges, but the text does not go that far.

[25] The sectarian affiliation of the *Śāriputrābhidharmaśāstra* is uncertain. It could be a Dharmaguptaka text (Willemen et al. 1998: 164-166).

問曰。優婆塞幾戒。答曰五。何等五盡壽不殺生。是優婆塞戒…盡壽受持。不得違犯。齊幾爲持戒優婆塞。若優婆塞。於此五戒中。常持戒護行近行。不缺行。不亂行。不濁行。不雜行。隨順戒行。齊是名持戒優婆塞。

Question: How many precepts for an *upāsaka*? Answer: Five. What five? 1. Until the end of one's life not to kill living beings. This is an *upāsaka*'s precept. 2. ... [same pattern for the other four precepts]. He takes them for life. He may not break them.

To what extent (cf. Pāli *kittāvatā*) is one an '*upāsaka* who keeps the precepts'? If an *upāsaka*, among these five precepts, always keeps the precepts, guards his conduct, keeps close to his conduct (?), is not lacking in conduct, is not faulty in conduct, does not stain his conduct, does not compromise his conduct, and follows the precepts, to this extent (cf. Pāli *ettāvatā*) is he called an '*upāsaka* who keeps the precepts'.

Here, between the paragraph on the refuges, which precedes the quoted passage, and the one on morality ("To what extent is one ..."), both of which are phrased in recognizable agreement with the *Mahānāmasūtra*, the author has inserted another paragraph ("How many precepts ..."), which explicitly states that *upāsaka*s who take the refuges are *ipso facto* supposed to take and observe all precepts. Therefore, according to the *Śāriputrābhidharmaśāstra*, the *śīlavat* or *śīlasampanna upāsaka* of the *Mahānāmasūtra* is merely a standard lay brother who is able to keep all precepts.

Against this strict interpretation, another version of the *Mahānāmasūtra* developed, available in the Sarvāstivādin *Dharma-*

[26] "To what extent is one called *upāsaka*? If a person is endowed with the *indriya*s and the male organ, his mind is not distracted, he is not forced by [fear of] pain ... if the Wheel of the Dharma is not in motion yet, he takes refuge in the Buddha, he takes refuge in the Dharma. ... Once the Wheel of the Dharma is in motion, he takes refuge in the Buddha, ... the Saṃgha, ... the Dharma. After having undertaken these three utterances, then he is called *upāsaka*", 齊幾名爲優婆塞。若人諸根男相具足。心無錯亂。不爲苦所逼。欲作優婆塞。向尊上心。向彼爲主依於捨彼喜樂彼法輪未轉。未有衆僧。口受二教。歸依佛。歸依法。受此二語已。即名優婆塞。… [verses] 法輪既轉。便有聖衆。即說三語。口受三教。 歸依佛。歸依法。歸依僧。受此三語已。即名優婆塞。 … [verses] (T.1548 XXVIII 573c13-26).

[27] T.1548 XXVIII 574a7-14.

skandha in the form of a long quotation. In this version the paragraph on *śīla* is expanded as follows:[28]

1. *kiyatā upāsakaḥ śikṣāsv* ***ekadeśakārī*** *bhavati / yataś copāsakaḥ buddhaṃ śaraṇaṃ gato bhavati dharmmaṃ saṃghaṃ śaraṇaṃ gato bhavati prāṇātipātāt prativirataḥ adattādānāt kāmamithyācārān mṛṣāvādād aprativirataḥ iyatā upāsakaḥ śikṣāsv ekadeśakārī bhavati /*
2. *kiyatā ...* ***pradeśakārī*** *... prāṇātipātād adattādānāt prativirataḥ ...*
3. *kiyatā ...* ***yadbhūyaskārī*** *... prāṇātipātād adattādānāt kāmamithyācārāt prativirataḥ ...*
4. *kiyatā ...* ***aparipūrṇṇakārī*** *... prāṇātipātād adattādānāt kāmamithyācārān mṛṣāvādāt prativirataḥ ...*
5. *kiyatā* ***paripūrṇṇakārī*** *... prāṇātipātād adattādānāt kāmamithyācārān mṛṣāvādāt surāmaireyamadyapramādasthānāt prativirataḥ ...*

This version envisions *upāsaka*s of five types according to how many precepts they take or, perhaps, they are able to keep. For the ambiguity is still there. The Chinese version of the *Dharmaskandha*, by contrast, is explicit and unambiguous[29]:

此何名爲能學一分。謂前所説鄔波索迦。歸佛法僧。發誠言已。唯能離殺。不離餘四。如是名爲能學一分。

How is one called 'able to train in one part' (*ekadeśakārin*)? It means that the previously mentioned *upāsaka*, who has gone for refuge to the Buddha, the Dharma, and the Saṃgha, has uttered the [following] sincere words: "I can only abstain from killing, not from the other four [precepts]". Thus he is called 'able to train in one part' (*ekadeśakārin*).

---

[28] Dietz 1984: 74-75.

[29] T.1537 XXVI 454a18-20. Because of differences in the order of chapters, it has already been suggested that the Chinese and Sanskrit versions represent two different recensions (Dietz 1985: 169; Willemen et al. 1998: 182). It has also been suggested that the Gilgit *Dharmaskandha* belongs to the Mūlasarvāstivāda (Dietz 1985) and that the traditional ascription of the Chinese version to the Sarvāstivāda (see the colophons at the end of each fascicule) must be taken "in its most general meaning" (Willemen et al. 1998: 70), i.e. it is not a specifically Vaibhāṣika recension. Indeed, as far as our passage on *upāsaka* is concerned, it is the Sarvāstivāda Chinese version that is more in line with the Sautrāntika doctrine (see below) that *upāsaka*s can take a partial *saṃvara*.

Here to different *upāsaka* statuses correspond different statements in the ritual of *upāsaka* ordination. According to the Chinese version, therefore, the distinction between different types of *upāsakas* is formal, just as in the *Gavesīsutta*, the *Ekottarāgama*, and the Mahāsāṃghika *Vinaya* (see above).

Another difference between the two versions lies in the number of types of *upāsaka*: five in the Sanskrit, but four in the Chinese. How can one explain this disagreement? In Table 3 I list the names of the types of *upāsakas* with reference to how many precepts they abstain from according to the two *Dharmaskandhas* and to other important post-canonical texts that happen to be explicit:

TABLE 3:
Correspondences between the Five Precepts and the Four *Upāsakas*

	Sanskrit *Dharma-skandha*	**Chinese *Dharma-skandha***	***Mahā-vibhāṣā*; Yaśomitra**	**Mppś**
ekadeśa-kārin	killing	killing	killing	killing
pradeśa-kārin	stealing	stealing	stealing	stealing **OR** stealing + sexual misconduct
yadbhūyas-kārin	sexual misconduct	sexual misconduct	sexual misconduct **OR** sexual misconduct + lying	lying
aparipūrṇa-kārin	lying	[missing]	[missing]	[missing]
paripūrṇa-kārin	drinking liquor	lying + drinking liquor	drinking liquor	drinking liquor

Only the Sanskrit *Dharmaskandha* mentions five types of *upāsaka*, adding the *aparipūrṇakārin* to the four mentioned in the other sources[30]. In other words, post-canonical sources knew a version of the *Mahānāmasūtra* attested in the Chinese *Dharmaskandha*, not in the Sanskrit. These texts had to solve a problem of classification: how do the five precepts correspond to the four *upāsaka* types? To one type they attributed two precepts: the *ekadeśakārin* only observes one precept, as the very term *ekadeśa* suggests, whereas the other types are defined by the specific observance of one or two precepts.

My impression is that the fourfold classification is earlier, and that it developed to determine how many types of *aparipūri* or *aparipūrṇa upāsaka*s (the only incomplete category mentioned in the *āgama/nikāya*s) there might be. In other words, originally the *ekadeśa-*, *pradeśa-*, and *yadbhūyaskārin* were all meant as *aparipūrṇakārin*; for this reason this term does not occur in the fourfold classification. To confirm this impression, one may notice that such an understanding of the term *aparipūrṇakārin* informs a passage from the *Saṃyuktābhidharmahṛdaya:* "Why is there no *upāsaka*

---

[30] For the Sanskrit *Dharmaskandha* see above. For the Chinese *Dharmaskandha* see T.1537 XXVI 454a18-27; in particular: "if he abstains from killing stealing, and sexual misconduct, but does not abstain from the other two, such [an *upāsaka*] is called *yadbhūyaskārin*", 離殺盜婬。不離餘二。如是名爲能學多分 (T.1537 XXVI 454a24-25). Yaśomitra: *yadbhūyaskārī. yas trīṇi catvāri vā rakṣati* (Wogihara 1932-35: 376, similarly 377 = Shastri 1970-73, II: 626, 627). *Mahāvibhāṣā*: "if one takes three [or] takes four [precepts], one is called *yadbhūyaskārin*", 受三受四名多分 (T.1545 XXVII 646a10; see also b10-11). Mppś: "A *pradeśakārin* takes either two precepts or three precepts", 少分行者。若受二戒若受三戒 (T.1509 XXV 158c26). The entire passage (T.1509 XXV 158c22-29) is translated by Lamotte in Mppś 821. In his *History of Indian Buddhism*, Lamotte (1958: 77) referred only to this classification. The Mppś (821) also adds the *samucchinnarāga*, i.e. the *upāsaka* who abstains from all sexual activities, also mentioned in the *Gavesīsutta*. In the Sanskrit *Abhidharmakośa* (Pradhan 1975: 215 = Shastri 1970-73, II: 626) only four *upāsakas* are mentioned, leaving out the *aparipūrṇakārin*, but Vasubandhu does not explain how the five precepts are distributed. Paramārtha's translation is not helpful: "Keeping one, *ekadeśa*; keeping two, *pradeśa*; keeping three, *yadbhūyaḥ*; keeping four, *paripūrṇa*", 一持一處。二持少處。三持多處。四持具處.

whose *saṃvara* is incomplete (*aparipūrṇa*)? ... If there isn't, why did [the Buddha] mention the *ekadeśakārin* and the other [three incomplete] *upāsaka*s?"[31], 何故無不具足律儀優婆塞...若無者何故說一行等優婆塞. Later, the Sanskrit *Dharmaskandha* came up with a neater classification, turning the *aparipūrṇakārin* into a separate category.

THE DEBATE IN THE *ŚĀSTRA*S

The treatises (*śāstra*) selected the *Mahānāmasūtra* as the one text where the Buddha defined *upāsaka* status[32], and they were confronted with the version attested in the *Dharmaskandha* and mentioning four types of *upāsaka*. The point of controversy was: does the *Mahānāmasūtra* say that there are *upāsakas* who choose how many precepts they want to take? The Chinese *Dharmaskandha*, as we have seen, is the only unambiguous canonical source: partial *upāsakas* actually take less than five precepts. This clarity, however, may come from the Chinese translators rather than the original Sanskrit version.

The *Mahāvibhāṣā* mentions three positions[33]. The masters of Gandhāra maintained that there are both *upāsaka*s without *saṃvara* (restraint), i.e. who do not take any precepts, and *upāsaka*s with an incomplete *saṃvara*, i.e. who take less than five precepts; the *ekadeśakārin* etc. mentioned by the Buddha are such *upāsaka*s. The masters of Kashmir maintained that there are neither *upāsaka*s without *saṃvara* nor *upāsaka*s with a partial *saṃvara*: even without uttering the formulas of the precepts, one who takes the refuges and declares himself an *upāsaka* is endowed with the complete *saṃvara* and must observe all precepts; the *ekadeśakārin* etc. are

---

[31] T.1552 XXVIII 951b11-12,14; see also 951c4-9.

[32] *idam utsūtraṃ vartate / kim atrotsūtram / upāsakatvābhyupagamād eva saṃvaralābho yasmāt prāṇātipātam ity āheti / na hy evaṃ sūtrapāṭhaḥ ukto yathā mahānāmasūtre pāṭhaḥ / tatraiva copāsakalakṣaṇopadeśo nānyatra* (*Abhidharmakośabhāṣya*, Pradhan 1975: 215 = Shastri 1970-73, II: 626)

[33] T.1545 XXVII 645c22-646b19.

upāsakas who happen to break one or more precepts. There was a third intermediate position, requiring at least one precept[34]:

> *Bhadanta* Saṃghavasu (僧伽筏蘇 Sēnggāfásū) has a theory in partial agreement with the two previous teachers. He says that one does not take just the three refuges to become an *upāsaka*, but one whose five-fold *saṃvara* is incomplete also becomes an *upāsaka*. This means that such a person, when he is about to take the precepts of an *upāsaka*, first has a detailed discussion with the master of the precepts, [such as]: "I can take such and such precept, but I cannot take such and such precept". After a detailed discussion, he goes for refuge to the Buddha, the Dharma, and the Saṃgha, takes the vow, and obtains such precepts. In accord with the previous detailed discussion, he can take some [precepts]. At this point he obtains the [partial] *saṃvara*. The number [of types of *upāsakas*] is also [to be explained] in this way. Therefore, [Saṃghavasu] says that the *upāsakasaṃvara* is called 'morality with a detailed discussion'. The morality of novices etc. does not get this name.

After the *Mahāvibhāṣā*, Vasubandhu in the *Abhidharmakośabhāṣya*[35] defended the position of the masters of Gandhāra, without using this term; by his times, this was the Sautrāntika position. Saṃghabhadra, by contrast, in the *Nyāyānusāra*[36] defended the position of the masters of Kashmir. Neither referred to the third position, which is the only one mentioned in the later *Abhidharmadīpa Vibhāṣāprabhāvṛtti*[37]:

---

[34] T.1545 XXVII 646b11-19.

[35] Pradhan 1975: 215-216 = Shastri 1970-73, II: 625-627. Xuanzang: T.1558 XXIX 76a1-b11. Paramārtha: T.1559 XXIX 233a5-b9.

[36] T.1562 XXIX 552a2-554a20. For a translation see Agostini 2002, Chapter Two.

[37] Jaini 1959: 124-125. The Dīpakāra in this case disagrees with Saṃghabhadra. Japanese scholars have pointed out that instances of disagreement between Saṃghabhadra and the Dīpakāra (references in Willemen et al. 1998: 253) "would challenge the hypothesis that the Dīpakāra is in the lineage of Saṃghabhadra" (Willemen et al. 1998: 253). Jaini (1959: 134) suggests dating the former between 450 AD and 550 AD. Shingyō Yoshimoto (reference in Willemen et al. 1998: 253) suggests a date of composition of AD 550-600. According to Bhattacharya (1992: 74), a reference to Uddyotakara's *Nyāyavārttika* would allow dating the verses and the commentary to the seventh century or later.

kaścit khalv akāryaikadeśaviratikṣamo bhavati | kaścid yāvat samagradauḥśīlyaviratikṣamaḥ | ity ato bhagavān akāryaikadeśaviratyāpy upāsakatvaṃ śāsti | na hi sarvaśīlavikalaḥ kaścic charaṇagamanecchāmātrakeṇopāsako bhavati ṣaḍaṅgoṣadhaikadvyaṅgavaikalyopayogāvad iti ||

Someone is indeed capable of a partial restraint from sins, someone [from more, and so on] – down to – capable of a total restraint from immorality. Therefore, the Blessed One teaches that one is an *upāsaka* even through a partial restraint from sins. For one who completely lacks morality does not become an *upāsaka* by merely wishing to go for refuge.

OTHER NON-THERAVĀDIN EVIDENCE

Other texts do not refer to a debate, which perhaps was going on only among Sarvāstivādins. They simply state their opinion, and most often agree with the masters of Gandhāra.

Indeed, only the *Vinayamātṛkā* agrees with the masters of Kashmir[38]: "an *upāsaka* does not stop at the three refuges, but further adds the five precepts. Henceforth he gets to be called *upāsaka*", 優婆塞者。不止在三歸。更加五戒。始得名爲優婆塞也.

Two Sarvāstivādin *karmavācanā*s from Turfan concern the *upāsaka* ordination: in one case the precepts are not uttered, in the other they are[39], which suggests that laypersons in that community had an option. Monks who revert to lay status have the same option according to a Vinaya text of the same school, the Sarvāstivāda *Vinaya Vibhāṣā*[40]:

---

[38] T.1463 XXIV 802b4-5. This text was probably translated at the beginning of the fifth century (Wang 1994: 172). It might be a Dharmaguptaka or Haimavata work (Nakamura 1980: 56, n. 24). Nakamura says that Hirakawa "criticized this opinion" (Nakamura 1980: 56, n. 24). Still, Hirakawa accepts a Dharmaguptaka affiliation in Bapat & Hirakawa (1970: xiv-xv, n. 2).

[39] See Härtel 1956: 25-29, 50-55. These texts belong to the Sarvāstivādins (Härtel 1956: 9).

[40] T.1440 XXIII 508a27-b2, b14-19. See also T.1440 XXIII 514c16-18. Hirakawa (1995: 20a) quoted an untraceable passage from this text teaching that *upāsaka*s who take the refuges must also keep the precepts.

若言我是沙彌非比丘。即失具戒。二種戒在。五戒十戒。若言我是優婆塞非沙彌。即失十戒。五戒在。若言。在家出家一切盡捨。我是三歸優婆塞。三種一時盡失。不失三歸...凡受優婆塞戒。設不能具受五戒。若受一戒乃至四戒。受得戒不。答曰。不得。若不得者。有經說。有少分優婆塞多分優婆塞滿分優婆塞。此義云何。答曰。所以作是說者。欲明持戒功德多少。不言有如是受戒法也。

If [a monk] says: "I am a novice, not a monk", then loses the full morality, but two types of morality remain: the five precepts [of *upāsaka*s] and the ten precepts [of novices]. If he says: "I am an *upāsaka*, not a novice", then he loses the ten precepts, but the five precepts remain. If he says: "I abandon the entire [morality] of householders and renouncers, I am a three-refuge *upāsaka*", then the three types of morality are lost at one time, but the refuges are not lost ... As for those who take the *upāsaka* precepts, if they cannot take all five precepts, but take one to four precepts, do they obtain the morality [of *upāsaka*s]? Answer. They don't. [Question] If they don't, a *sūtra* [the *Mahānāmasūtra*] mentions *upāsaka*s with some precepts, most precepts, and all precepts. What is its meaning? Answer. The reason for making this statement is that [the *sūtra*] wants to explain that in keeping [not taking] the precepts the qualities [of *upāsaka*s] may be more or less. It does not say that there is a teaching about taking the precepts in such a [partial] way".

Here, *upāsaka*s either take no precepts or take all of them, which is a position not mentioned in the *Mahāvibhāṣā* (see above). Haribhadra's commentary to the *Aṣṭasāhasrikāprajñāpāramitā-sūtra*[41] agrees:

triśaraṇagamanāt pañcaśikṣāpadaparigrahāc copāsakaḥ / tathopasiketi dvidhā bhedaḥ / triśaraṇagatam upāsakaṃ mām ācāryo dhārayatu / tathā triśaraṇagataṃ pañcaśikṣāpadagṛhītam upāsakaṃ mām ācāryo dhārayatv iti Vinaye dvividhāpāṭhāt /

By going to the three refuges and by taking the five precepts one is an *upāsaka*, and the same holds for an *upāsikā*. Thus, there are two types of *upāsaka*, because of the two readings in the *Vinaya*: 1. 'May the master consider me as an *upāsaka* who has gone to the three refuges' and 2. 'May the master consider me as an *upāsaka* who has gone to the three refuges and has taken the five precepts'

---

[41] Wogihara 1932-35: 331. I follow Lamotte in reading *mām* instead of *ma* (Mppś I 830, n. 3a).

The Gāndhārika and Sautrāntika position (see above) is found again in the Mahāyāna *Mahāparinirvāṇa Sūtra*[42]. Here the Buddha recalls his encounter with Mahānāman, who had asked for the meaning of *upāsaka* and *ekadeśa[kāry]upāsaka*. The Buddha says that he had answered that if one takes the three refuges, one is an *upāsaka* (若有善男子善女人。諸根完具受三歸依。是則名爲優婆塞也) and that "if one takes the three refuges and takes one precept, he is called *ekadeśa[kāry]upāsaka.*" 若受三歸及受一戒。是名一分優婆塞也.

The *Mahāprajñāpāramitā-śāstra*[43] is also explicit on at least one point: "The *ekadeśakārin* takes one precept from among the five precepts. He is not able to take the [other] four precepts." 一分行者。於五戒中受一戒。不能受持四戒.

The late *Upāsakasaṃvarāṣṭaka-vivaraṇa*[44] agrees:

> *'di ltar bslab pa'i yan lag lnga po 'di ni / dge bsnyen gyi sdom pa yongs su rdzogs par brjod do // thams cad las ldog par nus pa med na yang re re la yang nges pa sngon du song ba las log na 'bras bu chen po nyid do //*
>
> Thus, this fivefold group of limbs of morality is called 'complete vow of an *upāsaka*' (*paripūrṇopāsakasaṃvara*). Even if one is not able to abstain from them all, a great fruit [accrues] to one who is established in them one by one too, [progressively] abstaining from the preceding ones.

Other texts could be taken into account, but as they present some degree of ambiguity, I merely mention them: the *Satyasiddhi-*

---

[42] T.374 XII 568b11-12,13-14 (Northern version, translated by Dharmakṣema between 414-421 AD from a central Asian manuscript) and T.375 XII 815a18-19,21 (Southern version, based on Dharmakṣema's; see Bongard-Levin 1986: xix). The original text was compiled between AD 200 and 400 (Nakamura 1980: 212). The passage I quote should belong to the later section of the *sūtra* (Nakamura 1980: 213). So far, I have been unable to locate this passage in Faxian's translation of the Mahāyāna *Mahāparinirvāṇasūtra* made from an Indian manuscript found in Pāṭaliputra between 417-418 AD (Bongard-Levin 1986: xix-xx). For an English translation see Yamamoto 1973-75, III: 847.

[43] T.1509 XXV 158c25-26.

[44] *Tanjur*: Peking No. 5642, vol. U, pp. 192b7-8; Narthang No. 3633, vol. U, pp. 176b6-7; Derge No. 4141, vol. Su, 158a6-7; Cone, vol. Su, pp. 157a6-7.

śāstra[45], the *Abhidharmasamuccaya*[46], the *Saddharmasmṛtyupasthāna-sūtra*[47], and the **Upāsakapañcaśīlalakṣaṇa-sūtra*[48].

---

[45] "The Buddha spoke of *upāsakas* who have five precepts. Question: Some people say that if one takes all of them, one obtains the *saṃvara* of the precepts. How is this matter? Answer: Regardless of how many [precepts an *upāsaka*] takes, in all cases he obtains the *saṃvara*, but when taking them, there must be five [to choose from? uncertain translation]", 佛說優婆塞有五戒。問曰。有人言。具受則得戒律儀。是事云何。答曰。隨受多少皆得律儀。但取要有五 (T.1646 XXXII 300b9-11). The *Satyasiddhiśāstra* seems to be related on one side to Sautrāntika doctrine, on the other to Mādhyamika philosophy (Nakamura 1980: 113).

[46] "If one only practices one part of the *upāsaka* precepts (*śikṣāpada*), should we speak of 'possession' (*samanvāgama*) of the *upāsakasaṃvara* or of 'non-possession'? We should speak of 'possession', and yet it is called 'breaking the precepts'. 若唯修學鄔波索迦一分學處爲說成就鄔波索迦律儀爲說不成就。應說成就而名犯戒 (T.1605 XXXI 680a23-25). Does this passage refer to taking or to keeping less than five precepts? Walpola Rahula's translation (1971: 90-91) is completely different from mine and does not really adhere to the Chinese: "A l'égard du quelques disciples laïcs qui séjournent dans un établissement monastique *(śikṣāsthāna)*, elle (cette discipline) est appelée l'accompagnement *(samanvāgama)*; la discipline d'un disciple laïc est appelée non-accompagnement *(asamanvāgama)*, et le dit accompagnement est aussi appelé danger pour la moralité *(śīlavipatti)*, ...". He tried to understand the text as referring not to partial *upāsakas* but to two types of full *upāsakas*: 1. those who are particularly close to the monastery (something like the *dasasīlaupāsakas*), for whom one should speak of 'possession', and 2. ordinary laypersons, for whom one should speak of 'non-possession'.

[47] In order to stress the ambiguity of the following passages, I pedantically translate the character 受 (take) and the compound 受持 (take-keep) with the verb 'to take' (precepts), i.e. as Skt. *samādatte* or *gṛhṇāti*, and the character 持 (keep) with the verb 'to keep', i.e. as Skt. *rakṣati* or *pālayati* (a good translator should select one meaning): "Moreover, there are two types of morality: the morality of practicing one (*ekakāriśīla*?), and the morality of practicing more than one (*aneka*-). Practicing one: one precept. Practicing more than one: taking two or keeping three precepts", 復有二種戒。謂一行戒。非一行戒。一行者。所謂一戒。非一行者。或受二戒。或持三戒 (T.721 XVII 142c19-21); "Moreover, there are three types [of morality]: 1. minor morality (*pradeśaśīla*?), i.e., keeping one precept; 2. major morality (*yadbhūyaḥśīla*?), i.e., keeping two or three precepts; 3. complete morality of engagement (*paripūrṇasamādānaśīla*?), i.e., keeping all the precepts", 復有三種。一者少分戒。二者多分戒。三者盡受戒。少分戒者。持於一戒。多分戒者。或持二三。盡受戒者。持一切戒 (T.721 XVII 143a8-11); "How is one, by keeping the precepts, reborn in one or the other place? ... if one takes the precept 1. not to kill, one is reborn in the abode of the Four Gods, ... if one takes the precepts 1. not to kill and 2. not to steal, one is reborn among the Thirty-Three Gods, ... if one takes the precepts 1. not to kill, 2. not to steal, and

Finally, it may be worthwhile to recall that Buddhists outside India generally accepted partial morality: the Sautrāntika position was the one exported. Tsong kha pa (1352-1419), in a treatise of only four pages on the *Essence of the Ocean of the Vinaya*, referred to all possibilities: "Avoiding killing, stealing ... are the lay vows for men and women. Observing one, some, most, or all of these, together with pure conduct and the Refuge vows, are the six types of lay ordinations"[49]. In the nineteenth century an important Tibetan expert on *Vinaya*, Koṅ-sprul Blo-gros-mtha'-yas (1998: 93), listed the various types of *upāsaka* in his treatise on Buddhist discipline. As for contemporary Tibetan practice[50]:

> all the precepts are recited in a precept-giving ceremony, but lay people privately commit themselves only to those that they feel capable of fol-

---

3. not to indulge in sexual misbehavior ... one is reborn among the Yāma gods, ... because of a high degree of faith and knowledge, one is reborn among the gods of Tuṣita, ... if one does not 1. kill, 2. steal, 3. indulge in sexual misbehavior, [and does not practice] 4. false speech, 5. slanderous speech, 6. harsh speech, and 7. frivolous talk, one is reborn among the Nirmitavaśavartin gods ..." 云何持戒。生於何處。彼以聞慧。見此眾生。受不殺戒。生四天處...若受不殺不盜戒。生三十三天 ... 若受不殺不盜不婬。親近修習生夜摩天 ... 信智勝故。生兜率陀天 ... 不殺不盜不邪婬不妄語兩舌惡口綺語。生化樂天 ... 受持不殺不盜不邪婬不妄語兩舌惡口綺語。生於他化自在天中。 (T.721 XVII 142b29-c9; see also 142b23-28.).

[48] "If an *upāsaka*, although he has not taken any precept, commits an offence against a disciple (*śrāvaka*?) of the Buddha, a man of pure morality, even though there is no offence of breaking a precept, still in the future he will never obtain the five precepts and so on up to the minor ordination (*pravrajyā*) and the full ordination (*upasampadā*)", 若優婆塞。雖都不受戒。犯佛弟子淨戒人者。雖無犯戒之罪。然後永不得受五戒乃至出家受具足 (優婆塞五戒相經, T.1476 XXIV 943a19-21, translated by Guṇavarman in AD 431). There are no problems of translation in this interesting passage, but I am not certain of its Indian origin. It has been recognized that "this text is not a translation, but an excerpt from the *Daśabhāṇavāra-vinaya*", of the Sarvāstivādins (Nakamura 1980: 56, n. 24). The latter is preserved in Chinese (T.1435 XXIII, translated in AD 404-409; Nakamura 1980: 54, n. 24). However, I was not able to find the passage quoted above in any *Vinaya*. An almost identical passage occurs much later in the 法苑珠林 (T.2122 LIII, juan 88), but this is not an Indian text.

[49] *'Dul ba'i rgya mtsho snying po*, translated in Mullin & Ragbay 1978: 53.

[50] Harvey 2000: 83.

lowing, with those committed to only some of the five precepts still being known as *upāsaka*s or *upāsikā*s.

Chinese lay Buddhists, at least between 1900 and 1950, used to take partial vows: if one took one or two precepts, it was called a 'minor ordination' (少分戒 shāofēn jiè, **pradeśaśīla*); if one took three or four precepts, it was called a 'major ordination' (多分戒 duōfēn jiè, **yadbhūyaḥśīla*); if one took all five precepts, it was called a 'plenary ordination' (滿戒 mǎn jiè, **paripūrṇaśīla*). The type of ordination was registered on a certificate[51].

In contemporary Indonesia, different types of lay devotees are found in the Buddhayāna, also called Agama Buddha Indonesia, a syncretistic form of Theravāda: the *tisaraṇa* devotees stop at the refuges and are not called *upāsaka*s; the *bāla upāsaka*s take three precepts (not to kill, not to steal, not to lie); *upāsaka*s take all precepts. During certain ceremonies they wear different robes, and one can tell them apart[52].

EVIDENCE IN THERAVĀDA POST-CANONICAL TEXTS

Since partial *upāsaka*s seem to belong to all periods and to many schools of Buddhism in India, one would expect to find them mentioned in Theravāda commentaries too[53], and indeed there is some evidence that complicates our view of the laity in early Theravāda.

[51] Welch 1967: 361-362. He adds some important information on the seriousness and formality of a partial commitment: "The devotee who took the vow against killing could not, for instance, hunt or fish. So seriously were the vows looked upon, in fact, that not all five were necessarily taken ... Almost everyone, however, included the first vow ...".

[52] On the Buddhayāna see Bechert 1981: 11-12, 14. I owe the information on lay devotees to a personal informant, a well-educated Indonesian, academically trained in Buddhism, who kindly answered in written English to a questionnaire (see Agostini 2002: 29-30).

[53] The general Theravādin view is of course that an *upāsaka* must take all precepts. See for example the last section of the commentary to the *Sāmaññaphala-sutta* (DN-a 1.230 ff; *Chattha Sangayana* 1.205 ff), where the *Mahānāmasūtra* is quoted and interpreted.

The Pāli commentary to the *Vinaya* agrees with the Sarvāstivāda *Vinaya Vibhāṣā* (see above): a monk who disrobes (*sikkhāpaccakkhāna*) may choose to be recognized, among other options, as a three-refuge *upāsaka* or a five-precept *upāsaka*[54].

The young Sinhalese *upāsaka* Cakkaṇa is mentioned as the standard example of *sampattivirati*, the morality of those who do not take precepts[55], and yet abstain from bad actions. It is contrasted with *samādānavirati*, which entails taking the precepts[56]. The story goes that Cakkaṇa's mother was seriously ill. The doctor prescribed meat, and Cakkaṇa went hunting. He caught a hare, but when he was about to kill it, he felt that it was not the right thing to do, and let it go. His brother scolded him. Cakkaṇa told his mother that since he was born he had never consciously killed. Because of this act of truth, his mother recovered.

The *Paṭisambhidāmagga* says that the five precepts of *upāsaka*s and the ten precepts of novices are 'limited morality' (*pariyantapārisuddhisīla*)[57]. Mahāsena, in his commentary, added something he did not need to add[58]:

---

[54] *dvevāciko upāsako ti maṃ dhārehi, tevāciko upāsako, buddhaṃ saraṇagamaniko, dhammaṃ saṅghaṃ saraṇagamaniko, pañcasikkhāpadiko dasasikkhāpadiko upāsako ti maṃ dhārehī ti* (Vin-a 1.253; *Chattha Sangayana* 1.218).

[55] *asamādinnasikkhāpadānaṃ.*

[56] *Dhammasaṅgāni-a* 103, *Chattha Sangayana* 146 = SN-a 2.149-150, *Chattha Sangayana* 2.138-139 = MN-a 1.203-204, *Chattha Sangayana* 1.207.

[57] *Atthi sīlaṃ pariyantaṃ, atthi sīlaṃ apariyantaṃ. Tattha katamaṃ taṃ sīlaṃ pariyantaṃ? Atthi sīlaṃ lābhapariyantaṃ, atthi sīlaṃ yasapariyantaṃ, atthi sīlaṃ ñātipariyantaṃ, atthi sīlaṃ aṅgapariyantaṃ, atthi sīlaṃ jīvitapariyantaṃ. Katamaṃ taṃ sīlaṃ lābhapariyantaṃ? Idh' ekacco lābhahetu lābhapaccayā lābhakāraṇā yathāsamādinnaṃ sikkhāpadaṃ vītikkamati. idaṃ taṃ sīlaṃ lābhapariyantaṃ* ... (*Chattha Sangayana* 42; PTS I 43). Other examples follow to explain the other *pariyanta*s in term of a breach of the vow. The *Visuddhimagga* (Warren & Kosambi 1950: 37) quotes the *Paṭisambhidāmagga*, but not its commentary as this was yet to be written.

[58] *pariyantasikkhāpadānan ti ... Tattha ca dve pariyantā 1. sikkhāpadapariyanto ca 2. kālapariyanto ca. katamo sikkhāpadapariyanto? upāsakopāsikānaṃ yathāsamādānavasena ekaṃ vā dve vā tīṇi vā cattāri vā pañca vā aṭṭha vā dasa vā sikkhāpadāni honti. sikkhamānasāmaṇerasāmaṇerīnaṃ dasa sikkhāpadāni.*

For *upāsaka*s and *upāsikā*s there are either one, or two, or three, or four, or five, or eight, or ten precepts, depending on how many they take.

Mahāsena probably wanted to fill a gap in the written tradition and account for a custom still practised at his time[59].

The *Vibhaṅga* book of the *Abhidhammapiṭaka* has a section on the five precepts[60]. The commentary says that killing a big animal is worse than killing a little one; when it comes to killing men, the difference is based on moral standards, as one may kill

a man of bad morality ... a man who has the morality of cows [naturally good and inoffensive] ... one who has gone for refuge ... one who has taken the five precepts ... a stream-enterer ... a once-returner ... a non-returner ... one who has abandoned the defilements.[61]

---

ayaṃ sikkhāpadapariyanto. katamo kālapariyanto? upāsakopāsikā dānaṃ dadamānā parivesanapariyantaṃ sīlaṃ samādiyanti, vihāraṃ gatā vihārapariyantaṃ sīlaṃ samādiyanti; ekaṃ vā dve vā tayo vā bhiyyo vā rattindivāni paricchedaṃ katvā sīlaṃ samādiyanti. ayaṃ kālapariyanto. imesu dvīsu pariyantesu sikkhāpadaṃ pariyantaṃ katvā samādinnaṃ sīlaṃ vītikkamanena vā maraṇena vā paṭippassambhati, kālaṃ pariyantaṃ katvā samādinnaṃ taṃtaṃkālātikkamena paṭissambhati (*Paṭisambhidāmagga-aṭṭhakathā*: *Chattha Sangayana* I 188; PTS I 203-204).

[59] He completed his commentary, the *Saddhammapakāsinī*, probably in AD 499 or 559, in any case after Buddhaghosa (Hinüber 1996: 144).

[60] The chapter is the *Sikkhāpadavibhaṅga* (Vibh 284 ff; *Chattha Sangayana* 298 ff).

[61] *kunthakipillikassa hi vadho appasāvajjo. tato mahantatarassa mahāsāvajjo. so pi appasāvajjo. tato mahantatarāya sakuṇikāya mahāsāvajjo. tato godhāya. tato sasakassa. tato migassa. tato gavayassa. tato assassa. tato hatthissa vadho mahāsāvajjo. tato pi dussīlamanussassa. tato gorūpasīlakamanussassa. tato saraṇagatassa. tato pañcasikkhāpadikassa. tato sāmaṇerassa. tato puthujjanabhikkhuno. tato sotāpannassa. tato sakadāgāmissa. tato anāgāmissa. tato khīṇāsavassa vadho atimahāsāvajjo yeva* (Vibh-a 382-383; *Chattha Sangayana* 366-7). Cf. *Milindapañha*: *bhante nāgasena, katamaṃ buddhassa bhagavato gandhāpaṇan ti? Atthi kho pana, mahārāja, tena bhagavatā sīlavibhattiyo akkhātā, yena sīlagandhena anulittā bhagavato puttā sadevakaṃ lokaṃ sīlagandhena dhūpenti sampadhūpenti, disam pi anudisam pi anuvātam pi paṭivātam pi vāyanti ativāyanti, pharitvā tiṭṭhanti. Katamā tā sīlavibhattiyo? Saraṇasīlaṃ pañcaṅgasīlaṃ aṭṭhaṅgasīlaṃ dasaṅgasīlaṃ pañcuddesapariyāpannaṃ pātimokkhasamvarasīlaṃ. idaṃ vuccati, mahārāja, bhagavato gandhāpaṇan ti* (Mil 333; *Chattha Sangayana* 317).

This is a dangerous theory, especially if experts on Abhidharma should be appointed to decide law cases for householders, as indeed happened according to the commentary to the *Vinaya*[62]. In the *Mahāvaṃsa* this theory is applied to justify homicide. When the Cola prince Eḍāra invaded northern Sri Lanka in the second century BC, King Duṭṭha-Gāmaṇī defeated him, but was remorseful as he had caused the death of thousands. Eight *arhat*s comforted him, saying that he had only killed one man and a half: only one of his enemies had taken both the refuges and the precepts, so counting as one man; another one of his enemies had only taken the refuges, so counting as half a man; the other enemies were like beasts[63]. It was perhaps advisable at that time to take all precepts, as happens in modern Theravāda societies.

CONCLUSIONS

The primary evidence shows that *upāsaka*s in mainland India were encouraged but generally not obliged to take precepts. They could take as many precepts as they wanted, a practice that some monks (Vaibhāṣika Sarvāstivādins and probably Dharmaguptakas) did not want to accept. Our modern manuals, particularly influenced by contemporary Theravāda practice, unduly stress the importance of the five precepts as a requirement for achieving *upāsaka* status. Indeed, even some ancient Theravāda texts refer to partial *upāsaka*s.

More speculative is my interpretation of the debate: why was it important at all? In other words, the monks who wished to deny

---

[62] Hinüber 1995: 25-26.

[63] *kathaṃ nu bhante assāso mama hessati yena me / akkhohiṇīmahāsenāghāto kārāpito? iti // saggamaggantarāyo ca na 'tthi te tena kammunā / diyaḍḍhamanujā ve 'ttha ghātitā manujādhipa // saraṇesu hito eko pañcasīle 'pi cāparo / micchādi hī ca dussīlā sesā pasusamā matā //* (*Mahāvaṃsa* 25.108-109, Bhagwat 1936: 148). For the historical context see Rahula 1956: 79. The *Mahāvaṃsa* was written at the end of the fifth century AD (Norman 1983: 115; Hinüber 1996: 91). The commentary to the *Mahāvaṃsa*, centuries later, does not even try to soften this merciless position (suggested dates for the *Mahāvaṃsaṭīkā* range from the 8th century to 1000 AD; see Norman 1983: 139; Hinüber 1996: 92).

upāsaka status to laypersons who had taken only the refuges and some precepts were certainly not depriving them of the refuges and of the precepts: *upāsaka* status was something else.

The term *upāsaka* is derived from the root *ās-*, 'to sit', preceded by the prefix *upa*. The etymological meaning is simply 'to sit close, at the feet of'. This meaning hardly occurs in literature. The verb *upa-ās* is already attested in the oldest layer of Sanskrit literature, in the *Ṛgveda*, in the meanings 'to do service, to venerate'.[64] Later, in the *Upaniṣads*, it does not mean 'to venerate' in the same sense as in the *Ṛgveda*. In the *Bṛhadāraṇyaka Upaniṣad*, for example, we read: *prajñety enad upāsīta.*[65] Olivelle renders this as "One should venerate it [i.e. *brahman*] as knowledge".[66] He also explains that[67]

> the verb *upa-ās* ("to venerate") in the Upaniṣads has the meaning of 'to take as,' that is, take one thing as the same as another. The term thus establishes equivalences between components of different spheres, e.g., between bodily components and elements of the cosmos. This meaning is thus very similar to that of other technical terms, such as *bandhu* and *upaniṣad* ...

Przyluski argued that the meaning 'to take as something else' or 'to know as something else' only fits with the late philosophical literature based on the *Upaniṣads*, and that the semantic development from the meaning 'to venerate' to the purely intellectual meaning 'to know' went through an intermediate stage attested both in the *Upaniṣads* and in the Buddhist meaning of the term *upāsaka*. He quoted the beginning of the *Chandogya Upaniṣad*: *om ity etad akṣaram udgītham upāsīta | om ity udgāyati*, "Oṃ – one should venerate [or know] the High Chant as this syllable, for one

---

[64] ṚV 3.6 (Müller 1890-92): *pāvakaśoce tava hi kṣayaṃ pari hotar yajñeṣu vṛktabahirṣo naraḥ / agne duva icchamānāsa āpyam upāsate draviṇaṃ dhehi tebhyaḥ //* Sāyaṇa glosses *upāsate* as *sevante*. Griffith's translation (1896: 160a): "Around thy dwelling-plave, O brightly-shining Priest are men at sacrifice whose sacred grass is trimmed. Wishing to do thee service, Agni, they are there, desirous of thy friendship: grant them store of wealth".

[65] *Bṛhadāraṇyaka Upaniṣad* 4.1 (Olivelle 1998: 102).

[66] Olivelle 1998: 103.

[67] Olivelle 1998: 514.

begins the High Chant with Oṃ"[68]. He noticed that "here the most important point is not 'to know' that *oṃ* is the High Chant, but to act accordingly. For the author of this text, the essential point is to recite properly the formulae starting with the syllable *oṃ*"[69]. From this and other examples he concluded that "[the verb] *upa-ās* implies an act and not merely an idea, an opinion"[70]. In Buddhism, Przyluski continued, the term *upāsaka* also meant 'one who pays homage' by acting, first of all by reciting the formula of the three refuges.[71]

These observations bring us closer to the meaning of *upāsaka*, but they are still very generic. One would like to know what it meant to declare oneself an *upāsaka* in common Indian parlance, and compare this statement with the specifically Buddhist one. The term *upāsaka* occurs in an ancillary text to the *Atharva Veda*, the *Kauśikasūtra*, which is classified as *gṛhyasūtra*, i.e. as a text on domestic rituals. The twelfth chapter (*adhyāya*)

> deals with *madhuparka* which is offered to a preceptor, a guest or to the gods. The feet of the preceptor or the guest are washed, he is given a seat, and then a mixture of curds, honey and clarified butter is offered to him[72].

The guest can also be a wandering ascetic (*parivrājaka*), as the Buddha was, and in this case the fit offering (*madhuparka*) is oil and rice[73]. Those who pay this act of homage, the donors, declare themselves *upāsaka*s,[74] which in this context can only mean that

---

[68] Text and translation in Olivelle 1998: 170-171.

[69] Przyluski 1932: 144 (my translation).

[70] Przyluski 1932: 146 (my translation).

[71] More difficult is to follow Przyluski in his conclusions that originally the term *upāsaka* was used for both laypersons and monks, the community being relatively undivided yet, and that only later, when the contemplative life became the monopoly of monks, it only referred to the laity. There simply is no evidence for this.

[72] Modak 1993: 68.

[73] *tailaś ca piṇḍaś ca pārivrājako madhuparkaḥ* (*Kauśikasūtra* 92.10, Bloomfield 1890: 244).

they commit themselves to revere and assist, especially materially assist, the honorable guest.

The story of Trapuṣa and Bhallika, the first Buddhist *upāsakas*, seems to be modelled upon the common Indian understanding of how a layperson should honor a holy man according to the *madhuparka* ritual: they offered a rice cake and honey to the Buddha and declared themselves *upāsakas*. In the Buddhist formula, however, one also finds the important addition "for as long as I live" (*yāvajjīvam*)". Buddhist *upāsakas* committed themselves to a life of service to Buddhist clerics. Monks needed them not just because they were frequent donors, a role accessible to anybody, but also because they were the intermediaries between the clerics and society at large, a role not accessible to most laypersons. For gifts that monks may not directly receive (e.g., gold) should be temporarily entrusted to intermediaries (*veyyāvaccakara*, *kappiyakāraka*), and these are selected from among two categories of people: servants of the monastery (*ārāmika*) and *upāsakas*[75]. *Upāsakas*, therefore, had to be trustworthy in the eyes of the monks, who knew them, and in the eyes of the donors, who often did not know them. But how could a donor and a monk trust an *upāsaka* unwilling to take precepts (e.g., not to steal)? The prestige of the monks themselves was at risk. The Kāśmīri-Vaibhāṣika Sarvāstivādins maintained that if *upāsakas* do not explicitly utter the precepts, they are all the same supposed to keep them. The masters of Gandhāra and the Sautrāntikas were faithful to the letter (and to the spirit?) of the *sūtras*: *upāsaka* status is one thing, taking the precepts is another one.

---

[74] *athopāsakāḥ prāpyopāsakāḥ smo bho iti vedayante* (*Kauśikasūtra* 92.10, Bloomfield 1890: 245). For a sometimes free Hindi translation see Singha (1942: 222): "The donor should say: 'We are your *upāsakas*'" (*hamlog āpke upāsak haiṃ yah dātā kahe*).

[75] See the rule *Nissaggiya* 10, Pāli *Vinaya* 3.221.

REFERENCES

References to Pāli texts are to the editions of the Pāli Text Society. I have added references to the Burmese edition, available to me in the useful electronic format (see below: *Chattha Sangayana*). The very few abbreviations I use are immediately recognizable by scholars and conform to the indications found in Bechert 1990.

AGOSTINI, Giulio 2002. Precepts and Upāsaka Status: Indian Views of the Buddhist Laity. Unpublished PhD thesis, University of California, Berkeley.

AHIR, D. C. 1996. *The Status of the Laity in Buddhism.* (Bibliotheca Indo-Buddhica Series, 171.) Delhi: Sri Satguru Publications.

AKANUMA, Chizen 1929. *The Comparative Catalogue of Chinese Āgamas & Pāli Nikāyas.* (Bibliotheca Indo-Buddhica, 174.) Nagoya (Reprint: Delhi: Sri Satguru Publications, 1990).

ALLON, Mark 1997. Style and Function: A Study of the Dominant Stylistic Features of the Prose Portions of Pāli Canonical Sutta Texts and their Mnemonic Function. (Studia Philologica Buddhica, Monograph Series, 12.) Tōkyō: The International Institute for Buddhist Studies.

BAPAT, P. V. & A[kira] HIRAKAWA 1970. 善見毘婆沙 *Shan-Ch'ien-P'i-P'o-Sha: A Chinese Version by Saṅghabhadra of Samantapāsādikā.* Commentary on Pali Vinaya translated into English for the first time. (Bhandarkar Oriental Series, 10.) Poona: Bhandarkar Oriental Research Institute.

BAREAU, André 1966. Le bouddhisme indien. In: André Bareau, Walter Schubring & Christoph von Fürer-Haimendorf, *Les religions de l'inde*, III: *Bouddhisme, jaïnisme, religions archaïques* (Bibliothèque Historique): 13-246.

BECHERT, Heinz 1990. *Abkürzungsverzeichnis zur buddhistischen Literatur in Indien und Südostasien.* (Sanskrit-Wörterbuch der buddhistischen Texte aus den Turfan-Funden, Beiheft 3.) Göttingen: Vandenhoeck & Ruprecht.

—— 1981. The Buddhayāna of Indonesia: a Syncretistic form of Theravāda. *Journal of the Pali Text Society* 9: 10-21.

BHATTACHARYA, Kamaleswar. 1992. Realisme ontologique et opportunisme grammatical dans l'Abhidharmadīpa et la Vibhāṣa[*sic*]prabhāvṛtti. In: Ananda W. P. Gurugé (ed.), *Tenth International Conference of the International Association of Buddhist Studies. Unesco Headquarters, Paris, France. 18-21 July 1991. Summary Report.* Paris: The Permanent Delegation of Sri Lanka to Unesco.

BHAGWAT, N. K. 1936. *Mahāvaṃso or The Great Chronicle (of Ceylon)* (Devanāgarī Pālī Text Series, 2.) Bombay: University of Bombay.

BLOOMFIELD, Maurice 1890. The Kāuçika-sūtra of the Atharva-Veda. With Extracts from the Commentaries of Dārila and Keçava. *Journal of the American Oriental Society* 14: i-lxviii, 1-424.

BONGARD-LEVIN, G. M. 1986. *New Sanskrit Fragments of the Mahāyāna Mahāparinirvāṇasūtra (Central Asian Manuscript Collection at Leningrad)* (Studia Philologica Buddhica. Occasional Paper Series, 6.) Tokyo: The International Institute for Buddhist Studies.

CHAKRAVARTI, Uma 1987. *The Social Dimensions of Early Buddhism.* Delhi: Oxford University Press.

Chattha Sangayana = Burmese edition of Pāli scriptures and commentaries, available to me in electronic version: *Chaṭṭha Saṅgāyana CD-ROM version 3.* Dhammagiri, Igatpuri: Vipassana Research Institute, 1999.

DIETZ, Siglinde 1984. *Fragmente des Dharmaskandha: Ein Abhidharma-Text in Sanskrit aus Gilgit.* Herausgegeben und bearbeited. (Abhandanlungen der Akademie der Wissenschaften in Göttingen, Philologish-Historische Klasse, Dritte Folge, Nr. 142.) Göttingen: Vandenhoeck & Ruprecht.

—— 1985. Untersuchungen zur Schulzugehörigkeit der in Ujjain liegenden Gilgit-Fragmente. In: Heinz Bechert (ed.), *Zur Schulzugehörigkeit von Werken der Hīnayāna-Literatur*, I (Symposien zur Buddhismusforschung, 3.1 / AAWG, Phil.-Hist. Klasse, dritte Folge, Nr. 149): 163-179. Göttingen: Vandenhoeck & Ruprecht.

FREIBERGER, Oliver 2000. *Der Orden in der Lehre. Zur religiösen Deutung des Saṅgha im frühen Buddhismus.* (Studies in Oriental Religions, 47.) Wiesbaden: Harrassowitz.

GETHIN, Rupert 1998. *The Foundations of Buddhism.* Oxford: Oxford Universiy Press.

GRIFFITH, Ralph T. H. (transl.) 1896. *The Rig Veda.* 2nd edition. (Reprint: New York: Quality Paperback Book Club / Motilal Banarsidass, 1992.)

HÄRTEL, Herbert 1956. Karmavācanā: Formulare für den Gebrauch in Buddhistichen Gemeindeleben aus ostturkistanischen Sanskrit-Handschriften. (Sanskrittexte aus den Turfanfunden, 3.) Berlin: Akademie Verlag.

HARVEY, Peter 2000. An Introduction to Buddhist Ethics. Foundations, Values and Issues. Cambridge: Cambridge University Press.

HINÜBER, Oskar von 1995. Buddhist law according to the Theravāda-Vinaya: a survey of theory and practice. *Journal of the International Association of Buddhist Studies* 18.1: 7-44.

HINÜBER, Oskar von 1996. *A Handbook of Pāli Literature*. (Indian Philology and South Asian Studies, 2.) Berlin: Walter de Gruyter.

HIRAKAWA Akira 平川彰 1990. *A History of Indian Buddhism From Śākyamuni to Early Mahāyāna*. Transl. and ed. by Paul Groner. Honolulu: University of Hawai'i Press. (Reprint: Delhi: Motilal Banarsidass, 1993 [Buddhist Tradition Series, 19].)

—— 1995. The Formation of the Pañca-Śīla in Early Buddhism. (Translated by Paul L. Swanson). *World Fellowship of Buddhists Review* 32.3: 8-23.

JAINI, Padmanabh S. (ed.) 1959. *Abhidharmadīpa with Vibhāṣāprabhār*[sic]*tti*: Critically edited with notes and introduction. (Tibetan Sanskrit Works Series, 4). Patna: Kashi Prasad Jayaswal Research Institute.

KOṄ-SPRUL BLO-GROS-MTHA'-YAS 1998. *Buddhist Ethics. Jamgön Kongtrul Lodrö Tayé*. Transl. and ed. by the International Translation Committee founded by the V. V. Kalu Rinpoché. Ithaca, N.Y.: Snow Lion.

LAMOTTE, Étienne 1955. Le bouddhisme des laïcs. In: Gadjin M. Nagao & Jōshō Nozawa (eds.), Studies in Indology and Buddhology. Presented in Honour of Professor Susumu Yamaguchi on the Occasion of his Sixtieth Birthday / Yamaguchi Hakushi kanreki kinen Indogaku Bukkyōgaku ronso, Yamaguchi Hakushi Kanreki Kinenkai 山口博士還暦記念。印度學佛教學論叢: 73-79. Kyōtō: Ozokan 法藏館. [Japanese transl.: Zaike Bukkyō 31 (1956): 12-17.]

—— 1958. *Histoire du bouddhisme indien: Des origines à l'ére śaka*, I-II. (Bibliothèque du *Muséon*, 43.) Louvain: Institut Orientaliste.

—— 1960. *Lo spirito del Buddhismo antico*. Tradotto da Amalia Pezzali. (Le Civiltà Asiatiche, Quaderno, 1). Venezia: Istituto per la Collaborazione Culturale.

—— 1984. The Buddha, His Teachings and His Sangha. In: Heinz Bechert & Richard Gombrich (eds.), *The World of Buddhism: Buddhist Monks and Nuns in Society and* Culture: 41-58. London: Thames and Hudson.

LA VALLÉE POUSSIN, Louis de 1923-31. *L'Abhidharmakośa de Vasubandhu. Traductions et annotations*. Tome I: Introduction, chapitre 1 et 2; tome II: Chapitre 3; tome III: Chapitre 4; tome IV: Chapitres 5 et 6; tome V: Chapitres 7, 8 et 9. (Reprint: Bruxelles: Institut Belge des Hautes Études Chinois, 1971.)

—— 1925. Notes Bouddhiques VI – Notes sur le chemin du Nirvāna. § 3: Les fidèles laics ou *Upāsakas*. *Bulletin de la classe des lettres et des sciences morales et politiques*, 5e série, 11.1: 15-34.

LOPEZ, Donald S. Jr. 2001. The Story of Buddhism: A Concise Guide to Its History and Teachings. San Francisco: HarperSanFrancisco.

MAYEDA, Egaku 1985. Japanese Studies on the Schools of the Chinese Āgamas. In: Heinz Bechert (ed.), *Zur Schulzugehörigkeit von Werken der Hīnayāna-Literatur*, I (Symposien zur Buddhismusforschung, 3,1 / Abhhandlungen der Akademie der Wissenschaften in Göttingen, Philologisch-Historische Klasse, Dritte Folge, Nr. 149): 94-103. Göttingen: Vandenhoeck & Ruprecht.

MINAYEFF, I. P. 1894. *Recherches sur le bouddhisme*. Traduit du russe par R. H. de Pompignan. (Annales du Musée Guimet. Bibliothèque d'Études, 4.) Paris: Ernest Leroux.

MODAK, B. R. 1993. The Ancillary Literature of the Atharva-Veda: A Study with Special Reference to The Pariśiṣṭas. New Delhi: Rashtriya Veda Vidya Pratishthan.

Mppś = Lamotte, Étienne, *Le traité de la grande vertu de sagesse de Nāgārjuna (Mahāprajñāpāramitāśāstra)*. Tome I: Chapitres I-XV (1949); tome II: Chapitres XVI-XXX (1949); tome III: Chapitres XXXI-XLII (1970); tome IV: Chapitres XLII (suite)-XLVIII (1976). (I-II: Bibliothèque du *Muséon* 18; III-IV: Publications de l'Institut Orientalist de Louvain 2, 12.) Louvain: Université de Louvain, Institut Orientaliste, 1949-70.

MÜLLER, Max 1890-92. Rig-Veda-Samhitā. The Sacred Hymns of the Brāhmans together with the Commentary of Sāyanākārya, I-IV. London: Henry Frowde.

MULLIN, Glenn H. & Lobsang RABGAY 1978. Lama Mipam's Commentary to Nagarjuna's Stanzas for a Novice Monk together with Tsong Khapa's Essence of the Ocean of Vinaya. Dharamsala: Library of Tibetan Works and Archives.

NAKAMURA, Hajime 1980. *Indian Buddhism: A Survey with Bibliographical Notes*. Ogura, Hirakata City: Kufs Publications.

NORMAN, Kenneth Roy 1983. Pāli Literature. Including the Canonical Literature in Prakrit and Sanskrit of All the Hīnayāna Schools of Buddhism. (A History of Indian Literature, 7.2.) Wiesbaden: Otto Harrassowitz.

OLIVELLE, Patrick 1998. *The Early Upaniṣads*. Annotated text and translation. (South Asia Research Series.) New York: Oxford University Press.

PRADHAN, P. 1975. *Abhidharmakośabhāṣyam of Vasubandhu*. (Tibetan Sanskrit Works Series, 8.) Patna: K. P. Jayaswal Research Institute.

PRZYLUSKI, Jean 1932. Bouddhisme et Upaniṣad. *Bulletin de l'École Française d'Extrême-Orient* 32.1: 141-169.

PTS = Scholarly editions of Pāli scriptures and commentaries by the Pali Text Society, Oxford.

RAHULA, Walpola 1956. History of Buddhism in Ceylon. The Anurādhapura Period, 3rd Century BC – 10th Century AC. 2nd edition. Colombo: M. D. Gunasena.

—— 1971. *Le compendium de la super-doctrine (philosophie) (Abhidharmasamuccaya) d'Asaṅga*. Traduit et annoté. (Publications de l'École Français d'Extrême-Orient, 78.) Paris: École Français d'Extrême-Orient.

SCHLINGLOFF, D. 1962-63. *Die Religionen des Buddhismus*. Bd. I: *Der Heilsweg des Mönchtums*; Bd. II: *Der Heilsweg für die Welt*. (Sammlung Göschen, 174, 770.) Berlin: Walter de Gruyter.

SHASTRI, Dwarikadas 1970-73. Abhidharmakośa & Bhāṣya of Acharya Vasubandhu with Sphuṭārthā Commentary of Ācārya Yaśomitra, I-IV. Varanasi: Bauddha Bharati.

SINGHA, Thakur Udaya Narain 1942. *Atharvavedīya-Kauśika Gṛhyasūtram*. Kauśikācāryeṇa praṇītam. Dārilakeśavayos saṃkṣiptaṭīkayā yutam. Madhurapur, Bihar: Shastra Publishing House.

T. = Junjirō Takakusu & Kaigyoku Watanabe (eds.), *大正新修大藏經 Taishō shinshū Daizokyō*, I-LV. Tōkyō 1924-29.

WANG Bangwei 王邦維 1994. Buddhist Nikāyas through ancient Chinese eyes. In: F. Bandurski. et al., *Untersuchungen zur Buddhistischen Literatur*: 165-203. Göttingen: Vandenhoeck & Ruprecht.

WARDER, Anthony K. 1980. *Indian Buddhism*. 2nd edition. Delhi: Motilal Banarsidass.

WARREN, Henry Clarke & Dharmananda KOSAMBI (eds.) 1950. *Visuddhimagga of Buddhaghosācariya* (Harvard Oriental Series, 41.) Cambridge, Mass. (Reprint: Delhi: Motilal Banarsidass, 1989.)

WELCH, Holmes 1967. *The Practice of Chinese Buddhism, 1900-1950*. (Harvard East Asian Studies, 26). Cambridge, Mass.: Harvard University Press.

WILLEMEN, Charles, Bart DESSEIN & Collet COX 1998. *Sarvāstivāda Buddhist Scholasticism*. (Handbuch der Orientalistik / Handbook of Oriental Studies, 2.11.) Leiden: Brill.

WOGIHARA, Unrai 1932-35. *Abhisamayālaṃkār'āloka Prajñāpāramitāvyākhyā (Commentary on the Aṣṭasāhasrikā-Prajñāpāramitā) by Haribhadra*. Together with the text commented on. (Toyo Bunko Publications, D.2.) Tokyo: The Toyo Bunko.

YAMAMOTO, Kosho 1973-75. *The Mahāyāna Mahāparinirvāṇa-sūtra*. A complete translation from the classical Chinese language in 3 volumes. Annotated and with full Glossary, Index, and Concordance. (The Karin Buddhological series, 5). Tokyo: The Karinbunko.

Who is Afraid of Gold and Silver? A Study of the Rule against Monetary Gifts in the Various *Vinayas*

JUO-HSÜEH BHIKKHUNĪ

1. INTRODUCTORY REMARKS

The issue of gold and silver has attracted considerable attention from scholars. It appears mainly in the broader context of the Buddhist councils, particularly the second one, the Council of Vesālī, which is said to have been occasioned by ten illicit practices.[1] Accepting gold and silver is the last in the list and is considered the most important one by scholars; some even take it to have been the only issue.[2]

[1] The ten illicit practices or ten points are enumerated in *Cullavagga* XII (Vin II 294-308). A summary of these practices can be found in Prebish 1974: 246-247 (also Lamotte 1988: 126; Mayeda 1964: 576): (1) *Siṅgiloṇakappa* – preserving salt in a horn; (2) *Dvaṅgulakappa* – taking food when the shadow is beyond two fingers wide; (3) *Gāmantarakappa* – after finishing a meal, going to another village for another meal; (4) *Āvāsakappa* – holding several *uposatha* within the same *sīmā*; (5) *Ānumatikappa* – confirming an act in an incomplete assembly, only later having it confirmed by monks who were not present; (6) *Āciṇṇakappa* – carrying out an act improperly, citing as authority its habitual performance in this way; (7) *Amathitakappa* – after eating, drinking unchurned milk which is somewhere between the states of milk and curd; (8) *Jalogiṃ* – drinking unfermented wine; (9) *Adasakaṃ nisīdanam* – using a mat without a border; (10) *Jātarūpatajatam* – accepting gold and silver. For a full discussion, see Hirakawa 1970: 699-733. Also, Mitsuo 1972: 595-602.

[2] The Mahāsāṅghika *Vinaya* does not record "the ten points", but it does mention the issue concerning gold and silver, which is the last of the ten points. This

Much has been written about the Buddhist councils and no discussions on the Council of Vesālī miss out this issue. Scholars' attention, however, has been focused on the history/historicity of the councils, or on the historical value of the *Vinaya* texts, or on the cause of the original schism between the Theravāda and Mahāsāṅghika. Study of the original schism has given rise to debates on the *Vinaya* practices of the Theravāda and Mahāsāṅghika.[3]

A review of the works published shows that very few of them are devoted solely to the study of the rule proper. An initial survey of the rules in the various *Vinaya*s and the relevant texts indicates that there is still much to work on.[4] This study does not intend to

---

has led scholars to different suggestions. Some say that it indicates laxity in the Mahāsāṅghika *Vinaya*, because the fact that it only deals with the point regarding gold and silver suggests that it does not object to the other nine. However, Bareau claims that far from indicating laxity, the fact means that only one point was involved in the Second Council. Pachow, followed by some Japanese scholars, argues that actually it was the tenth point that caused the Second Council; the other nine are a different issue and somehow they were added into the account of the Second Council (Pachow 1955: 27 ff). La Vallée Poussin (1976: 52) regards the tenth point to be "of the utmost importance", and this is the only one of which one may "believe with relative security that it brought into conflict Yaśas and the Vajjiputtakas".

[3] The Pāli *Vinaya* contains an extended discussion on the origin of the Second Council, whereas the Mahāsāṅghika merely gives an extremely brief account. This led Demiéville to the conclusion that the Mahāsāṅghika *Vinaya* "appears infinitely more lax than the Pāli Vinaya" (Pachow 1955: 244). But Prebish and Nattier (1977) disagree with Demiéville; to them the brevity of the Mahāsāṅghika account "may well be attributable to its high antiquity rather than simple laxity". They further survey the ten practices "on a point by point basis", and conclude that there is nothing less than a "complete and absolute concord" between the Pāli and Mahāsāṅghika *Vinaya*s. Hence Demiéville's conclusion, according to them, is unfounded. They adopt the account given by "a text of extreme importance for understanding the initial schism" (Prebish 1994: 60), *Śāriputraparipṛcchā-sūtra* (T1465[24]899c ff), and suggest that unwarranted *Vinaya* expansion by the future Sthaviras was responsible for the initial schism. To buttress this theory, Prebish further examines in another piece of work (1996: 258-270) the section of *śaikṣa-dharma*s of the Mahāsāṅghika-Lokottaravādin *Prātimokṣa-sūtra* and the parallel of the Pāli text. Cousins (1994: 48) is also of the opinion that "the Mahāsāṅghikas were essentially a conservative party resisting a reformist attempt to tighten discipline."

tackle the issues of the Buddhist councils or the original schism, but it attempts a more fundamental task, a study of the rule proper as it is presented in the various *Vinaya*s.

To gain an overall view, it is necessary to look into the canonical texts of the various *Vinaya* traditions. The different versions of the Maṇicūḷaka episode, including that in the *Sutta*s, and the relevant passages in the post-canonical commentaries will also be consulted. Apart from the *Bhikkhu-Vibhaṅga*s, texts elsewhere in the *Vinaya*, particularly the *Bhikkhunī-Vibhaṅga*s are significant. In the case where the information given by some *Bhikkhu-Vibhaṅga*s is fairly limited, the texts for nuns make up for the deficiency. Reference to all these texts enables one to discern the course of changes.

---

[4] To give some instances: La Vallée Poussin's work – *The Buddhist Councils* – is a thorough study and gives a relatively detailed discussion on the subject of gold and silver, which he regards as the most important issue. Nevertheless, his study basically relies on the Pāli texts. Demiéville ("A propos du concile de Vaiśālī", 1950-51) consults the *Vinaya*s preserved in the Chinese languages, but his attention centers on the Mahāsāṅghika, which is in sharp contrast with the Theravāda. He draws the conclusion that the Mahāsāṅghika *Vinaya* is extremely lax. Prebish and Nattier ("Mahāsāṃghika origins: The beginnings of Buddhist sectarianism", 1977) seem to have based their examination merely on the *Pātimokkha* texts, which, on a superficial level, produces an image of concordance. But in studying the full *Vibhaṅga*s of the various traditions and some later commentarial texts, one finds no "complete and absolute concord" but, quite on the contrary, astonishing variations. In dealing with the rule against taking gold and silver, Akira Hirakawa gives in his work (*A Study of the Vinaya-Piṭaka*, 1970) a detailed discussion in comparative perspective. Yet he has not exhausted the relevant materials. For instance, some post-canonical commentaries are not consulted, nor are the differing versions of the Maṇicūḷaka episode in the *Sutta*. Moreover, his discussion overlooks the significant variations in the concluding passage of the episode. His earlier work, *Monastic Discipline for the Buddhist Nuns* (1982), gives no discussion on the gold-and-silver issue; nor does his late work, *A Study of the Bhikkhunī Vinaya* (1998), pay attention to the historical value of the texts for nuns concerning the practice of the rule against monetary gifts. He points out that both the *Bhikṣuṇī Vinaya*s of the Sarvāstivāda and Mūlasarvāstivāda contain an additional rule prohibiting nuns from begging for gold and silver. Nevertheless, we read no further discussion beyond the remark that it is not clear why this rule, similar to the one against taking gold and silver, was added (Hirakawa 1998: 324).

2. THE ORIGIN OF THE PRESCRIPTION REGARDING GOLD AND SILVER

2.1. The immediate cause according to the *Vibhaṅga*

The rule prohibiting taking gold and silver (*jātarūparajata*) is present in all the extant *Vinaya*s, but their background stories vary. Compared with the counterparts in some Chinese *Vinaya*s, the Pāli version of the story (Vin III 236,34–237,35) appears to be relatively primitive. It has a simpler plot and indicates no development. The text recounts that the monk Upananda regularly depended on a certain family for alms food. One day when he approached his supporting family, he was told that a portion of meat was saved for him but was eventually given to their son, who was hungry at midnight and thus asked for Upananda's share of meat. The householder then hinted at offering Upananda a *kahāpaṇa*.[5]

In the beginning Upananda hesitated, saying that he, presumably as a monk, had given up the use of *kahāpaṇa*. The householder agreed to what Upananda said.[6] Nevertheless, Upananda later changed his mind and asked for that *kahāpaṇa*. This incurred the householder's criticism and led to the laying down of this rule.

According to the text, Upananda was surely aware of the proscription against accepting gold and silver. This would suggest that such a proscription predated the actual laying down of the training rule, and was probably operative as a principle common to ascetics.

Among the other *Vinaya*s, the Mahīśāsaka and Sarvāstivāda in fact give no introductory story. The Mahīśāsaka (T1421[22]37a27 ff) recounts that two monks, Nanda and Upananda[7] by name, took

---

[5] Monetary unit made of gold, silver or copper. For more discussion, see BD II 100, fn. 1.

[6] Vin III 237,22 f: *pariccatto me āvuso kahāpaṇo ti. āma bhante pariccatto ti.*

[7] The Chinese reads 難陀、跋難陀。 The Mahāsāṅghika also has two monks 難陀、優波難陀， the latter being obviously the transliteration of Upananda. I presume that 跋難陀 and 優波難陀 are two slightly different transliterations for Upananda. The Dharmaguptaka text supports my presumption in that its background story is almost the same as that of the Pāli and the monk is also 跋難陀 by name.

with their own hands gold and silver; they both took them, and caused them to be taken when they were offered. This is next to a plain statement of the rule. The Sarvāstivāda (T1435[23]51a27 ff) merely says that the group of six monks took treasure with their own hands. Note that here only one factor constitutes an offence, but the rule contains two factors: taking treasure with one's own hands, and causing it to be taken.

The story of the Mūlasarvāstivāda[8] (T1442[23]740a19 ff) starts with the Maṇicūḷaka episode (recounted in section 2.3 below). To conclude this episode, the text spells out that on the issue of gold and silver there was no formal proscription yet. Following this is a brief account similar to that of the Mahīśāsaka. It relates that the group of six monks either took with their own hands gold, silver and money or had them taken for the purpose of building houses. This led to the laying down of the rule.

Among the Chinese *Vinaya*s, the Dharmaguptaka (T1428[22] 618c22 ff) is the only tradition that shares the framework of the Upananda story found in the Pāli text. There are several variations in the Dharmaguptaka text, some of which are not insignificant. In the Pāli, the householder intended to offer him a *kahāpaṇa*, but Upananda hesitated, which implies that it was already the practice for a monk to refrain from receiving monetary gifts.

A similar but more advanced implication can be discerned from the Dharmaguptaka text. Here one reads that the son of the householder, a high official in this case, gave his mother five *māsaka* in exchange for Upananda's portion of meat, telling her to purchase meat for Upananda in the market. When Upananda learnt that the money was intended for him, he straightforwardly asked for the money, not the meat. Then the housewife gave him the money by placing it on the ground. Having taken the money, Upananda deposited it in a certain shop in the market. This account presupposes the existence of some proscription against possessing gold and silver.

[8] This refers to the *Vinaya* preserved in the Chinese canon throughout this study.

What is interesting is that in the Dharmaguptaka *Vinaya* the Upananda story is followed by the Maṇicūḷaka episode. The text says that Upananda's misconduct not only caused discussion at the royal court but also incurred criticism from other monks. Those monks reported this matter to the Blessed One and he laid down the rule. Apparently the *Vinaya* redactor(s) included this episode to account for this rule. As mentioned above, refraining from keeping gold and silver was already the practice at that time. Supported by this, Maṇicūḷaka argued at court against the use of money by Buddhist monks.

According to the story, what Upananda did was to accept a monetary gift, which was placed on the ground, and he took it with his own hands. Thus the rule was laid down in this formula: "Should any monk take with his own hands money or gold and silver, or should he have them taken, or accept what has been placed on the ground, he commits an offence of expiation involving forfeiture."[9] Nevertheless, the insertion of the Maṇicūḷaka episode here makes the text contradictory. As we shall see in the following section, the concluding remarks of this episode had undergone modification. The Buddha was made to have allowed monks to receive monetary donations for the sake of the *Saṅgha*, but nothing in the rule proper, the casuistry or the non-offence section indicates such permission.

The background story to the corresponding rule of the Mahāsāṅghika recension (T1425[22]310c5 ff) elaborates, showing steps through which the rule had been revised several times until it took its final shape. Like the Mūlasarvāstivāda, it starts with the Maṇicūḷaka episode, which concludes with the following remarks: "You should train in this way: No gold and silver can be saved. By no means do I allow gold and silver to be saved."[10]

---

[9] T1428 [22]619b23: 「若比丘自手捉錢、若金銀，若教人捉，若置地受者，尼薩耆波逸提。」

[10] T1425[22]310c29 ff: 「佛告諸比丘，汝等當如是學，不得畜金銀，我無有方便得畜金銀。」

Following the Maṇicūḷaka episode is an account of a case of misconduct by Nanda and Upananda. The text relates that they counted "money" so that they were seen by the Buddha to have dirt on their hands. This led to the prohibition against taking gold and silver in one's own hands (T1425[22]311a9). Another prohibition to close a legal loophole was caused by Udāyin. On his almsround, he was told by a housewife that he had missed a feast the day before; presumably in compensation, he was given money to exchange for food in the market. To avoid taking it with his own hands, he tied it into a corner of his robe. On seeing this, people in the market place were cynical. They teased him, asking him to untie the corner, take the money with his own hand and pay for the food. As a result, this story led to a further revision of the rule: it is not allowed to take gold and silver, even indirectly by means of one's robe.

The last case has it that a monk was quite emaciated due to illness. No one offered him suitable food[11] or medicine, and he was not allowed to take gold and silver, so there was no way to get food or medicine for his illness. The Blessed One prescribed, on account of this situation, that an ill monk may have a legitimiser (*kappiya-kāraka*)[12] keep money for him, but the monk himself was not to get greedy and attached to it. Thus the rule reaches its final shape. What is noteworthy is that the institution of legitimiser, which is a later development, is incorporated into the story and the final shape of the rule is the consequence of an exception.

[11] Suitable food for illness is considered as a sort of medicine, such as oil, honey, raw sugar or condensed juice of sugar cane (*phāṇita*), milk, ghee, fish and meat. Cf. T1425[22]316c28.

[12] *Kappiya-kāraka* literally means one who makes allowable; this normally refers to a person who serves the monastery or a lay devotee. From a historical point of view, the institution of legitimiser was a later development. It is not unusual for the Chinese *Vinaya*s to present the role of a legitimiser in their *Vibhaṅga*s. For further discussion, see below sections 3.1 and 5.

2.2. The remote cause recorded in the *Khandhaka*

By incorporating the Maṇicūḷaka episode into their background stories, the Mahāsāṅghika and Mūlasarvāstivāda have clearly shown that prior to the actual laying down of the training rule, an informal proscription against taking gold and silver was already in practice. This is hinted at in the Pāli background story and one finds confirmation from the *Khandhaka*, where the Maṇicūlaka episode appears in the context of the Second Council – the Council of Vesālī. The concluding chapter (chapter twelve) of the *Cullavagga* (Vin II 294 ff) records the illicit practices of the monks who were Vajjis of Vesālī. On the Observance day (*uposatha*), they put a bronze pot filled with water in the midst of the *Saṅgha*, and they asked for donations in the name of the *Saṅgha*: "There will be some work to be done for the *Saṅgha* with the requisite."[13] In its very early use, "requisite" (*parikkhāra*) refers to the "set of necessities" of a Buddhist monk, the four indispensable articles of a mendicant: robe, alms-bowl, seat and bed, medicine. Later the "set of necessities" was extended to comprise from eight to twelve items.[14]

The "requisite" in this context is obviously not the requisite in that special sense. In its later use, this had become a generic term for any funds donated to the *Saṅgha*, to a group of monks or nuns, or to an individual, through which things necessary for the monastic life, including for repairing or building houses, could be obtained. This is presumably why "requisite" is used generically in place of "funds for such-and-such".

In *Nissaggiya-Pācittiya* 10 for monks, the term for robe-fund is *cīvara-cetāpana*, not *parikkhāra*. It is interesting to note that "requisite" in the generic sense is found only in this context (the Council of Vesālī), but more instances can be seen in the *Vibhaṅga* for nuns. A set of five rules, *Nissaggiya-Pācittiya* 6-10 (Vin IV 250,22 ff), prohibits nuns from misusing the requisite donated for a

---

[13] Vin II 294,16 f: *bhavissati saṅghassa parikkhārena karaṇīyan ti.*

[14] Cf. *Sumaṅgala-Vilāsinī* (the commentary on the *Dīgha-Nikāya*) I 206,33 f for details.

certain purpose. There one reads of requisites for robe-cloth, rice-gruel, medicine and even a cell.

The devotees presumably put their coins into the water. No explanation is given for that. It could be due to the purifying character of water, which might make the donation more valuable. On top of that, it seems to be a device to avoid taking a monetary donation with one's own hands. Let us now have a look at the corresponding passages of the other *Khandhaka* texts.

The Dharmaguptaka (T1428[22]968c19 ff) says nothing but that monks obtained gold and silver on the Observance day and the donation was shared among them. The Mahīśāsaka (T1421[22]192a27 ff) resembles the Pāli to a great extent. Its text says that on the Observance day (the eighth, fourteenth and fifteenth) the monks often sat down at a place to which many devotees came, and placed in front of them their bowls filled with water. When people walked by, they pointed to the water, saying: "Here this is auspicious, [you] may give funds for robes, leather sandals and medicine."

The Mūlasarvāstivādin recension (T1451[24]407c26 ff) of the Council of Vesālī mentions a similar device. The text says that the monks at Vesālī converted their bowls into auspicious objects by decorating them with flowers and other ornaments, and devotees were told that it was meritorious to deposit money in such bowls.[15] But in this tradition monks had novices hold the bowls while begging door by door, which implies that the monks were aware of the prohibition against taking gold and silver with their own hands.

The Mahāsāṅghika (T1425[22]493a25 ff) gives a slightly different account. Instead of resorting to merit-making, the monks of this tradition were said to have besought the laity to make monetary donations to the *Saṅgha*. They related with bitter lamentation that when the Blessed One was still alive they had enjoyed abundant

[15] T1451[24]412a5 ff: 「十者、諸苾芻躬持好缽塗拭香華，即令求寂持以巡門，普告諸人，作如是語：『遍廣嚴城現在人物，及四[方]遠來商客之類，若有布施，若金若銀貝齒之類置缽中者，得大利益富樂無窮。』 … 何謂金寶淨法？答曰：『此諸苾芻莊飾妙缽，持以巡門，乞諸金寶貝齒之類。』」

supplies from the laity, but since his *parinibbāna* they were like orphans and were short of requisites. So people gave money of various amounts, depending on their finances, and on the Observance day the monks collected all the coins and shared them out, considering them as a fund for medicine.

Now let us come back to the Pāli text. When the monks at Vesālī made an appeal to the laity for donations, the venerable Yasa tried to dissuade them from giving coins but failed. At night those monks collected and distributed the gold coins; they offered the venerable Yasa his share but he declined it. As a consequence, they accused the venerable Yasa of endangering the devotees' faith by reviling and abusing them, and hence carried out a legal act of reconciliation (*paṭisāraṇiyakamma*) against him.

According to the first chapter of the *Cullavagga* (Vin II 17,33 ff), where proceedings of reconciliation are described, the venerable Yasa had to apologize to the lay devotees. It was on that occasion that the venerable Yasa defended himself by referring to the Maṇicūḷaka episode. The text tells that once the king's assembly, while engaged in conversation, shared the view that Buddhist monks were allowed to receive gold and silver. But in the assembly there was a village headman, Maṇicūḷaka by name; he spoke against this wrong view, basing himself on the Buddha's teachings. After so doing, Maṇicūḷaka went to the Blessed One for confirmation. The Blessed One spoke in praise of him and then restated that in no way should Buddhist monks accept or ask for gold and silver.

It was obvious that although Buddhist monks were admonished not to receive or ask for gold and silver, there was no formal proscription. Then the venerable Yasa went on to explain that it was in Rājagaha when Upananda accepted gold and silver that the Buddha laid down the rule.

In collating the relevant passages in both the *Khandhaka* and the *Bhikkhu-Vibhaṅga*, one finds that the Maṇicūḷaka episode plays a crucial role for understanding the rule concerning monetary donation. In the *Khandhaka*, this episode is used to buttress the view that the Blessed One does not allow his monks to receive gold and silver. In the *Bhikkhu-Vibhaṅga*, this episode is incorporated by some *Vinaya* traditions into the procedure through which the rule gradually takes its shape.

The Maṇicūḷaka episode appears either in the background story to the rule about gold and silver, or in the context of the Second Council. The Dharmaguptaka is the only exception: both the *Vibhaṅga* and the *Khandhaka* contain this episode. In the Mahīśāsaka, it appears in the *Khandhaka* but not the *Vibhaṅga*, and likewise in the Pāli and Sarvāstivāda. On the contrary, in the Mahāsāṅgīka and Mūlasarvāstivāda, the Maṇicūḷaka episode appears in the *Vibhaṅga* but not the *Khandhaka*.

2.3. Various versions of the Maṇicūḷaka episode: the significance of the variations

Apart from in the *Vinaya*, the Maṇicūḷaka episode also exists in the *Sutta*.[16] In the Pāli tradition, this episode can be found in the *Saṃyutta-Nikāya*,[17] and it reads nearly the same as in the *Vinaya*. There are two corresponding texts in the Chinese canon. One is *sūtra* 911 of the *Saṃyuttāgama* (T2[99]228b4 ff; SĀ 1 hereafter), and the other is *sūtra* 126 of the collection entitled *Separate Translation of the Saṃyuttāgama* (《別譯雜阿含經》 T2[100] 421b11 ff; SĀ 2 hereafter).

All these different versions of the Maṇicūḷaka episode share the same basic framework, but one crucial concept marks a fundamental divergence. For convenience of discussion, we may classify these stories into two groups. Group A includes the texts of the Pāli (*Sutta*, *Vinaya Vibhaṅga* plus *Khandhaka*), Mahīśāsaka (*Vinaya Khandhaka*), Mahāsāṅghika (*Vinaya Vibhaṅga* plus *Khandhaka*),

[16] La Vallée Poussin (1976: 54) takes Maṇicūḷaka to be a "fictitious personage" and he is "only a double of Yaśas". Besides, the Maṇicūḷaka episode in the *Sutta* is unknown to him.

[17] SN 42: *Gāmaṇisaṃyutta*, *sutta* 10; SN IV 325 ff; in the Chaṭṭhasaṅgāyana electronic edition this *sutta* is entitled *Maṇicūḷaka-suttaṃ*.

Mūlasarvāstivāda (*Vinaya Vibhaṅga*), and Sarvāstivāda (*Vinaya Khandhaka*). Group B contains only two texts, namely, that of Dharmaguptaka (*Vinaya Vibhaṅga* plus *Khandhaka*) and SĀ 1. There is some ambiguity in SĀ 2, so it will be dealt with separately.

This section does not intend to make a detailed comparison of the versions of the Maṇicūḷaka episode. The most significant divergence appears in the final passage, so I shall focus my discussion on that.

In the Pāli *Vinaya*, the Blessed One concludes this episode by making a decisive statement:

> And even though I, village headman, said that grass may be sought for by one who needs grass; wood may be sought for by one who needs wood; a wagon ... needs wagon; a man ... needs a man, I, village headman, have never said that for any reason whatever gold and silver can be accepted or sought for.[18]

The Maṇicūḷaka episode in the *Sutta* has the same concluding remarks. As it is an independent *sutta*, there is nothing earlier in the text which relates to the remarks about the necessaries for construction. Hence the remarks in the *Sutta* look somehow out of place. But not so in the *Vinaya*. We recall the previous discussion on the illicit practice of the monks at Vesālī: they asked for donations because the *Saṅgha* needed to do some work, which required "requisites". Though not explicit, this probably referred to repairing or building houses. The Mūlasarvāstivāda spelt this out: "In cases of repairing and building houses, grass, wood, wagon and manpower should be sought for, but not gold, silver or money ..."[19]

---

[18] Vin II 297,28 ff: *api cāhaṃ gāmaṇī evaṃ vadāmi: tiṇaṃ tiṇatthikena pariyesitabbaṃ dāruṃ dārutthikena pariyesitabbaṃ sakaṭaṃ sakaṭatthikena pariyesitabbaṃ puriso purisatthikena pariyesitabbo, na tv evāhaṃ gāmaṇī kenaci pariyāyena jātarūparajataṃ sāditabbaṃ pariyesitabban ti vadāmīti.*

[19] T1442[23]740a19 ff: 「沙門釋子不應受捉金銀錢等。是故諸苾芻，若爲修營房舍等事，應求草木車乘人功；然不應求金銀錢等，我不說言得有方便，令諸苾芻畜捉金等。」

Following this line of thought, one may discern a causal connection between the conclusion of the Maṇicūḷaka episode and the Vesālī episode: the Vesālī episode led to the conclusion of the Maṇicūḷaka episode. But the problem lies with the dating of these two texts. If the Maṇicūḷaka episode predates the Vesālī episode as it is presented in the Pāli *Khandhaka*, then the above-mentioned reasoning reverses cause and effect. More discussion below under 2.4.

The *Vibhaṅga* of the Mahāsāṅghika contains the Maṇicūḷaka episode in the background story. The concluding remark of the episode is the least elaborate:

> The Buddha said to the monks: "You should train in this way: No gold and silver can be saved. By no means do I allow gold and silver to be saved."[20]

Compared with the other *Vinaya*s, the Mahāsāṅghika account of the Second Council is extremely brief. The Maṇicūḷaka episode does not appear in that context, but this may well be that the episode was omitted due to the abbreviated structure of the *Khandhaka* text. At the end of the account one does read the typical remarks which conclude the Maṇicūḷaka episode:

> Bowls should be sought for by those who need bowls, robes by those who need robes and medicine by those who need medicine, [but] by no means should gold, silver and money be sought for."[21]

The discrepancy between the two quotations deserves attention. In the first place, the verb used in the former is "to save", whereas that in the latter is "to seek for", which is more aggressive. Secondly, the former is a plain prohibition against saving gold and silver, whereas the latter is more than that. The context suggests that the need for requisites had become an excuse for seeking monetary gifts. Thus the implication of the latter is clear: no exception

---

[20] See above footnote 10.

[21] T1425[22]493c8 ff: 「須缽者求缽、須衣者求衣、須藥者求藥，無有方便得求金銀及錢。」

allowed to the practice of forsaking gold and silver. The account of the Second Council starts with the story of how the monks at Vaiśālī asked for monetary donations in the name of requisites for the *Saṅgha*, and concludes by disallowing such an excuse. Hence the conclusion of the account corresponds quite well to its start.

Salient compromise of the Dharmaguptaka

The Maṇicūḷaka episode is recorded in the *Vibhaṅga* of the Dharmaguptaka *Vinaya* as part of the story introducing the rule against taking gold and silver. Having confirmed Maṇicūḷaka's view, the Blessed One said:

> Now you should understand, high official,[22] if you see Śakyan ascetics who take me as their teacher but take gold, silver, money or treasured objects, you should definitely know this is not the [right] practice of the Śakyan ascetics. I have ever said that a monk may accept [it] if he searches for wood, bamboo, grass and bark for house-building; he should not accept [it] for the sake of himself.[23]

There is some literal ambiguity here in that the text does not spell out the object of the verb "accept". Judging from the context, I take the object to be gold or silver. This is confirmed by textual evidence. The same story appears in the account of the Second Council and it leaves no room for ambiguity. The concluding remarks by the Blessed One read:

> Elder, should you see a Śakyan ascetic taking gold and silver, [you] should definitely know this is not the [right] practice of the ascetics. I have said that [one] is allowed to beg for gold and silver for [getting] bamboo, reeds, grass and wood, [but] one should not accept [or] take gold and silver [for] himself.[24]

---

[22] Maṇicūḷaka is presented here as a high official (大臣), but elsewhere in the *Khandhaka* he is just an elder (長者) with no official status.

[23] T1428[22]619b1 ff: 「大臣，汝今當知，若見沙門釋子以我爲師，而捉金銀若錢珍寶，則決定知非沙門釋子法。我有如是言，比丘若爲作屋故求材木竹草樹皮得受，不應自爲身受。」

As is shown previously, in the case where building materials or requisites are needed, the Pāli and Mahāsāṅghika insist that monks should just seek for exactly what they need, but the Dharmaguptaka relaxes with certain condition. The context suggests a distinction between "for one's own sake" and "for the sake of the *Saṅgha*", though the latter is not spelt out.

It appears that "for one's own sake" was a new concept. No such concept occurs in the text except in the concluding passage, so its presence there is probably the result of later modification.

Consistency of the SĀ 1

One point is distinctive to SĀ 1: the concept "for one's own sake" occurs throughout the text. That is to say, right at the beginning, the controversy is over whether or not a Buddhist monk should keep gold and silver for his own sake, not merely over whether or not he should keep gold and silver.

SĀ 1 tells a slightly different story. Maṇicūḷaka came to visit the Buddha, reporting to him that the king convened his ministers for a discussion. The king posited the question whether or not it was legitimate for Buddhist monks to accept and keep gold and silver for personal purposes. Some answered in the positive and some in the negative. To Maṇicūḷaka, the answer in the positive seemed suspect. So he visited the Blessed One to find out whether that was their own opinion or they had heard it from the Blessed One.

The Blessed One replied in the negative, that accepting and taking gold and silver for one's own sake was by no means allowed. Maṇicūḷaka was very much pleased. After he left with joy, the Blessed One related to the monks what had happened, then went on to prescribe:

---

[24] T1428[22]969a21 ff: 「長者，汝若見沙門釋子捉持金銀，決定應知非沙門法。我作是説，聽爲竹葦草木故求乞金銀，終不應自受取金銀。」

> From now on, monks, you [may] seek for wood when wood is needed, grass when grass is needed, a wagon when a wagon is needed, a workman when a workman is needed. Be cautious not to accept and take, for one's own sake, gold, silver, and all sorts of valuables.[25]

We notice that the concluding passage of SĀ 1 stands in between that of the Pāli and the Dharmaguptaka. On the one hand, it agrees with the Pāli on seeking for building materials when needs occur, but on the other hand, it agrees with the Dharmaguptaka on the additional phrase "for one's own sake".

For the Dharmaguptaka, such an addition makes good sense, as it allows an exception when seeking for gold and silver is not motivated by personal interest. Unlike the Dharmaguptaka, SĀ 1 does not spell out such an exception. But why is the expression "for one's own sake" here? If, like the Pāli, monks are allowed to seek for building materials only, it would mean that by no means can they seek for gold and silver instead, regardless of whether the gold and silver are for a personal or communal purpose. This is why in the Pāli the Blessed One concludes his remarks in such a decisive tone that he has never said gold and silver can be accepted or sought for for any reason whatever.

By comparison, the concluding remark of SĀ 1 appears weaker in that the additional expression "for one's own sake" implies some compromise: it would be all right if one accepts gold and silver "not for one's own sake". In opposition to "for one's own sake" is "for the sake of the *Saṅgha*". There is, therefore, no substantial difference between the Dharmaguptaka and SĀ 1. The Dharmaguptaka spells out its compromise straightforwardly, whereas the SĀ 1 beats around the bush.

[25] T99[2]228c11 ff: 「諸比丘，汝等從今日須木索木、須草索草、須車索車、須作人索作人；愼勿爲己受取金銀種種寶物。」

Ambiguous SĀ 2

The concluding remarks of SĀ 2 are fairly interesting, though at the same time ambiguous enough. Again at the end of the text, after Maṇicūḷaka has left with joy, the Blessed One relates to the monks what has happened and says to them:

> From now on, monks, when he who is in need of [treasures] wants to take [them], he should have the thought of grass-and-wood and of taking excrement, thinking "[I] would rather take excrement and the foul than take treasures.[26]

It is difficult to determine what this passage precisely means. There are at least two possible interpretations and the divergence lies in how one takes the phrase "should have the thought of grass-and-wood and of taking excrement" (當作草木及捉糞想). Without the original text, the exact reading is hard to establish. In the following, I shall attempt to interpret this phrase from different angles.

Interpretation I:

1. The phrase "should have the thought of grass-and-wood and of taking excrement" can be understood as "one should call to mind the images of grass-and-wood and of grasping excrement."

2. Why does one need to call to mind these images when he is in need of treasures? The reasons could be: (1) Treasures are used to exchange for grass and wood, which one actually needs. The image of grass-and-wood is to remind him that he should just look about for what he actually needs, not treasures; (2) Excrement is disgusting, but to an ascetic, treasures are even more disgusting. He would rather grasp the former than take the latter. Thus the image of grasping excrement serves as a reminder that he should not take treasures.

3. All in all, the images of grass-and-wood and of grasping excrement serve to debar the monk from taking treasures.

---

[26] T100[2]421c20 ff: 「汝諸比丘，從今已後，若有所須欲捉之者，當作草木及捉糞想：寧捉糞穢，不捉寶物。」

Interpretation II:

1. The phrase "should have the thought of grass-and-wood and of taking excrement" can be rendered as: one should conceive [them] as grass-and-wood and formulate the thought of grasping excrement.

2. Why does one need to conceive treasures as grass-and-wood? The reason could be: Treasures are nothing but a means of getting grass-and-wood, which are what the monk will get eventually. So, by conceiving the former as the latter, the monk will not become greedy and attached. This could be seen as a speculative strategy.

3. Why does one need to formulate the thought of grasping excrement? The reason could be: Treasures are favorable while excrement is disgusting. By formulating the thought of grasping something disgusting, the monk becomes detached; speculative strategy again. A monk should not take treasures, but if he has to when he is in need of them, there should be some protective devices in order to prevent him from getting greedy and attached. This is reminiscent of the Mūlasarvāstivādin *Vinaya*, where one reads such instruction by the Blessed One: "When a robe-fund is offered [to you] by someone, [you] may accept if you are in need of it. Having accepted, you may keep it with the thought that this belongs to that person."[27] So, a monk may receive and keep a monetary gift, but by means of some speculative strategy he ascribes ownership to a "ritual donor" (see section 3.4).

The two interpretations lead to totally different consequences. In the former case, there is no way of taking treasures while in the latter taking treasures is allowable with some protective devices.

One cannot fail to tell the purport of the Maṇicūḷaka episodes of Group A: no gold and silver, and moreover, no excuse at all. There exists inconsistency in the episodes under Group B: compromise is either spelled out or hinted at in the last statements of the final

[27] T1442[24]741b14 ff: 「若有他施衣價，欲須便受，受已即作彼人物心而持畜之。」

passage. But if one sets aside this bit, the rest of the text is no different from the episodes of Group A.

Considering the consistency of the text, one may take the first interpretation. But now that the text holds such a firm stance, it could have just concluded with a straightforward forbiddance, as do the other texts of Group A. Moreover, SĀ 2 presupposes a problem (or situation), that is, one is in need of treasures and wants to take them, then a solution (or instruction) follows. Note that what this text regards is one needs treasures, not building materials as is presented in the other texts. If it purports to prohibit from taking treasures, there seems to be no need to posit such a situation; in the end the problem is left unsolved.

The previous discussion demonstrates that some texts had undergone modification due to compromise, which was presented in a circuitous way. As we remember, the texts of Group B allow one to accept and take or even beg for monetary donation in the case where one needs building materials. This implies one does so for the sake of the *Saṅgha*. Following this line of thinking, one may take the final remarks here as a further revised version. This may have taken place at the time when compromise was already accepted. Thus SĀ 2 went a step further to straightforwardly tackle the case where one is in need of treasures. In order to solve the problem, one is allowed to take treasures (not for one's own sake) but some protective devices must be applied to help maintain mental purity. This is the second interpretation.

2.4. Comparative notes

The Maṇicūḷaka episode is the core of all the materials related to the issue of gold and silver. Our examination of the materials has shown that before it was included into the *Pātimokkha*, the issue of gold and silver was not purely a *Vinaya* matter. It came under the category of the Dhamma; that is why it appears in the *Sutta*. When Maṇicūḷaka the village headman went to see the Blessed One for confirmation, he said that he hoped to have "explained in accordance with the Dhamma" (*dhammassa vā anudhammaṃ vyākaromi*). Having given his confirmation to Maṇicūḷaka, the Blessed One further made the following comments: "If gold and silver are allowable for anyone, the five cords of sensual pleasure are allowable for him. If the five cords of sensual pleasure are allowable for anyone, you can definitely consider him to lack the character of an ascetic or of a follower of the Sakyan son."[28]

A careful examination of the episode as a whole and a collation of its various versions point us to the assumption that the concluding statement of the episode presented in the Mahāsāṅghika *Vibhaṅga* is comparatively primitive; and that the concluding statement as we have it in the other texts is a revised version. If one takes forsaking gold and silver to be the practice in the early days, it is plausible to believe that the early version was a plain admonishment. The discussion on the two different versions of the concluding remarks in the texts of the Mahāsāṅghika has shown that the one starting with "Bowls should be sought for ... robes ... medicine ..." is a later version. This version is more than a plain proscription: it purports to stop monks from seeking for monetary gifts in the name of requisites for daily living. The version starting with "Grass may be sought for … wood … wagon … man …" may have been even later. The need for building materials suggests that this was a matter of the community. Acting in the name of the *Saṅgha* would be more justified. The distinction between "for one's own sake" and "for the sake of the *Saṅgha*" prevailed at the time when Buddhist monasticism well developed. Nevertheless, one notice that the Maṇicūḷaka episodes of Group A did not give way to the consideration "for the sake of the *Saṅgha*", whereas for the episodes of Group B, the reason "for the sake of the *Saṅgha*" gave rise to compromise.

Later the modification by the *Vinaya* was adopted by the *Sutta* and thus the text was updated. Then when the concept of *Saṅgha*

---

[28] Translation from Bhikkhu Bodhi 2000: 1347.

predominated, the conduct motivated by the interest of the *Saṅgha* became legitimated. As a consequence, the practice of forsaking gold and silver relaxed. Some versions of the Maṇicūḷaka episode were further updated to reflect this compromise. These are the texts which come under Group B.

A different view is not impossible. By the time of the Second Council, the rule against taking gold and silver existed already but not in the present form. The factor for an offence could be just taking gold and silver, and this allowed the monks at Vesālī to make use of a legal loophole. Remember that the coins were thrown into the water and that they asked for donation in the name of the *Saṅgha*. What the monks at Vesālī had done demonstrated that the rule was somewhat insufficient. One of the tasks of the Second Council was to revise the rule, making it more comprehensive to forestall legal loopholes. It is, however, quite a different matter that in the course of time the practice became more and more relaxed. The text of the Dharmaguptaka and SĀ 1 are two of the instances; we shall see more in the subsequent discussion.

3. THE PRACTICE OF THE RULE: UNDERLYING CONCERN AND FURTHER DEVELOPMENT

3.1. The rule of the Pāli *Vinaya*

Nissaggiya-Pācittiya 18 in the Pāli reads:

> Should any monk take gold or silver, or have it taken [on his behalf], or accept what is placed down [for him], he commits an offence of expiation involving forfeiture.
>
> (*Yo pana bhikkhu jātarūparajataṃ uggaṇheyya vā uggaṇhāpeyya vā upanikkhittaṃ vā sādiyeyya, nissaggiyaṃ pācittiyan ti.* Vin III 237,36 ff)

According to the formulation of the rule, an offence may be committed by any of the three deeds, bodily, verbal and mental, respectively: 1) taking gold or silver; 2) having it taken; 3) accepting what is placed down [for him]. There is physical contact with the objects involved in the first case, whereas "touching" is avoided in the latter two. The second case involves verbal but not bodily deed (i.e. taking with one's own hands), while in the third case "accepting" is a mental attitude, but no offence is committed by mental deed alone. I shall come back to this point shortly.

The absence of bodily deed in the second and third cases indicates that avoiding physical contact does not nullify an offence, for the point here is possession or ownership of monetary gifts. Thus whether or not the action of "taking" leads to an offence depends on the motive of the agent. The non-offence section makes this point clear. It says that it is no offence for a monk to pick up gold or silver left lying around the monastery or a house where he is visiting if he means to keep it safe for the owner.[29] This may explain why the emphatic expression "with one's own hands" (*svahastaṃ*) present in the training rules of all the *Vinaya* traditions is absent from the Pāli and Mahīśāsaka. As opposed to "should have it taken", the first factor of the Mahīśāsaka reads "should he himself take", not "should he take with his own hands". "Should he himself take" is exactly the gloss on "should take" made by the Pāli canonical commentary, so it seems there is less emphasis on physical contact in both traditions.

The underlying concern of this rule is crystal clear. As Mōhan Wijayaratna puts it:

> [T]he Pāli Vinaya did not attribute any impurity to physical contact with money ... In Buddhism purity and impurity are not concepts which apply at the material, physical and external level. On the contrary, purity is always expounded as an internal virtue related to the mind.[30]

There is no doubt that for the Pāli tradition physical contact with gold and silver is not the main concern here; what matters is whether or not one acts with a pure mind.

---

[29] Vin III 237,7-8: *Anāpatti ajjhārāme vā ajjhāvasathe vā uggahetvā vā ugghāpetvā vā nikkhipati yassa bhavissati so harissatīti.*

[30] Wijayaratna 1990: 83-84.

The third case may take place when a lay devotee, being aware of the proscription on gold and silver, offers a monetary gift by placing it near/for a monk. If he accepts that, he commits an offence. An independent *Prātimokṣa-sūtra* belonging to the Kāśyapīya Nikāya is preserved in the Chinese canon.[31] It is interesting to note that its corresponding rule involves only one factor: "Should any monk take treasures with his own hands, he commits an offence of expiation involving forfeiture."[32] As is shown above, the expression "should take" implies, in fact, possessing or ownership. Nevertheless, if one takes it in its literal sense, one can manage to obtain monetary gifts without touching them. Hence the inclusion of the latter two factors makes the rule more comprehensive in order to close loopholes.

By "should take" the canonical commentary simply means "if he himself takes" (*ugganheyyā ti sayaṃ gaṇhāti.* Vin III 238,5). But in the post-canonical commentaries further discussions can be found. According to the *Kaṅkhāvitaraṇī*, a monk incurs a full offence only when he is taking gold and silver "for his own sake", or when he picks up gold and silver which are ownerless.[33] The *Samantāpāsadikā* further gives an exposition in detail; whether or not a monk incurs a full offence depends on two things: 1) the object he accepts; 2) his motive.

The text distinguishes three kinds of object, namely, *nissaggiya* objects (*nissaggiya-vatthū*), *dukkaṭa* objects (*dukkaṭa-vatthū*) and allowable objects (*kappiya-vatthū*). The last one refers to articles which are allowable to a monk, such as oil, ghee, honey, medicine and others. *Nissaggiya* objects are gold, silver and monetary units, which entail a full offence of *Nissaggiya-Pācittiya* when accepted. *Dukkaṭa* objects are articles such as pearls, precious stones, un-

[31] This text (T1460[24]659a7~665b9), known as *Chieh-t'o-chieh-ching* (解脱戒經), is translated by Prajñāruci in 543 AD.

[32] T1460[24]662a1:「若比丘自手取寶，尼薩耆波逸提。」

[33] <u>*Ugganheyya vā*</u> *ti attano atthāya diyyamānaṃ vā katthaci ṭhitaṃ vā nipparigga haṃ disvā sayaṃ gaṇheyya vā.* (Maskell 1956:71)

husked grain, orchards, slaves and livestock, which entail an offence of wrong-doing when accepted. *Nissaggiya* objects are by no means to be accepted, whether for one's own sake or for the sake of the *Saṅgha*, groups of monks, an individual, a shrine and so on. A monk commits a full offence only when he accepts *Nissaggiya* objects for his own sake. It is an offence of wrong-doing to accept them for other purposes. But *dukkaṭa* objects only entail an offence of wrong-doing when accepted, regardless of the purpose.[34]

The distinction of purpose, that is, for one's own sake or for the sake of others, deserves attention. This is reminiscent of our discussion on the different versions of the Maṇicūḷaka episode (see above section 2.3). In both the Dharmaguptaka *Vinaya* and SĀ 1, one finds the expression "for one's own sake"; its opposite, "for the sake of the *Saṅgha*", was implied and that gave rise to compromise. Apparently at the time of the post-canonical commentaries, relaxation took place even in the Theravāda tradition.[35] More evidence will be given below, where we shall see the motive "for the sake of the *Saṅgha*" used to justify the deed of accepting and even asking for monetary donations. One point worthy of notice is that the contents of the Chinese canonical *Vinaya*s are of the strata similar to those of the Pāli post-canonical commentaries.

In commenting on the phrase "or accept what is placed down [for him]" (*upanikkhittaṃ vā sādiyeyya*), the *Samantapāsādikā* says that when being offered a monetary gift, the monk should avoid transgressing the rule by refusing it either verbally, mentally or physically. Refusal through any of the three doors will do.[36] If a

---

[34] Sp 690,15-19: *tattha nissaggiyavatthuṃ attano va saṅghagaṇapuggalacetiyānaṃ va atthāya sampaṭicchituṃ na vaṭṭati, attano atthāya sampaṭicchato nissaggiyaṃ pācittiyaṃ hoti* (add *hoti*, adopting the *v.l.*), *sasānaṃ atthāya dukkaṭaṃ, dukkaṭavatthuṃ sabbesam pi atthāya sampaṭicchato dukkaṭam eva.*

[35] Thanissaro Bhikkhu (1994: 216) points out that this goes beyond the *Vibhaṅga*; he writes: "[T]here is no mention of this in the Vibhaṅga, so the added factor does not seem warranted. Thus whether the bhikkhu takes the money for himself or for others is not an issue here."

[36] Sp 691,2-3: *tīsu dvāresu hi yena kenaci paṭikkhittaṃ paṭikkhittam eva hoti.*

monk rejects the gift through verbal or physical action even though he has the intention to accept it, he commits no offence.[37] In the opposite case, where the monk, being of a pure mind, makes no verbal or physical refusal, but does not consent to it in his heart, [thinking]: "This is not allowable for us," the mental refusal too makes him not guilty of an offence.[38]

According to the theory of the six origins of offence (*cha āpattisamuṭṭhānā*), no offence originates from the element of thought alone.[39] Although "accepting" is a mental attitude, it is not a mere thought without any context, but is a positive mental response to something which is not allowed. In such a context, a negative response is expected and should be expressed either physically or verbally. Thus a monk is guilty of an offence not because he has done something, but on the contrary because he has failed to do what he is supposed to. This is technically called an offence originating from inaction (*akiriyā*). In an opposite case where actual action is involved, it is called an offence originating from action (*kiriyā*).

In the case where neither bodily nor verbal actions can be discerned, whether a monk is guilty of an offence depends on his mentality. If he refuses in his heart, such mental refusal alone exempts him from an offence. Nevertheless, once the message of

---

[37] Sp 690,30-33: *upanikkhittasādiyane pana idaṃ ayyassa hotū ti vutte sace pi cittena sādiyati gaṇhitukāmo hoti, kāyena vācāya vā na yidam kappatīti paṭikkhipati anāpatti.*

[38] Sp 690,33-691,2: *kāyavācāhi vā apaṭikkhipitvāpi suddhacitto hutvā na yidaṃ amhākaṃ kappatīti na sādiyati anāpatti yeva.*

[39] According to the fourth chapter of the *Parivāra* (Vin V 92,10 ff), the six origins of offences (*cha āpattisamuṭṭhānā*) are the six possible combinations of the three elements body, thought, and speech; that is to say, an offence may originate from (1) body only; (2) speech only; (3) body and speech only; (4) body and thought only; (5) speech and thought only; (6) body, speech and thought. The third chapter of the *Parivāra* (Vin V 86 ff) – *samuṭṭhāna* (origin) – classifies all training rules into six types: from one-origin rules to six-origin rules. The rule against taking gold and silver is a six-origin rule, which means an offence may arise from any of the six origins of offences listed above. Cf Shih 2000: 61, fn. 68.

refusal is conveyed through either bodily or verbal action, then one's mental state is disregarded. As is stated above, according to the *Samantapāsādikā*, a monk commits no offence so long as he clearly expresses rejection even though he actually wants to take a monetary gift. Thus an offence is entailed only when the monk accepts the gift in his heart and at the same time expresses no rejection in words or bodily action. The *Samantapāsādikā* says that he commits an offence due to inaction of the doors of speech and body.[40]

It seems inevitable that as Buddhist monasticism developed the monastics would accept monetary offerings. The *Vibhaṅga* proper has evidence of such tendency. *Nissaggiya-Pācittiya* 10 concerns appropriate behaviour of a monk towards his steward (*veyyāvacca-kara*), who handles a robe-fund offered to the monk.

A further exemption can be found in the *Mahāvagga* (VI 34,20-21; Vin I 244,32–245,7). Gold (coins) could be deposited with a certain legitimiser (*kappiya-kāraka*) so that the latter could procure for the monk provisions for a journey which were allowable: milk, curds, butter-milk, butter, ghee.[41] In this circumstance, it was all right for the monks to accept whatever was allowable. However, the Buddha stressed that in no circumstances should gold or silver be accepted or sought for:

> I prescribe, monks, that you may accept whatever is allowable through that, but I do not say that in any way gold or silver should be accepted or sought for.
>
> (*anujānāmi bhikkhave yaṃ tato kappiyaṃ taṃ sādituṃ. na tv evāham bhikkhave kenaci pariyāyena jātarūparajataṃ sāditabbaṃ pariyesitabban ti vadāmīti.* Vin I 245,4-7).

---

[40] Cf Sp 691,3 ff: *sace pana kāyavācāhi apaṭikkhipitvā cittena adhivāseti kāyavācāhi kattabbassa paṭikkhepassa akaraṇato akiriyasamuṭṭhānaṃ, kāya-dvāre ca* (emend from *kāyadvāre*, adopting the *v.l.*) *vacīdvāre ca āpattim āpajja-ti, manodvāre pana āpatti nāma n' atthi.*

[41] Vin I 244,33-34: *anujānāmi bhikkhave pañca gorase khīraṃ dadhiṃ takkaṃ navanītaṃ sappiṃ.*

The above discussion shows that a monk must have confronted difficulties in his daily life: on the one hand, he is in need of requisites, but on the other he has to observe the rule against taking gold and silver. Some reconciliation is needed for a monk to obtain what he needs and at the same time not to breach the rule.[42] Hence the institution of the role of "legitimiser", with whom the donor deposits his/her monetary gift. In order not to violate the rule, the monk has to phrase it with care; for instance, he should just point out a legitimiser but is not to give orders to either the donor or the legitimiser concerning the gift. Such verbal purity is not merely an expedient means of avoiding an offence, but also serves as a safeguard against the thought of "ownership". In other words, the money still belongs to the donor; what the monk has is the right to obtain allowable articles from that donation. He is not the "recipient" or "owner" of any monetary gift; this is the real point. Thus the underlying concern was still there even where an exception had been made.

One point deserves attention. We do not see the technical term legitimiser (*kappiya-kāraka*) in the *Vibhaṅga*. A legitimiser is someone who makes allowable behaviour originally not allowed to monks. It is rendered as 「淨人」 (lit. one who makes purity in the sense of making [things] allowable) in the Chinese *Vinaya* texts. In the rule at stake, it is the attendant of the monastery (*ārāmika*) or a lay devotee (*upāsaka*) who exchanges the forfeited gold and silver for goods allowable to monks. In *Nissaggiya-Pācittiya* 10 the person with whom the donor deposits his money is called a steward (*veyyāvaccakara*, 執事人 in Chinese), not a legitimiser (*kappiyakāraka*), but the *Samantapāsādikā* glosses the former with the latter: *veyyāvaccakaro ti kiccakaro kappiyakārako ti attho.* (Sp

[42] Olivelle (1974: 57 ff) is of the opinion that the material sources of the *Vinaya* were all related with the development and organization of monastic living. Practical needs or practical difficulties of common living were "at the root of most of the rules and their progressive amendations (sic!)". He has examined some monastic rules and customs to show the gradual transformation from the wandering to sedentary living. Cf. also Frauwallner 1956: 5 f.

672,22-23). It would seem that *veyyāvaccakara* is not a technical term, whereas *kappiyakāraka* is and comes to replace the former.

The absence of this technical term here suggests that the idea was a later institution. It is, however, interesting to notice that in the Chinese *Vinaya*s, the role of legitimiser (淨人) frequently appears to aid the management of forfeited gold and silver. Moreover, considerable development in dealing with forfeited gold and silver can be discerned in the various *Vinaya* traditions.

The institution of steward, later legitimiser, must have made life easier for individual monks and also for lay devotees who wished to be generous. According to *Nissaggiya-Pācittiya* 18, gold or silver was prohibited not only to an individual monk but also to the *Saṅgha*. Later, funds for robe-cloth and journey-provisions became exceptions to the rule.

As pointed out above in our discussion on the term "requisite", a set of five rules in the *Bhikkhunī-Vibhaṅga* demonstrates that there were funds for various purposes intended for either the *Saṅgha*, a group of nuns, or an individual nun. In those cases the funds were deposited with a shop-owner. There was, however, one exception. *Nissaggiya-Pācittiya* 10 (the rule peculiar to nuns) gives the case where the nun Thullanandā's cell had fallen apart, so she was in need of necessaries for building, including workmen. For that purpose her devotees collected a voluntary donation (*chandakaṃ*) and gave it to the nun.

Two points are worth mentioning. Firstly, in this set of five rules, the fund (or "requisite" in a technical sense) offered is called a "voluntary donation" collected by devotees. This term is not glossed in the *Vibhaṅga*, but the *Samantapāsādikā* writes:

> *A voluntary donation*: saying: "Let us do this religious duty; give whatever you can afford", [they] have created agreement and pleasure in others. This [term] is a synonym for a requisite obtained in this way.[43]

---

[43] Sp IV 918,1-3: *chandakan ti idaṃ nāma dhammakiccaṃ karissāma yaṃ sakkotha taṃ dethā ti evaṃ paresaṃ chandañ ca ruciñ ca uppādetvā gahitaparikkhārass' etaṃ adhivacanaṃ.*

When we come to discuss the Sarvāstivādin *Vibhaṅga* for nuns, we shall see a rule prohibiting nuns from begging for gold and silver, but there is no offence in her merely accepting a voluntary gift. There is no corresponding rule in the Pāli counterpart, but the above discussion has shown that accepting such a gift was also a practice in this tradition. Secondly, the case of Thullanandā tells us that a fund for building materials can be offered to an individual; thus one may accept a monetary gift "for one's own sake". We recall that the Maṇicūḷaka episodes of the Dharmaguptaka *Vinaya* and SĀ 1 warned monks against accepting a monetary gift "for one's own sake".

Nevertheless, in commenting on *Nissaggiya-Pācittiya* 10, the *Samantapāsādikā* has extended the allowance to cover all funds. Apart from funds intended for an individual monk, there are also funds for the *Saṅgha*, groups of monks and buildings in a monastery. In addition to money, jewels and other valuables, commodities, livestock and even land can also be donated as funds.[44]

In order not to transgress the rule against receiving inappropriate funds, the donor has to follow the principle of verbal purity, that is to say, one has to phrase one's donation carefully: never to mention any individual monk or the *Saṅgha* as recipients of the donation. For instance, instead of "I am giving this to the *Saṅgha*", the donor should say: "This is for the purpose of the four requisites", or "Accept whatever is allowable coming from this."[45]

By this indirect means, a monk accepts, on behalf of the *Saṅgha*, that which is allowable coming from the various types of funds, provided the donation is correctly phrased. This is the same as accepting the funds "for the sake of the *Saṅgha*". This practice would not strike us as strange when we come to the *Vibhaṅgas* of some Chinese *Vinayas*. But one should take note of this discrepancy: post-canonical *vs* canonical texts.

---

[44] For a summary of other funds, cf. Thanissaro Bhikkhu 1994: 202 ff.

[45] Thanissaro Bhikkhu 1994: 202 ff.

3.2. The Mahīśāsaka and Dharmaguptaka

The corresponding rule of the Mahīśāsaka is the least elaborate one. The rule says: "Should any monk himself take gold, silver or money, or have it taken, or have the intention of accepting it, he commits an offence of expiation involving forfeiture."[46] The canonical commentary discusses nothing but the proceedings of forfeiture.

Nevertheless, the *Vibhaṅga* for nuns provides us with some information. In all the nuns' *Vibhaṅga*s there exists a set of rules for the rightful use of donations.[47] There are, in the Mahīśāsaka tradition, four rules under the category of *Nissaggiya-Pācittiya* (N-Pāc 25-28; T1421[22]84c10 ff). In surveying these rules, one finds the following practices: for the sake of building an *uposatha* hall (for the sake of the *Saṅgha*), nuns went out to beg for funds everywhere; an individual nun accepted funds for a dwelling-place (for her own sake). The underlying concern of these rule is that a nun/nuns should not misuse the funds. This implies that accepting or even begging for funds for one's own sake or for the sake of the *Saṅgha* was not an issue at the time of the nuns' *Vibhaṅga*.

The rule of the Dharmaguptaka says:

> Should any monk take with his own hands money or gold or silver, or should he have it taken, or accept what is placed on the ground, he commits an offence of expiation involving forfeiture.[48]

---

[46] T1421[22]37b4: 「若比丘自捉金銀及錢、若使人捉、若發心受，尼薩耆波逸提。」

[47] There is no agreement among the various traditions on the numbers and formulas of these rules, the introductory stories and other matters. Chatsumarn Kabilsingh gives in her work (1984: 79 ff) full quotations of the set of these rules in the various *Vinaya* traditions, yet her attention is focused on the discrepancies among them. Cf. also Hirakawa 1998: 353-366 for a detailed discussion. A study of these rules will be presented in another piece of work; in this paper I shall just touch upon what is related to the subject in question.

[48] T1428 [22]619b23: 「若比丘自手捉錢若金銀、若教人捉、若置地受者，尼薩耆波逸提。」

Apart from the procedure of forfeiture, one reads in the casuistry no discussion on the practice of the rule.

Again, we have to turn to the nuns' text. Four rules (N-Pāc 20-23; T1428[22]729a25 ff) relate the nuns' practices in terms of monetary or non-monetary donations. Two of them (N-Pāc 20 and 23) concern funds for the *Saṅgha*. In the former (N-Pāc 20) a voluntary fund for an *uposatha* hall was given to nuns, whereas the latter (N-Pāc 23) relates that in order to build houses, nuns went out to look for funds. Another rule (N-Pāc 22) has it that an individual nun accepted a voluntary fund for building a separate cell. Apart from buildings, N-Pāc 21 concerns provisions for a visiting nun. It says that a certain nun was coming from afar, so the resident nuns begged for funds from house to house in the name of the guest nun: they needed funds for her meals.

3.3. The Sarvāstivāda

It is characteristic of the Sarvāstivāda to name the object "treasure" (*pao* 寶) and this term is glossed as gold and silver. The Chinese and Sanskrit versions of the rule read as follows:

Chinese Sarvāstivāda:

> Should any monk take with his own hands treasure, or have it taken, he commits an offence of expiation involving forfeiture.[49]

Sanskrit Sarvāstivāda:

> Should any monk take with his own hands treasure, or have it taken, or accept what is laid down [for him], he commits an offence of expiation involving forfeiture
>
> (*yaḥ punar bhikṣuḥ svahastaṃ rūpyam udgṛhṇīyād vā udgrāhayed vā nikṣiptaṃ vā sādhayen niḥsargikā pātayantikā.*)[50]

---

[49] T1435[23]51b6:「若比丘自手取寶、若使他取，尼薩耆波夜提。」

[50] Finot 1913: 498.

One reads the same term – treasure – in the Kāśyapīya *Prātimokṣa*. From the Sanskrit version of the Sarvāstivādin *Prātimokṣa-sūtra*, one learns that its Sanskrit equivalent is *rūpya*. This is reminiscent of the Pāli *Vinaya*, where the term used both in the introductory story and the canonical commentary is *rūpiya*, but in the rule itself, it is *jātarūparajata*.[51]

Although the training rule *per se* says "take with his own hands", the canonical commentary, in defining taking, distinguishes five direct and indirect manners involving physical or verbal actions. They are: (1) taking from others' hands; (2) taking by means of clothing from others' clothing; (3) taking by means of appliances from others' appliances; (4) [taking in the sense of] saying: "Place it here"; (5) [taking in the sense of] saying: "Give it to the legitimiser so-and-so".

The last two manners do not involve physical action, but verbal instruction. Although the monk does not touch the gift with his own hands, by giving orders he already assumes ownership. Clearly, for the Sarvāstivāda touching is not the main point; what matters is indeed possession of treasures. This view is buttressed by the casu-

[51] It is worth noting that here *rūpiya* is not glossed, but according to the post-canonical commentary, *rūpiya* appears to be a generic term for all precious objects, such as gold, silver, other splendid metals, mother-of-pearl, precious stones, coral and so on (Sp 689,25-26: *rajataṃ pana saṅkho silā pavāḷaṃ rajataṃ jātarūpan ti ādīsu rūpiyaṃ vuttaṃ*). In the next rule, *Nissaggiya-Pācittiya* 19, which prohibits monks from engaging in "various types of monetary exchange" (Thanissaro Bhikkhu 1994: 220), the term *rūpiya* is used throughout the whole text and is glossed as gold or coins used in business exchange (Vin III 240,1-2: *rūpiyaṃ nāma satthuvaṇṇo kahāpaṇo lohamāsako dārumāsako jatumāsako ye vohāraṃ gacchanti*). The post-canonical commentary further identifies the term with *jātarūparajata* (Sp 696,24-25: *rūpiyasaṃvohāran ti jātarūparajataparivattanaṃ*.) We read the mere term "silver" in the *Upālipariprcchā-sūtra,* a text preserved in the Chinese canon. T1466[24]904c27 ff reads: 「取銀，犯二事 … 種種賣銀行，犯二事 …」 and from the Pāli parallel we learn that the corresponding term is *rūpiya* (Stache-Rosen 1984: 55: *rūpiyaṃ paṭigaṇhanto dve āpattiyo āpajjati ... nānappakārakaṃ rūpiyasaṃvohāraṃ samāpajjanto dve āpattiyo āpajjati ...*) For more discussion on the terms in question, cf. Hirakawa 1993: 331 ff; also BD II 100 ff, where Horner calls attention to variations due to redaction.

istry following the commentary on what entails a full offence of *Naiḥsargika-Pātayantika*. The text goes on to say that it is an offence of wrong-doing should a monk take with his own hands money made of iron, copper, and other materials. The principle for decision is thus clear: the lower the value of the accepted articles, the lighter the guilt. We recall a similar discussion in the Pāli *Vinaya*, but it is in the post-canonical commentary, not the *Vibhaṅga*.

Another point deserves full attention. As this rule about gold and silver is common to both monks and nuns, it is included in the complete text of the *Bhikṣunī-Prātimokṣa* (i.e. a text containing both those rules which are common to monks and those peculiar to nuns). Nevertheless, one finds in the text of the Chinese Sarvāstivādin *Vinaya* for nuns another rule prescribing that a nun should not ask for gold and silver "for her own sake".[52]

In the non-offence section some exceptions to this rule are given. There is no offence for a nun if she begs for [gold and silver] not for her own sake but for the sake of a *stūpa* or the *Saṅgha*. What is more interesting is that there is also no offence when gold and silver are given to her without her begging for them.[53] Thus it is all right for a nun to accept a monetary gift, whether for personal or communal use, provided it is a voluntary gift. Apparently at the time when the *Bhikṣunī-Vibhaṅga* was composed, nuns were allowed to accept monetary gifts, but not to beg for them unless they did so for the sake of the monastery.

The *Vibhaṅga* for nuns is later than that for monks,[54] so is likely to contain later developments. One may thus infer that what applied to nuns at that time applied also to monks in that the gold-and-silver issue is gender-free. Such allowance is not recorded in the

---

[52] The rule (N-Pāt 24) says: "Should a nun, for her own sake, beg for gold and silver, she commits an offence of expiation with forfeiture." (T1435[23]315a29 ff: 「若比丘尼自爲身乞金銀者，尼薩耆波夜提。」

[53] T1435[23]315b3 ff: 「若比丘尼自爲乞金銀，得尼薩耆波夜提。隨乞隨得爾所，尼薩耆波夜提。若爲佛圖乞、若爲僧乞、若不乞自與，不犯。」

[54] Cf. Shih 2000: 22 ff for more discussion.

Vinaya for monks, but this probably means only that the text was not updated. Thus prior to the composition/compilation of the *Vinaya* for nuns, accepting monetary gifts, or even begging for them, for the sake of the community must have been current practice among the Sarvāstivādin monastics, both monks and nuns.

Moreover, in the set of three rules (*Naiḥsargika-Pātayantika* 26-28; T1435[23]315c7 ff) concerning the rightful use of funds, the practice seems to relax a step further. Three rules relate that nuns begged for funds in order to build houses for the *Saṅgha*, a group of nuns and for one's own sake, respectively. Here the distinction between "for one's own sake" and "for the sake of the *Saṅgha*" is disregarded.

Among the Chinese *Vinayas*, the Mūlasarvāstivāda and the Sarvāstivāda are the only two traditions that contain a rule of this sort. The rule (*Naiḥsargika-Pāyantika* 24) of the Mūlasarvāstivāda says that a nun commits an offence of expiation with forfeiture should she beg for gold and silver,[55] but no exemption from an offence is given in the text. This does not necessarily mean that the Sarvāstivāda is more relaxed. On the contrary, by the time the rule forbidding nuns to beg for gold and silver was laid down, accepting a monetary gift must have been allowed. It would otherwise not appear in the non-offence section as an exception to the rule.

[55] T1443[23]964c6: 「若復苾芻尼乞求金銀者，泥薩祇波逸底迦。」 The background story relates that a certain goldsmith was newly married, and put his wife to a test to see whether she would be competent in running the household. He placed a gold ring near his wife and went out. Then the nun Thullanandā on her alms-round came into the goldsmith's house for food. When the wife of the goldsmith was going to offer her some noodles, the nun Thullanandā saw the gold ring and said to her: "It would be inauspicious if you offered me noodles first, [you] may give me gold." Hearing this, the wife of the goldsmith fell silent. The nun Thullanandā said: "Give me gold", took the gold ring and left. The goldsmith got back home and learnt what had happened. He went to seek the nun out and said to her: "Why did you steal my gold?" The nun Thullanandā replied: "How dare I take it if it is not given [to me]?" Then the goldsmith asked the nun Thullanandā to return the gold ring to him, but she put the gold ring into her mouth. So the goldsmith struck her, forcing her mouth open to get back the gold ring. This incurred criticism from the laity and led to the laying down of the rule.

The Mūlasarvāstivāda merely prohibits a nun from begging for gold or silver; it does not say that she may accept a voluntary gift. This is presumably because accepting monetary gifts was already in practice by the time the rule for nuns was laid down. The rule against taking gold and silver contains only two factors for an offence: taking with one's own hand or having them taken. With the aid of a legitimiser (or donor), one is able to avoid violating the rule. Moreover, as we shall see in the following section, the Blessed One is said to have made exceptions over and over again in response to situations. In the end, one may accept monetary gifts, regardless of whether a ritual donor is available or not.

3.4. The Mūlasarvāstivāda

The rules of the Chinese and Sanskrit Mūlasarvāstivādin texts respectively read:

Chinese Mūlasarvāstivāda:

> Should any monk take with his own hands gold, silver, money and others, or have them taken, he commits an offence of expiation involving forfeiture.[56]

The Sanskrit Mūlasarvāstivāda has the same formulation :

> Should any monk take with his own hands gold or silver, or have it taken, he commits an offence of expiation involving forfeiture.
>
> (*yaḥ punar bhikṣuḥ svahastaṃ jātarūparajataṃ udgṛhṇīyād vā udgrāhanasat vā naisargikā pāyantikā*)[57]

The Mūlasarvāstivādin *Vinaya* lays stress on the phrase "have them taken", distinguishing eighteen possible modes of verbal instruction which entail an offence. The factors for a full offence include not only "taking" money, gold and silver, but also "touching" gems, precious stones, lapis lazuli and others. This would suggest that the

[56] T1442[23]740c5: 「若復苾芻自手捉金銀錢等、若教他捉，泥薩祇波逸底迦。」

[57] Banerjee 1954: 18.

Mūlasarvāstivāda takes both "ownership" and "physical contact" into consideration. The gravity of guilt depends on the value of the articles taken; for example, it is a full offence if one takes money which is in use in one's own country, but only an offence of wrong-doing to take money which is not the currency in one's own country. There is no offence in taking iron, copper or other metals.

Actual vs ritual donor

The casuistry first accounts for the exception to the proscription on accepting gold and silver. The story tells that there was in Campa a certain elder who was wealthy and generous. He built a dwelling for the Blessed One and the *Saṅgha*. Once some monks who had spent the rains in this dwelling asked for robes after the rain retreat. The elder needed more time to prepare hemp robes of good quality, but those monks, with no care about quality, did not want to wait. Then the elder suggested that he offer robe-funds as an alternative, yet accepting gold and silver was not allowed. As a consequence, those monks left obtaining nothing.

This led to the first exception to this rule concerning gold-and-silver. The Blessed One was said to have instructed thus: "When a robe-fund is offered [to you] by someone, [it] may be accepted if you are in need of it. Having accepted it, you may keep it with the thought that this belongs to that person."[58] This can be regarded as a sort of strategy for safeguarding against the consciousness of "ownership". Nevertheless, a monk is not to take a robe-fund with his own hands, but should look for an attendant of the monastery or a lay devotee to serve as his "donor" by keeping the robe-fund on his behalf. Thus the Mūlasarvāstivāda distinguishes two types of donor: one who is the real or actual donor, whereas the one who is appointed to handle money for monks is a donor in the ritual sense – a "ritual donor". It is, however, not crystal clear how a "ritual donor" differs from a legitimiser.

[58] See above footnote 27.

One notices that at this point in time the *Vibhaṅga* was well aware of the first factor constituting an offence, so that a monk was advised not to take a robe-fund with his own hands. Nevertheless, the *Prātimokṣa* commentary[59] preserved in the Chinese *Vinaya* literature goes a step further. The text says that when obtaining gold etc. a monk is not guilty of an offence to take it so long as he bears in mind that the gift belongs to the donor.[60]

Another point in the canonical commentary is that once such a "ritual donor" is appointed, his relation with the monk lasts forever, even though the latter goes elsewhere. Without further exposition, it is not clear what this persistent relation between them may affect. Fortunately the above-mentioned post-canonical commentary has made this point clear: in the case where a monk and his "ritual donor" are far separated, when the monk obtains a monetary gift he may receive and keep it to himself but must conceive it as belonging to his donor. So long as the donor is still alive, their relation continues, and there is no offence for the monk, no matter how long the monk keeps the money.[61] In brief, distance makes no difference.

In the *Vibhaṅga* further exceptions have been made. The text goes on to relate that a certain monk had no "ritual donor", so when a monetary gift was offered to him, he was in doubt and did not dare to accept it. Hearing the monk's report, the Blessed One was said to have given these instructions: "[You] should accept it. Having accepted it, take it to the presence of a certain monk and say to him: 'Venerable sir, [please] bear this in mind. I, the monk so-and-so, have got this article which is not allowable; I will use it to exchange for articles which are allowable.' Having uttered this thrice, [you] may make use of it at will without any doubt."[62]

---

[59] The *Prātimokṣa* commentary is entitled *Kên-pên sa-p'o-to-pu lü-shê* (根本薩婆多部律攝： T1458[24]525a1-617a26), translated into Chinese by I-Ching around 700 AD.

[60] T1458[24]560c16 「苾芻若得金等物時，作施主物想，執捉無犯。」

[61] T1458[24]560c16 f: 「縱相去遠得不淨物，遙作施主物心持之，乃至施主命存以來，並皆無犯。」

Though not indicated in the text, violation of the first factor was implied in the context. Since the monk had no donor, he had to take a monetary gift with his own hands. The post-canonical commentary again does not hesitate to spell this out. In commenting on this case, it says that having uttered thrice his intention of undertaking an exchange, the monk should himself take up or have another take up the monetary gift.[63] Thus both the first and the second factors for an offence are violated. Another case is given, in which a monk obtains gold, silver and others on his journey. The commentary says that for the sake of provisions, he should accept and take them with him. Alternatively he may have them taken by a legitimiser or novice.[64] Here a legitimiser does not seem to play an absolute role. Another point concerns novices. The commentary explains that for a novice it is prohibited only to keep gold or silver for his own sake but not to take it.[65]

The *Vibhaṅga* goes on to relate another exception, but one valid only at a time of emergency. When a monastery suffers from robbers, all gold, silver and other treasures belonging to the *Saṅgha* or *stūpa* should be moved to a secure place. This should be done by the attendants of the monastery or lay devotees, otherwise by novices. Should no one be available, then the monks themselves may undertake this task. It is obvious that the *Saṅgha* does possess and own articles which were originally prohibited. The institution of "inexhaustible property" (*wu-chin-wu* 無盡物) (see below section 4.5) has best demonstrated this point.

---

[62] T1442[23]741b25 ff: 「佛言：應受。受已持物對一苾芻作如是說：『具壽存念，我苾芻某甲得此不淨物，我當持此不淨之物，換取淨財。』如是三說，隨情受用，勿致疑心。」

[63] T1458[24]560c18 ff: 「若無施主可得者，應持金銀等物，對一苾芻隨住隨立，作如是說：『具壽存念，我苾芻某甲得此不淨財，當持此不淨財換取淨財。』如是再三，應自持舉、或令人舉。」

[64] T1458[24]560c22 ff: 「若苾芻於行路中得金銀等，爲道糧故，應自持去、或令淨人等及求寂持去。」

[65] T1458[24]560c24 f: 「應知求寂於金銀等，但制自畜，不遮執捉。」

Since the text for monks is already full of innovations, what we read in the text for nuns does not strike us as strange. In the latter there are a set of six rules (*Naiḥsargika-Pāyantika* 25-30; T1443 [23]964c9 ff) against misuse of funds. Only one rule (N-Pāy 28) is about a fund for repairing a house; three of them (N-Pāy 25-27) are about funds for robe-cloth, dying or sewing robes and bedding. In these four cases, funds are donated voluntarily. Two rules (N-Pāy 29-30) recount that the nun Thullanandā begged for offerings (monetary and non-monetary) for the *Saṅgha* and for a group of guest nuns.

3.5. The Mahāsāṅghika

Now we come to the tradition of the Mahāsāṅghika. Its training rule reads:

> Should any monk take with his own hands unworked [gold or] similar valuables, or have it taken, getting greedy and attached, he commits an offence of expiation involving forfeiture.[66]

By contrast, the Sanskrit *Prātimokṣa-sūtra* of both the Mahāsāṅghika and the Mahāsāṅghika-Lokottaravādin has a more elaborate formulation:

> Should any monk take with his own hands gold or silver, or have it taken, or even say "lay it down here" or accept what is being placed down [for him], he commits an offence of expiation involving forfeiture.
>
> Mahā: *yo puna bhikṣuḥ svahastaṃ jātarūparajataṃ udgṛhṇeya vā udgṛhṇāyeya* (sic!) *antamasato iha nikṣipehīti vā vadeya, upanikṣiptaṃ vā sādiyeya, niḥssargika* (sic!) *pācattikaṃ*. (Pachow 1956: 18)
>
> Mahā-L: *yo puna bhikṣuḥ svahastaṃ jātarūparajataṃ udgṛhṇeya vā udgṛhṇāpeya vā antamasato iha nikṣipehīti vā vadeya, upanikṣiptaṃ vā sādiyeya, nissargikaṃ pācattikaṃ*. (Tatia 1975: 16)

---

[66] T1425[22]311b15: 「若比丘自手捉生色似色、若使人捉舉，貪著者，尼薩耆波夜提。」

The forbidden object in the various *Vinayas*, except for the Sarvāstivāda, is expressed by the term *jātarūparajataṃ*. It is rendered as "gold, silver, money and others 「金銀錢等」" in the Chinese Mūlasarvāstivāda. We read the similar rendering: gold, silver, money in the Mahīśāsaka and Dharmaguptaka, so presumably it is the same term *jātarūparajataṃ* in their original texts. In contrast to *suvaṇṇa*, which refers to worked gold, *jātarūpa* refers to gold in its natural state, i.e. unworked gold. In the Pāli, *jātarūpa* is glossed as "the colour of the teacher" (*satthuvaṇṇo*) and *rajata* as coins made not only of silver but also of copper, wood, or lac, or whatever is used for exchange in business.[67]

The *Samantapāsādikā* gives a further explanation. It says that *jātarūpa* refers to gold and the colour of gold is similar to that of the Blessed One, that is why it is called the colour of the teacher. But the text goes on to note that any splendid metals which have the colour of the teacher can be called *jātarūpa*. On the other hand, the denotation of *rajata* is further extended to include "bones, pieces of hide, fruit, seeds of trees used as currency, whether they have been stamped with a figure or not" (Thanissaro Bhikkhu 1994: 215).[68]

In the Chinese Mahāsāṅghika, we have these two peculiar terms 「生色」 (literally: "natural/genuine colour") and 「似色」 (literally: "resembling colour"). In collating with the Sanskrit *Prātimokṣa-sūtra* of the Mahāsāṅghika (Pachow 1956: 18), one finds that their corresponding term is *jātarūparajata*. The canonical commentary glosses 「生色」 as gold and 「似色」 as silver. Both gold and silver refer to "money and other articles used in the

[67] Vin III 238,2: *jātarūpaṃ nāma satthuvaṇṇo vuccati. rajataṃ nāma kahāpaṇo lohamāsako dārumāsako jatumāsako ye vohāraṃ gacchanti.*

[68] Sp 689,21–690,7: *jātarūparajatan ti ettha jātarūpan ti suvaṇṇassa nāmaṃ, taṃ pana yasmā tathāgatassa vaṇṇasadisaṃ hoti tasmā sattuvaṇṇo vuccatīti padabhājane vuttaṃ, tass' attho yo satthuvaṇṇo lohaviseso idaṃ jātarūpaṃ nāmā 'ti. rajataṃ pana ... idha pana yaṃ kiñci vohāragamanīyaṃ kahāpaṇādi adhippetaṃ ... antamaso aṭṭhimayo pi cammamayo pi rukkhaphalabījamayo pi samuṭṭāpitarūpo pi asamuṭṭāpitarūpo pi sabbo saṅgahīto.* Cf. BD II 102 f; Hirakawa 1993: 343 f.

market".[69] The commentary tells us what these terms refer to but not their meanings.[70] In the following I shall attempt some interpretations.

The term 「生色」 is the Chinese rendering in its literal sense for *jātarūpa*, for *jāta* means born or produced and that is what the Chinese word 「生」 means. Apart from this, *jāta* also means natural, true, or good, likewise, in Chinese 「生」 also means bright and lively. Thus 「生色」 can be taken to mean natural or genuine colour, which often has the implication of excellence. This is reminiscent of the Pāli canonical and post-canonical commentaries, in which *jātarūpa* is glossed as "the colour of the teacher" (*satthuvaṇṇo*). The next term 「似色」 (resembling colour), however, is not a literal translation for *rajata*. Although *rajata* is glossed as silver, it actually refers to coins made of all materials except gold. The "colour" in "resembling colour" would seem to refer to the first term (i.e. natural/genuine colour) and "resembling colour" refers to other coins, which, similar to gold, are also used as monetary exchange in business. That is why they are said to be resembling the natural/genuine colour, i.e. gold.

Alternatively, a simpler interpretation is possible. In the case of metals, the Chinese character 「生」 means "unworked" as opposed to "worked"; 「色」 has the meaning of "class, kind ...". Thus 「生色」 means the unworked class [of gold], and 「似色」 means the similar class: the class [of valuables] similar to 「生色」 in terms of their value and use as currency in the market.

---

69 T1425[22]311b21 f: 「生色者是金也；似色者是銀。生色似色者，錢等市用物。」

70 In an English translation of the Chinese Mahāsāṅghika *Bhikṣuṇī Vinaya* (Hirakawa 1982: 194), we read "gold and silver" for 「生色、似色」. Another work by Hirakawa (1993: 362 ff) gives a detailed discussion on the rule against monetary gifts but offers no explanation for the Chinese renderings for *jātarūparajata*. The English translation of the rule by Kabilsingh (1991: 52) has "the like thing and valuable things" for 「生色、似色」. It remains unclear how to understand these two peculiar terms.

As shown previously, the rule concerning gold and silver has undergone several revisions. The initial proscription was against keeping gold and silver; then the first revision included in the rule the emphatic expression "with one's own hands". This is followed by another addition: neither was it allowed to tie gold and silver into one's robe. In collating the various formulations of the rules, one finds that the Mahāsāṅghika is unique in that the rule ends with psychological elements – getting greedy and attached. By contrast, the rule of the Sanskrit Mahāsāṅghika and the Mahāsāṅghika-Lokottaravādin elaborate a bit more but is basically of the same formulation as that of the other *Vinaya*s.

The *Vibhaṅga* contains a lengthy passage (T1425[22]311c5 ff) on how monks, when receiving monetary gifts, should endeavour to avoid physical contact with them. The following is a summary of some interesting and important points. In the first place, monks obviously own money other than robe-funds. This passage starts with the statement that whenever a monk obtains "money" (*ch'ien* 錢) or when a robe-fund is offered to him at the end of the rains, he is not to take it with his own hands. Instead, he should have a legitimiser take charge of it.[71] In another case, one reads that a monk has lots of gold, silver and money, in that he takes charge of the business for the *Saṅgha* and the Buddha-[shrine]. Later in the passage, more instances are given in the context of verdict-making. Each account starts with a conditional presupposition: that if a monk has lots of gold, silver and money ... There is no clear indication of whether the monk is keeping monetary gifts for the *Saṅgha* due to his administrative position or they are his personal property. The final case has it that a monk is ill and obtains funds for medicine. Since he is ill, he is allowed to put the money under the bedding. When in the dark he searches for it to make sure it is still there, he touches it. In this situation, he is not guilty of an

---

[71] T1425[22]311c5 f: 「比丘凡得錢，及安居訖得衣直時，不得自手取，當使淨人知。」

offence. This case seems to imply that keeping money for one's own sake is an exceptional case.

Secondly, the role of legitimiser is not necessarily taken by a lay devotee, or by an adult. He can be a child at a fairly tender age, presumably a small novice.[72] It is interesting to note that the legitimiser is not expected to be mature enough to be responsible for taking charge of or making financial arrangements for the monks. He serves, however, as an intermediary between the monk and his funds. In other words, his main function is to help him avoid touching money.

Thirdly, much stress is placed on physical purity. Apart from gold and silver used as money in trading, the text elaborates on how monks should avoid touching anything made of gold and silver. There may be cases where the devotees get newly-made gold/silver dishes, foot-stools or other utensils, and monks are invited to initiate the use of them. In order not to have direct contact with them, the monks should have the devotees cover them with grass, leaves, or blankets. The same principle applies in the monastery: there may be gold/silver incense burners, Buddha statues ... and even anything with a gold/silver coating. In the cases where they may have to be moved, monks are not to take them; they should have the legitimisers do so instead.

Finally, let us have a look at the text for nuns. It contains three rules (*Niḥsargika-Pācattika* 11-13; T1425[22]524b9 ff) against misuse of funds. The nun concerned was Thullanandā. In one case she begged for bedding for the *Saṅgha* and obtained a fund for that instead. In another case she obtained a voluntary fund for robe-cloth and alms-bowl. The final rule recounts that she induced the devotees to offer a meal to the *Saṅgha* and was given a fund for that. Note that there is no mention of building houses, but of basic requisites for monastic life. There are three rules, also *Niḥsargika-*

---

[72] The text gives no indication who they are, but Akira Hirakawa (1970: 354) regards them as novices. This makes good sense and explains why a legitimiser at a tender age has such close contact with a monk as to travel with him.

Pācattika 11-13, in the *Bhikṣuṇī Vinaya* of the Mahāsāṅghika-Lokottaravādin (Roth 1970: 168-172). In collating these two texts, one finds that they largely agree with each other.

3.6. Comparative notes

Generally speaking, there exists a rule against taking gold and silver in the extant *Vinayas* of all traditions. But the formulation of the rule varies, mainly in two aspects. Firstly, there are variations in the objects of prohibition: gold and silver in the Pāli *Vinaya*, yet in some of the Chinese *Vinayas*, the Dharmaguptaka, Mahīśāsaka and Mūlasarvāstivāda, money is spelt out and added to gold and silver. The Sarvāstivāda has merely the one word "treasures"; the Mahāsāṅghika has the peculiar expressions "natural/genuine colour and resembling colour" in a literal sense (or, the unworked [gold or] similar valuables).

Regardless of the terms used in the rule proper, the canonical commentaries of all the Chinese *Vinayas* make it clear that the objects concerned include not only gold, silver and various sorts of precious stones, but also monetary units made of different materials.

Another variation lies in the factors constituting an offence of *Nissaggiya-Pācittiya*. According to the various versions of this training rule, each of the following acts makes a monk guilty of a full offence:

A. Taking (with his own hands) gold and silver.
B. Causing gold and silver to be taken.
C. Saying: "Put it here."
D. Accepting what is being placed down for him, or, saying: "Give it to legitimiser so-and-so."[73]

[73] T1435[23]51b10: 「若言與是淨人。」 This is peculiar to the Sarvāstivādin *Vinaya*.

C and D make no fundamental difference, for they either imply or indicate acceptance of gold and silver. The following chart gives us a clear view of the variations.

	Pāli	Mahī	Dha	C Sar	Skt Sar	C Mūla	Skt Mū	C Mahā	Skt Mahā Mahā-L	Kāś
P	ABD	ABD	ABD	AB	ABD	AB	AB	AB	ABCD	A
Cc				CD		C				

P = Pātimokkha/Prātimokṣa; Cc = Canonical commentary; Mahī = Mahīśāsaka; Dha = Dharmaguptaka; C Sar = Chinese Sarvāstivāda; Skt Sar = Sanskrit Sarvāstivāda; C Mūla = Chinese Mūlasarvāstivāda; Skt Mū = Sanskrit Mūlasarvāstivāda; C Mahā = Chinese Mahāsāṅghika; Skt Mahā = Sanskrit Mahāsāṅghika; Mahā-L = Mahāsāṅghika-Lokottaravādin; Kāś = Kāśyapīya

The Kāśyapīya *Prātimokṣa* stands at one extreme,[74] the Sanskrit Mahāsāṅghika and Mahāsāṅghika-Lokottaravādin at the other. But as C and D are not much different, the Pāli, Mahīśāsaka, Dharmaguptaka, and Sanskrit Sarvāstivāda can be included into the latter group. Thus in the respect of *Pātimokkha/Prātimokṣa*, only three *Vinaya* traditions, i.e. Chinese Sarvāstivāda and Mahāsāṅghika, Chinese and Sanskrit Mūlasarvāstivāda, stand in between these two extremes. On the other hand, it is interesting to find that the Sanskrit/Prakrit texts are more elaborate than the Chinese except for the Mūlasarvāstivāda. Although the *Prātimokṣa* texts of the Sarvāstivāda and Mūlasarvāstivāda involve only two factors, their canonical commentary makes up the insufficiency. A and B must be fundamental in that they appears in every version of the *Pātimokkha/Prātimokṣa* rule proper except the Kāśyapīya.

Regarding the practice of the rule against taking gold and silver, our discussion has demonstrated that considerable variations exist in the various traditions as presented in their texts. Among the Chinese *Vinaya*s, the Mahīśāsaka, Dharmaguptaka and Sarvāstivāda

[74] See footnote 32 above.

offer almost no information on the practice of the rule. In this respect, the *Vibhaṅga* for nuns helps a lot. A survey of the relevant rules of the various traditions shows that at the time of the *Vibhaṅga* for nuns, accepting or begging for monetary funds for various purposes must have been a common practice, and whether they did so for the sake of the *Saṅgha*, a group of nuns or their own individual sakes was not an issue. Likewise, the Pāli post-canonical commentaries have gone beyond the *Vibhaṅga*, but this tradition endeavours not to transgress the rule by preserving verbal purity.

The *Vibhaṅga*s of the Mahāsāṅghika and Mūlasarvāstivāda show a step-by-step relaxation of the rule. The Mūlasarvāstivāda had innovated so much as to totally go against the rule, and all innovations were ascribed to the Blessed One himself. Monks of the Mahāsāṅghika owned monetary gifts, but that could be for the sake of the *Saṅgha*. By contrast to the Pāli, physical instead of verbal purity was the essential concern. Nevertheless, verbal purity was not completely unknown to the Mahāsāṅghika. In the next rule, *Naiḥsargika-Pācattika* 19 (T1425[22]312c3 ff), prohibiting monks from engaging in various types of transactions, the offence of buying or selling could be nullified by careful phraseology.

4. THE PROCEEDINGS OF FORFEITURE

This section looks into the issue of forfeiture and its administrative variations as shown in the various *Vinaya*s. The Mūlasarvāstivāda is the only *Vinaya* to pay no attention to the procedure for forfeiture; the canonical commentary is primarily concerned with how exceptions were made when need occurred. The redactor(s) had relaxed the rule to the extent that so long as mental purity was maintained, the two factors for an offence could be disregarded. As a consequence, it was hard to transgress the rule, and this presumably explains the absence of a procedure for forfeiture in this *Vinaya*.

4.1. Two alternatives in the Pāli *Vibhaṅga*: exchange or abandonment

When gold or silver is improperly or illegally obtained, it has to be forfeited. The canonical commentary says: "It has to be forfeited in the midst of the *Saṅgha*" (*nissaggiyaṃ hoti saṅghamajjhe nissajjitabbaṃ*, Vin III 238,8 f). In general, the rules in the category of *Nissaggiya-Pācittiya* have two characteristics: each rule involves forfeiture of the articles procured illegally, and the offender against the rule should forfeit such an article to either the *Saṅgha* or a group (*gaṇa*), or even to an individual (*puggala*). As a matter of fact, to whom it may be forfeited does not really matter, for the forfeiture is generally symbolic: the forfeited articles are eventually returned to the offending monk.

Three training rules[75] are exceptions, that is to say, the forfeiture in these rules is not merely symbolic. In the case of the rule under discussion, gold or silver is not to be possessed by anyone whatever, so the text does not say "forfeited to the *Saṅgha* or a group, or an individual", but says "in the midst of the *Saṅgha*". According to the Pāli canonical commentary, there is an alternative way of dealing with the thing forfeited. In the first place, if an attendant of the monastery (*ārāmika*) or a lay devotee (*upāsaka*) happens to come, it is an appropriate occasion for the forfeited gold and silver to be made use of in an allowable manner. He or she may exchange what is forfeited for requisites which are allowable to monks. On such an occasion, however, a principle of verbal purity is operative. The *Saṅgha* is not to give a direct instruction what should be done. Instead, this is what should be said: "Sir, you should know about this" (*āvuso imaṃ jānāhīti*, Vin III 238,17). This presumably means: "You should know about the proper way of dealing with this." It would seem that this has become a protocol, for in this

---

[75] They are the rules against accepting gold and silver (*Nissaggiya-Pācittiya* 18), undertaking monetary exchange (*Nissaggiya-Pācittiya* 19), and asking for a new alms bowl when the old one has less than five repairs (*Nissaggiya-Pācittiya* 20).

situation the lay devotee knows that monks and nuns are not allowed to own or use gold and silver, so the monks need give no further instructions.

Secondly, when the lay devotees ask what they should bring, the monks are not to tell them straightforwardly to bring such-and-such. They should just name the items wanted. In the post-canonical commentary this example is given: "Lay devotee, ghee or oil is fine with the wanderers."[76] Thirdly, there is also a restriction on the articles to be acquired by the exchange: only oil, ghee, honey or molasses are allowable. When the lay devotee has undertaken an exchange and brought what is allowable, all except the offender against this rule may partake.[77]

The *Samantapāsādikā* explains that what has been forfeited is just gold and silver and not the articles coming from an exchange. In order to show that the articles are to be shared by all members of the *Saṅgha* except for the offender, the text says "in the midst of the *Saṅgha*".[78] In the instruction on the procedure for forfeiture, the text goes on to relate that the offender should approach the *Saṅgha* and say: "I, honoured sirs, accepted gold and silver, which is to be forfeited by me. I forfeit it to the *Saṅgha*." This does not mean that the *Saṅgha* is the only party that can possess it,[79] but the *Saṅgha*

---

[76] Sp 691,31 ff: *kappiyaṃ ācikkhitabbaṃ sappiṃ vā ti pabbajitānam sappi vā telaṃ vā vaṭṭati upāsakā ti evaṃ ācikkhitabbaṃ.*

[77] Vin III 238,20 f: *sace so tena parivattetvā kappiyaṃ āharati, rūpiya-paṭiggāhakaṃ ṭhapetvā sabbeh' eva paribhuñjitabbaṃ.*

[78] Sp 691,27 ff: *saṅghamajjhe nissajjitabban ti ettha yasmā rūpiyaṃ nāma akappiyaṃ tasmā nissajjitabbaṃ, saṅghassa vā gaṇassa vā puggalassā ti na vuttaṃ, yasmā pana taṃ paṭiggahitamattam eva na tena kiñci kappiyabhaṇḍaṃ cetāpitaṃ tasmā upāyena paribhogadassanatthaṃ saṅghamajjhe nissajjitabban ti vuttaṃ.*

[79] The BD (II 103, fn. 2) says: "*VA*. 691 points out that as the *rūpiya* is not legally allowed (*akappiya*), neither a group nor an individual may possess it, but only the Order. Therefore it can only be forfeited to the Order." According to the commentary quoted above in footnote 78, the Sp (i.e. VA in the BD) does not say the *Saṅgha* can possess gold and silver; on the contrary, it implies that gold and silver are not to be possessed at all, which is why "forfeiture to the *Saṅgha* or a group or an individual" is not said in this case. The quotation just cited is a

serves as the authority in determining which to do: exchange the forfeited gold and silver or remove them.

If for any reason the transaction cannot be done in such an appropriate way, the forfeited articles should be abandoned. Should the lay devotee volunteer to do so, it is good, but should this not be the case, one of the monks should be chosen as the "money-discarder" (*rūpiyachaḍḍaka*). The appointed monk should be endowed with five virtuous qualities[80] so that he is reliable for this duty, that is to say, throwing it away without taking any note of where it falls. Should he take note, it is a wrong-doing on his part.

4.2. Two alternatives in the Mahīśāsaka: abandonment or exchange

Among the various *Vinaya* traditions, the Mahīśāsaka agrees to the greatest extent with the Pāli. In the first place, the text[81] specifies the procedure for forfeiture: the items (gold, silver or money in general) should be forfeited in the midst of the *Saṅgha*, not to a group or an individual. Secondly, there are in the Mahīśāsaka, as in the Pāli, two alternative ways of dealing with the forfeited articles. The only difference lies in the order. In the Pāli the proceeding of exchanging comes first, hence this seems to be the preferred option.

---

typical expression used to gloss "should be forfeited" (*nissajjitabbaṃ*). But in our present case, "in the midst of the *Saṅgha*" is applied in place of "to the *Saṅgha*" to make a distinction.

[80] *pañcah' aṅgehi samannāgato bhikkhu*. The text (Vin III 238,24 ff) goes on to specify the five qualities: *yo na chandāgatiṃ gaccheyya, na dosāgatiṃ gaccheyya, na mohāgatiṃ gaccheyya, na bhayāgatiṃ gaccheyya, chaḍḍitā-chaḍḍitañ ca jāneyya.* (He must be one who would not be unfair out of partiality, hatred, delusion, or fear, and he should know what is and is not to be thrown away.)

[81] In the Mahīśāsaka *Vinaya*, the rule against taking gold and silver is the last – the thirtieth – of the *Nissaggiya-Pācittiya* chapter. Compared with the corresponding rules in the other recensions, the Mahīśāsaka is extremely brief. The text omits the commentary on the rule but refers readers to the commentary on the preceding rule, which is against various sorts of trading with gold and silver. There full discussion of the procedure for forfeiture etc. is given.

Only if this proceeding does not work for some reason are the forfeited articles to be abandoned.

On the contrary, the Mahīśāsaka first presents the proceeding of abandonment. Only if this proceeding does not work will an alternative be considered. The text says that the *Saṅgha* will appoint a monk as the money-discarder, to throw the forfeited items away into a hollow, fire, water or the wilderness. While fulfilling this duty, he is not to pay any attention to where it falls, nor is he to pick it up again once he has laid it down somewhere. Should he not fulfill this duty, he is not to ask the *Saṅgha* how to deal with the forfeited items, nor should the *Saṅgha* give him relevant instructions.

Following this passage is a second choice, appearing as an alternative. If the above-mentioned arrangement is not carried out, the monk may have a legitimiser exchange the forfeited article for robes and food. The latter may be accepted by the *Saṅgha* and shared among all the monks except the offender.

4.3. Symbolic forfeiture of the Dharmaguptaka

For the Pāli, Mahīśāsaka and Mahāsāṅghika, the articles illegally obtained must be forfeited in the midst of the *Saṅgha*. The forfeiture in the Pāli and Mahīśāsaka is substantial: the forfeited gold and silver will not be returned to the offender. The Mahāsāṅghika has a different treatment: what is forfeited goes to the *Saṅgha*. Concerning this point, more discussion will come up shortly.

By contrast to these three traditions, the Dharmaguptaka gives a completely different account of forfeiture; it is not only personal but also symbolic. According to the *Vibhaṅga*, it involves two proceedings. Firstly, gold or silver is to be forfeited to an individual, either a faithful attendant of the monastery or a pious lay devotee. The offending monk should say thus: "As you understand, this is not what I should [take]."[82] This is reminiscent of the above di-

---

[82] T1428[22]619b28 f: 「此是我所不應，汝當知之。」

scussion on the Pāli text, where the monk should carefully phrase his request. In the text of the Sarvāstivādin *Vinaya*, however, the monk explicitly tells the legitimiser to take gold and silver on his behalf.

So here the attendant of the monastery or lay devotee should already know how to behave. The text then goes on to say that if the lay devotee takes the money and returns it, the monk should accept that, but he should have a legitimiser (*kappiya-kāraka*) handle it on his behalf. This is the second proceeding. The legitimiser is supposed to exchange the returned money for requisites, such as robes, alms-bowl, sitting cloth and so on, then give them to the monk. It is to be noted that the Pāli text uses no technical designation but ordinary terms such as monastery attendant or lay devotee.

Alternatively, instead of returning the money to the offending monk, the lay devotee may himself keep the money, undertake the exchange and give the monk articles allowable in return. Nevertheless, if he does not do so, the monk should have another monk speak to the lay devotee on his behalf: "It is given to you on the Buddha's instruction for the sake of making it allowable. You should give the monk articles in return."[83] If this does not work, the offending monk should himself go to persuade the lay devotee to give the forfeited articles to the *Saṅgha* or the *stūpa* or to instructors or others, or even return the money to the original donor, in order that his donation will not be lost.

One point deserves attention. The above-stated treatment implies that accepting a monetary donation in the name of the *Saṅgha* or the *stūpa* presumably was already in practice.

4.4. Abandonment or symbolic forfeiture of the Sarvāstivāda

The proceeding of forfeiture presented in the Sarvāstivādin *Vinaya* is as peculiar as that in the Dharmaguptaka. In the case where a monk has already committed a full offence, there are two alterna-

[83] T1428[22]619c5 f: 「佛有教爲淨故與汝，應還彼比丘物。」

tives in dealing with the treasure, depending on the quantity. If it is a small quantity, it should be thrown away. If it is large, and the monk has a legitimiser of agreeing heart (*t'ong hsin ching-ren* 同心淨人), then he should say to him: "As this is not allowable to me, I should not take it. You should take it."[84] The Mahāsāṅghika and Sarvāstivāda agree on this point: whether or not the forfeited articles are to be abandoned depends on the quantity.

Thus the offending monk may forfeit to an individual in a private way, and then confess his offence to the *Saṅgha*. Before acknowledging his offence, the *Saṅgha* should ask him whether or not he has forfeited the treasure. If the answer is negative, the *Saṅgha* should have him do so, otherwise every member of the *Saṅgha* incurs an offence of wrong-doing.

Like in the Dharmaguptaka, here we have the technical term legitimiser. Besides, the monk gives direct instruction to the legitimiser, spelling out that he should take the forfeited article. It is an interesting contrast with the texts of the Pāli and Dharmaguptaka, where the principle of verbal purity (i.e. avoid giving direct instructions) is observed even in the proceeding of forfeiture.

Having taken the forfeited treasure, the legitimiser then returns it, saying: "I give it back to the monk." The monk says: "This is an article not allowable to me. [I] would accept [what is] allowable."[85] In the case where no such legitimiser is available, the forfeited treasure should be used to exchange for bedding for the universal *Saṅgha*.[86] So when a legitimiser is available to the offending monk, he himself may make use of the forfeited article. It is only when no legitimiser is available that the forfeited article goes to communal

---

[84] T1435[23]51b19 f: 「我以不淨故，不應取是寶，汝應取。」

[85] T1435[23]51b21: 「比丘言：『此是不淨物；若淨當受。』」

[86] *Cātuddisa-saṅgha* (四方僧伽) as opposed to *sammukhībhūta-saṅgha* (現前僧伽). These are the twofold structure of the *Saṅgha*. The former is a universal concept beyond temporal and spatial confinement, whereas the latter refers to any local *Saṅgha* in actuality. Cf. Hirakawa 1946: 293 ff for a detailed discussion. Here there is no indication of how the forfeiture should be performed when no legitimiser is available or of who is supposed to undertake the exchange.

use. This is another practice different from that of the Pāli and Mahīśāsaka. We recall that for these traditions the forfeiture is to be performed amidst the *Saṅgha*, and the exchanged articles are to be shared by all members of the *Saṅgha* except for the offending monk.

By saying "[I] would accept [what is] allowable", the monk seems to apply the principle of verbal purity. Instead of giving a direct instruction such as "Exchange this for such-and-such", the above-quoted remark gives the hint that the legitimiser takes what is not allowable to him and gives what is allowable in return, but the monk avoids spelling this out. It would seem that for the Sarvāstivāda, the principle of verbal purity is still there, but may not be observed as strictly as by the Pāli.

4.5. "Inexhaustible property" of the Mahāsāṅghika and Mūlasarvāstivāda

Like the Pāli and Mahīśāsaka, the Mahāsāṅghika says that any unduly received gold and silver should be forfeited in the midst of the *Saṅgha*. But unlike the Pāli, the text does not say much about the subsequent arrangements. It merely says that the forfeited articles, regardless of their quality and quantity, should not be returned to the offender, nor should they be shared among the monks. Apparently the Mahāsāṅghika has a unique course not shared by the other traditions.

If the amount is great, it should be ascribed to the so-called "inexhaustible property" (*wu-chin-wu* 無盡物). This seems to imply that when what is forfeited is of small value, it should be thrown away. "Inexhaustible property" refers to monetary or non-monetary gifts donated to the *Saṅgha*. Later, when the monastic lending institution was established, it was used as a sort of capital from which the interest or profit produced may be used for construction or robes, but not for food.

As stated previously, the Mūlasarvāstivāda records no procedure for forfeiture, but one reads elsewhere in the text of the institution of "inexhaustible property". Its origin appears in the casuistry of *Naiḥsargika-Pāyantika* 19, a rule prohibiting monks from making a profit on various types of transaction, including monetary exchange.[87] The text relates that the lay devotees in Vaiśālī built several dwellings for monks. When they saw those houses gradually falling apart as time went by, they worried that after their deaths no one would have the houses repaired or rebuilt. Considering long-term maintenance, they made a donation to the *Saṅgha* so that the monks might repair their houses as need occurred. They termed such a donation "inexhaustible property". The monks did not accept that, for taking gold and silver was prohibited. So the Blessed One modified the proscription, ruling that "inexhaustible property" could be accepted when the *Saṅgha* needed to repair or build houses.[88]

A further exception to *Naiḥsargika-Pāyantika* 19 had thus been made. The text goes on to relate that the monks, having received "inexhaustible property", left it in the storage room. The donors suggested that the monks do business with it for profit. Then the Blessed One is said to have announced: "Profit should be pursued if it is for the sake of the *Saṅgha*."[89]

4.6. Comparative notes

An examination of the various *Vinaya*s shows that with regard to forfeiture the Pāli and Mahīśāsaka unambiguously hold the following position: (1) the forfeiture is public; (2) the forfeited articles are used to exchange for allowable items, or otherwise abandoned; (3) the exchanged articles are to be shared among all members of the *Saṅgha* except the offender; (4) no one may make personal use of the forfeited articles.

[87] T1442[23]743a26: 「若復苾芻種種出納求利者，泥薩祇波逸底迦。」
[88] T1442[23]743b17 f: 「佛告諸苾芻：『若爲僧伽有所營造，受無盡物。』」
[89] T1442[23]743b27 f: 「世尊告曰：『若爲僧伽應求利潤。』」

On this point the Dharmaguptaka and Sarvāstivāda appear more relaxed: (1) the forfeiture is to a person; (2) unlike the Pāli, Mahīśāsaka and Mahāsāṅghika, the forfeiture is symbolic; (3) the forfeited articles should be exchanged for requisites which are allowable; (4) the offending monk makes personal use of the forfeited articles.

The discrepancy in the procedure of forfeiture between the Dharmaguptaka and Sarvāstivāda lies in the person to whom the offending monk forfeits. According to the text of the Dharmaguptaka, the monk forfeits to an attendant of the monastery or a lay devotee; then he has a legitimiser handle the forfeited items, which is returned to him. Thus the attendant of the monastery and the legitimiser function differently, although the former may do the same service as a legitimiser does, that is, give the offending monk allowable requisites in return.

There is only one role in the Sarvāstivādin text. It is the legitimiser who receives the forfeited treasure from the monk, exchanges it for allowable requisites, and then gives the requisites to the monk.

The *Vibhaṅga* of the Mūlasarvāstivāda sees the transition from the term "monastery attendant" to "legitimiser". In the context of accepting a robe-fund (T1442[23]741b11 ff), the Blessed One gives the instruction that a steward may be sought for. Being asked who can serve as a steward, the Blessed One says that a monastery attendant or a lay devotee may be sought for. Following this instruction is the gloss on "monastery attendant" as "legitimiser".[90] It is apparent that the institution of "legitimiser" comes later. In the subsequent discussion, the term "legitimiser" is used throughout in place of "monastery attendant".

In comparing the Pāli and Chinese *Vibhaṅgas*, one finds that the term "legitimiser" does not appear in the Pāli text, in which it is a

[90] T1442[23]741b17 ff: 「佛言：『應求寺家人，或鄔波索迦。』寺家人者，謂是淨人；鄔波索迦者，謂受三歸五戒。」 The term 寺家人 (*ssu-chia-ren*) is the Chinese equivalent to the Pāli *ārāmika*, and here a lay devotee (*upāsaka*) is defined as one who has taken the three refuges and five precepts.

monastery attendant or a lay devotee who performs the service of exchanging. On the other hand, one reads in the Sarvāstivādin text the single term "legitimiser", who acts in the symbolic forfeiture by accepting the treasure and giving the offending monk in return robes or food.

The *Vibhaṅga*s of the Dharmaguptaka and Mūlasarvāstivāda contain both the old and the new term. Nevertheless, the Mūlasarvāstivādin text uses the new term to gloss and subsequently replace the old one, whereas in the Dharmaguptaka "monastery attendant " and "legitimiser" co-exist to fulfill different duties. This appears to me to be synchronization of the diachronic development of administrative personnel. Some *Vinaya*s updated their texts, adopting the new term throughout, whereas some presented both terms.

In the Mahāsāṅghika the forfeited article is not to be returned to the offending monk, nor is it exchanged for daily requisites, so there is nothing about the procedure for forfeiture. It can be inferred from the context that the forfeited articles are abandoned if they are of little amount or value; otherwise they are kept as the "inexhaustible property" from which interest or profit may be produced. This indicates that gold and silver can be possessed by the *Saṅgha.*

For an individual monk, the rule against taking gold and silver as presented in some *Vinaya*s had considerably relaxed. Through some expedient means, personal use of the forfeited gold and silver had become allowable. If gold or silver was accepted not for a personal purpose but for the sake of the *Saṅgha*, this was more justified. Indeed, the Mahāsāṅghika and Mūlasarvāstivāda developed the institution of "inexhaustible property". Although the Dharmaguptaka mentions no such term as "inexhaustible property", it does hint that the *Saṅgha* or the *stūpa* can keep a monetary donation.

5. CONCLUDING REMARKS

Our study of the rule against taking gold and silver has demonstrated that the practices presented in the various *Vinaya*s are rich in diversity. The *Vibhaṅga*s of both the Mahāsāṅghika and the Mūlasarvāstivāda are most informative, and they appear to have been carefully updated. Within the same text, one sees practice develop diachronically. The Mūlasarvāstivāda is astonishingly innovative, and all the innovations are ascribed to the Blessed One. But that seems implausible. Relaxation to the extent of contravening the rule must be the result of later development. If the Blessed One were the author of those relaxations, the rule itself would have been revised.

One finds nothing contradictory to the rule in the Pāli and Mahīśāsaka. Although the Dharmaguptaka and Sarvāstivāda do not have much discussion on the practice of the rule either, their texts are more recent than the Pāli and Mahīśāsaka in that the institution of legitimiser was already well known to them, and in the case of the Sarvāstivāda a legitimiser functioned as the recipient of the articles forfeited by a monk. Further relaxation is found in the Dharmaguptaka. The context of forfeiture suggests that monetary gifts were accepted in the name of the *Saṅgha* or a *stūpa*. Moreover, the Maṇicūḷaka episode included in the introductory story indicates that gold and silver are not always forbidden. If the *Saṅgha* is in need of building materials, monks are allowed to accept or even ask for gold and silver instead. So the *Vibhaṅga*s of the Dharmaguptaka, Mahāsāṅghika and Mūlasarvāstivāda can be considered as more updated.

The concept of "*Saṅgha*" plays an important part in the development of the gold-and-silver issue. As our discussion has shown, no *Vinaya* tradition remained unchanged in its application of the rule against monetary gifts, and exceptions were made "for the sake of the *Saṅgha*". The Pāli post-canonical commentary, the *Samantapāsādikā*, has a lengthy discussion on different kinds of fund donated to the *Saṅgha*. This obviously goes beyond the *Vibhaṅga*, although violation of the rule can be avoided when the donation is correctly phrased.

Nevertheless, when we come to the *Bhikkhunī-Vibhaṅga*, the distinction between "for the sake of the *Saṅgha*" and "for one's own sake" seems to have been disregarded. Nuns accepted or, in most cases, begged for funds in the name of the *Saṅgha*, of a group of nuns, or even of an individual nun. The funds could be for an *uposatha* hall, a cell, houses in the monastery, food, robes or other things. In collating the various recensions of the *Vibhaṅga*s for nuns, one finds that they largely agree, despite some minor discrepancies, on practice in respect of monetary donations. These appear to be ordinary practices, and presumably would not be unique to nuns. As mentioned above, some *Vibhaṅga*s for monks contain very limited information, but the corresponding *Vibhaṅga*s for nuns make up for the deficiency.

A survey of the various *Vibhaṅga*s shows that the underlying concern of the rule, possession or ownership, was well understood by all traditions, but in the course of time the rule was relaxed step by step. When changes occurred, strategies were invented to try to retain the underlying concern or to switch the focus. The Pāli insisted on mental purity – being completely free of ownership and responsibility – by resorting to verbal purity. By contrast, the Mahāsāṅghika placed extreme stress on physical purity, although the principle of verbal purity was applied under a different rule. At the outset the Mūlasarvāstivāda appeared to be strict in monastic discipline, taking both "ownership" and "physical purity" into consideration. In the course of time it innovated considerably, but concern with ownership was still discernable. By means of the strategy of ascribing the ownership to a ritual donor, mental purity was retained.

The application of the rule was doubtlessly subject to changes, as were the texts. There seems to have been mutual borrowing between the *Sutta* and *Vinaya*, and some Chinese versions of the

Maṇicūḷaka episode may haye modified the concluding remarks of the text to tally with practice then current.

The various texts in their present forms cannot be considered as synchronous. One finds that not only are the various *Vinaya*s of different strata, but within one and the same *Vinaya*, materials of different strata can be discerned. There is no way to date the various *Vinaya*s as a whole, or the materials of differing strata within one text. It is therefore not possible to tell with certainty which tradition was stricter or more relaxed at a certain period of time. But one may be sure of the relative antiquity of the Pāli recension. Quite often one finds that the discussions contained in the Chinese canonical texts appear not in the Pāli canon, but in its post-canonical commentaries.[91]

REFERENCES

BANERJEE, A. C. (ed.) 1954. *Prātimokṣa-Sūtram*. Calcutta: Calcutta Oriental Press Ltd.

BD = I. B. Horner (transl.), *Book of the Discipline*. Oxford: The Pali Text Society, 1993.

BODHI BHIKKHU, 2000. *The Connected Discourses of the Buddha. A New Translation of the Saṃyutta Nikāya*, I-II. Boston: Wisdom Publications.

COUSINS, L. S. 1994. The "five points" and the origins of the Buddhist schools. In: Tadeusz Skorupski (ed.), *The Buddhist Forum*, II.: 27-60. London: School of Oriental and African Studies, University of London.

Dharmaguptaka Vinaya T1428[22].

DEMIÉVILLE, P. 1950-51. A propos du concile de Vaiśālī. *T'oung Pao* 40: 239-296.

FRAUWALLNER, Erich 1956. *The Earliest Vinaya and the Beginnings of Buddhist Literature*. Rome: Instituto per il Medio ed Estremo Oriente.

FINOT, M. L. 1913. Le Prātimokṣasūtra des Sarvāstivādins. Texte Sanskrit. *Journal Asiatique* 1913: 465-558.

[91] I am indebted to the National Science Council for the one-year research grant, which includes a subsidy for attending international conferences. This article is part of the result of the research and has already been presented at the 12th World Sanskrit Conference (13-19 July, 2003) held in Helsinki, Finland.

GEIGER, Wilhelm (transl.) 1934. *The Mahāvaṃsa*. London: Luzac & Co.

HIRAKAWA, Akira 1946. *Studies on Early Buddhism*. Tokyo: Shunjūsha.

—— 1970. *A Study of the Vinaya-Piṭaka*. Tokyo: Sankibo Busshorin.

—— 1982. *Monastic Discipline for the Buddhist Nuns*. Patna: Kashi Prasad Jayaswal Research Institute.

—— 1993. *Studies on the Two Hundred and Fifty Precepts*, II. Tokyo: Shunjūsha.

—— 1998. *A Study of the Bhikkhunī Vinaya*. Tokyo: Shunjūsha.

KABILSINGH, Chatsumarn 1984. *A Comparative Study of the Bhikkhunī Pātimokkha*. Varanasi: Chaukhabha Orientalia.

—— (transl.) 1991. *The Bhikkhunī Pātimokkha of the Six Schools*. Bangkok: Thammasat University Press.

Kên-pên sa-p'o-to-pu lü-shê (根本薩婆多部律攝) T1458[24]525a1–617a26.

LAMOTTE, E. 1988. *History of Indian Buddhism*. Translated by Sara Webb-Boin. Louvain: Université catholique de Louvain, Institut orientaliste.

LA VALLÉE POUSSIN, Louis de 1976. *The Buddhist Councils*. Calcutta: K. P. Bagchi & Company.

Mahāsāṃghika Vinaya T1425[22]

Mahīśāsaka Vinaya T1421[22]

MASKELL, Dorothy (ed.) 1956. *Kaṅkhāvitaraṇī nāma mātikaṭṭhakathā. Buddhaghosa's Commentary on the Pātimokkha*. London: Luzac & Co.

MASUDA, Jiryo (transl.) 1978. *Origin and Doctrines of Early Indian Buddhist Schools. A Translation of the Hsüan-Chwang Version of Vasumitra's Treatise*. New York: AMS Press.

MAYEDA, Egaku 1964. *A History of the Formation of Original Buddhist Texts*. Tokyo: Sankibo Busshorin.

MITSUO, Sato 1972 *A Study of the Early Buddhist Order in the Vinaya Piṭaka*. Tokyo: Sankibo Busshorin.

Mūlasarvāstivādin Vinaya T1443[24]

OLIVELLE, Patrick 1974. *The Origin and the Early Development of Buddhist Monachism*. Colombo: M.D. Gunasena.

PACHOW, W. 1955. *A Comparative Study of the Prātimokṣa*. Santiniketan: Sino-Indian Cultural Society.

PACHOW, W. & R. MISHRA (eds.) 1956. *The Prātimokṣa-sūtram of the Mahāsāṅghikās*. Allahabad: Ganganatha Jha Research Institute.

PREBISH, Charles S. 1974. A review of scholarship on the Buddhist councils. *Journal of Asian Studies* 33.2: 246-247.

—— 1994. *A Survey of Vinaya Literature*, I. Taipei: Jin Luen Publishing House.

PREBISH, Charles S. 1996. Śaikṣa-dharmas revisited: further considerations of Mahāsāṃghika origins. *History of Religions* 35: 258-270.

PREBISH, Charles S. & Janice J. NATTIER 1977. Mahāsāṃghika origins: the beginnings of Buddhist sectarianism. *History of Religions* 16: 237-272.

ROTH, Gustav (ed.) 1970. *Bhikṣuṇī-Vinaya. Including Bhikṣuṇī-Prakīrṇaka and a Summary of the Bhikṣu-Prakīrṇaka of the Ārya-Mahāsāṃghika-Lokottaravādin.* (Tibetan Sanskrit Work Series, 12.) Patna: KP Jayaswal Research Institute

SHIH, Juo-hsüeh Bhikkhuṇī 2000. *Controversies over Buddhist Nuns*. Oxford: The Pali Text Society.

Sp = *Samantapāsādikā, Vinaya-aṭṭhakathā*, I-VII. Edited by J. Takakusu & M. Nagao (vols. V and VII by Mizuno). London: The Pali Text Society 1924-47. [Index volume by H. Kopp, London: The Pali Text Society, 1977.]

Sumaṅgalavilāsinī (*Dīghanikāya-aṭṭhakathā*). Ed. by T. W. Rhys Davids & J. E. Carpenter. London: The Pali Text Society, 1886-1932.

T = *Taishō Shinshū Daizōkyō*. 100 vols. Tokyo 1924-.

TATIA, N. 1975. *Lokottaramahāsāṃghikānāṃ Prātimokṣasūtram*. Patna: Nava Nalanda Mahavihara.

THANISSARO BHIKKHU 1994. *The Buddhist Monastic Code*. Valley Center, CA: Metta Forest Monastery.

Upālipariprcchāsūtra. Ein Text zur buddhistischen Ordensdisziplin. Aus dem Chinesischen übersetzt und den Pāli-Parallelen gegenübergestellt von Valentina Stache-Rosen, hrsg. Heinz Bechert. (Abhandlungen der Akademie der Wissenschaften in Göttingen, Philologisch-historische klasse, 3.140.) Göttingen: Vandenhoeck & Ruprecht, 1984.

Vin = Hermann Oldenberg (ed.), *Vinaya-Piṭaka*, I-V. London: Williams & Norgate, 1879-83.

WIJAYARATNA, Mōhan 1990. *Buddhist Monastic Life*. Translated by Claude Grangier & Steven Collins. Cambridge: Cambridge University Press.

Preliminary Observations on Compositional Methods in Haribhadra's *Ālokā*

ILONA MANEVSKAIA

INTRODUCTION

This paper is intended as a preliminary report on the compositional techniques used by Haribhadra in the first chapter of his *Aṣṭasāhasrikā-Prajñāpāramitā-vyākhyā-Abhisamayālaṃkāra-ālokā* (briefly *Ālokā*). I will also briefly compare the methods found in the *Ālokā* with those in treatises from different traditions, specifically the *Nyāyabhāṣya* and *Yuktidīpikā*, in order to show that a similar use of heterogeneous techniques and methods can be demonstrated for these three texts.

In India great attention was always devoted to the rules of composition of texts. In early times, a list of special compositional devices for *śāstra*s, i.e. technical treatises in Brahmanical scholastics, generally called *tantrayukti*, was developed.[1] Enumerations of *tantrayukti*s are found in Kauṭilya's *Arthaśāstra* (a work on statecraft, c. 3rd century BCE), *Suśruta-saṃhitā* (a medical treatise, c. 1st-3rd century CE), and the *Caraka-saṃhitā* (a medical treatise, c. 1st century BCE). In addition to listing the *tantrayukti*s the first two treatises provide definitions and examples of their application.

[1] For more information on *tantrayukti*s, see Oberhammer 1967-68: 600-616; Oberhammer, Prets & Prandstetter 1991-96; Lele 1981.

For the list of the *tantrayukti*s, see Appendix I. For their Sanskrit definitions provided by the *Arthaśāstra* and *Suśruta-saṃhitā*, see Appendix II.

As for Buddhist literature, the para-canonical Pāli treatises *Nettippakaraṇa* and *Peṭakopadesa* (both before the 5th century CE) were manuals for commentators to interpret the *Theravāda* canon,[2] while the *Vyākhyā-yukti* ("Principles of Exegesis") by Vasubandhu (c. 4th-5th century CE) served the same purpose for the *Mahāyāna* tradition. The *Vyākhyā-yukti* was originally written in Sanskrit, yet has been preserved as a whole only in Tibetan translation.[3] In India, as well as later in Tibet, this text often served as the methodological basis for writing a commentary.[4]

ABHISAMAYĀLAṂKĀRA-ĀLOKĀ OF HARIBHADRA

Haribhadra, a Buddhist scholar,who lived in the 8th century under the Pāla dynasty, was a pupil of Śāntarakṣita and belonged to the *Yogācāra-mādhyamika-svātantrika* school. He wrote two commentaries on the *Abhisamayālaṃkāra* (AA), the *Ālokā*, which is at the same time a commentary on the *Aṣṭasāhasrikā-prajñāpāramitā-sūtra*, and the *Abhisamayālaṃkāra-kārikā-śāstra-vṛtti*.[5] The latter is a concise version of the former, but with a different ordering of material within the chapters. Both commentaries became important for the study of the *Prajnāpāramitā* literature in Tibet and served as a model for the later Tibetan commentators on the AA and the *Prajnāpāramitā-sūtra*s.

In the first chapter of the *Ālokā*, Haribhadra introduces two commentarial methods and in addition to that also uses special

---

[2] Hinüber 1996: 77-82.

[3] For quotations from *Vyākhyā-yukti* in works which have been preserved in the original language, the original Sanskrit is available, as for instance is the case in the verse quoted in *Ālokā*, discussed below.

[4] For details see Skilling 2000; Cabezon 1992; Verhagen, this volume.

[5] Nakamura 1980.

devices, the latter possibly in some form associated with *tantra-yukti* lists.

I. At the outset of his commentary Haribhadra lists four *anubandhas*[6] to introduce his exposition:[7]

1. *Sambandha* ('connection')
2. *Abhidheya* ('subject-matter')
3. *Prayojana* ('purpose')
4. *Prayojana-prayojana* ('purpose of the purpose').

The number of *anubandhas* varies in different texts. Some *sūtra* commentaries recognize a set of four or five *anubandhas* while others list six.[8] Compared to the longest list of six *anubandhas*, two are not found in Haribhadra's list, namely *abhidhāna* 'text' and *prayojana-niṣṭhā* 'ultimate purpose'.

Haribhadra first explains the meaning of these terms in general and subsequently shows their application in the context of the AA. Although *sambandha* 'connection' opens his list of *anubandhas*, Haribhadra does not discuss it in detail. He merely states the following:

> *Sambandha* ('connection') should not be indicated separately from *prayojana* ('purpose') because [this will give] no [additional] result. Since only that which is not understood from the explanation of other things deserves to be stated separately. For example, when something like *abhidheya* 'subject-matter' is indicated, no understanding of the remaining things follows. But it is impossible to indicate *prayojana* and not to indicate *sambandha* [implicitly at the same time].[9]

---

[6] See Schoening 1996: 32-37; Broido 1983.

[7] Haribhadra himself does not use the term *anubandha* for these four.

[8] Schoening 1996: 32-37.

[9] Ālokā, p. 3, ll. 14-18: *ko 'sya sambandhādiḥ | tatrocyate | sambandhas tāvan na prayojanāt pṛthag upadarśanīyo niṣphalatvāt | sa hi nāma pṛthagupādānam arhati yo yasminn abhihite 'pi na gamyate, yathābhidheyādyanyatarābhidhāne netarāvagatir bhavati | na ca sambhavo 'sti prayojane 'bhihite sambandho nābhihita iti*. Kamalaśīla in his commentary on *Tattvasaṃgraha* lists *sambandha* as the third element with *abhidheya* and *prayojana* as the first two. Like Hari-

Further Haribhadra says that

> Indeed, in *Prajnāpāramitā* [*sambandha*] between *śāstra* and *prayojana* should be characterized as the relation between the means of accomplishing and that which is to be accomplished ... And this relation between the means of accomplishing and that which is to be accomplished becomes clear by indicating the *prayojana.*[10]

After that Haribhadra continues to explain *abhidheya*, *prayojana*[11] and *prayojana-prayojana*[12]. Let me summarize his discussion. He says that *abhidheya*, 'subject-matter', is the path of the Bodhisattva to attainment of Enlightenment and the eight *abhisamaya*s are the stages on this path[13]. The *prayojana*, 'purpose', is to facilitate understanding of this 'subject-matter'[14]. The 'purpose of the purpose' is to make progress in this practice[15]. Concluding these brief explanations, Haribhadra cites the first two ślokas of the AA[16].

---

bhadra, he does not explain *sambandha*. In *Śālistamba[ka]-ṭīkā sambandha* opens the list of *anubandha*s and it is explained as the connection between *Śālistamba-sūtra* and its *Kārikā*, and also as the connection with the Buddha and not with works of non-Buddhists; see Schoening 1996: 33.

[10] Ālokā, p. 3, ll. 18-21: *Tathā hi sa Prajñāpāramitā-pradarśyamāṇaḥ śāstra-prayojanayoḥ sādhya-sādhana-bhāva-lakṣaṇo darśanīyaḥ | nānyo guruparva-kriyādilakṣaṇaḥ | tasyārthipravṛtter anaṅgatvāt | sa ca sādhya-sādhana-bhāvaḥ prayojanābhidhānād eva darśitaḥ* |. The section on *anubandha*s in Haribhadra's *Ālokā* was probably partly derived from *Tattvasaṃgraha* of Kamalaśīla, see Funayama 1995: 181-182. See also *Tattvasaṃgraha* of Kamalaśīla (Jha 1937: 3-15).

[11] Ālokā, p. 4, l. 20: *Kriyā-phalaṃ prayojanaṃ* .

[12] Ālokā, p. 4, l. 30: *Kriyā-phalasya phalaṃ prayojanaṃ.*

[13] Ālokā, p. 4, ll. 10-15.

[14] Ālokā, p. 4, ll. 16-20.

[15] Ālokā, p. 4, ll. 21-30.

[16] Skt. *Sarvākārajñatā-mārgaḥ śāsinā yo atra deśitaḥ | dhīmanto vīkṣiṣīraṃs tam anālīḍhaṃ parair iti || smṛtau cādhāyā sūtrārthaṃ dharma-caryāṃ daśātmikāṃ | sukhena pratipatsīrann ity ārambha-prayojanam || iti* (Ālokā, p. 5, ll. 1-5).

Tib. *Rnam-pa-thams-cad-mkhyen-nyid-lam | ston-pas-'di-las-bshad-pa-gang | gzhan-gyis-myong-ba-ma-yin-te | chos-spyod-bcu'i-bdag-nyid-kyi || mdo-don-dran-pa-la-bzhag-nas | blo-dang-ldan-pas-mthong-'gyur-phyir | bde-blag-tu-ni-*

Haribhadra considers 'purpose' in the AA to be twofold and to include 'purpose of the purpose'. This is evident from the following: the AA when discussing 'purpose' concludes with "... they will be able to make quick progress in the tenfold practice of the Dharma", which in Haribhadra's interpretation amounts to 'purpose of the purpose'.

II. After this, Haribhadra quotes from Vasubandhu's *Vyākhyā-yukti*. This famous verse, often cited and referred to in Indo-Tibetan commentarial literature, formulates a five-fold system for explanation of the *sūtra*s.

> Those who wish to explain the meaning of *sūtra*s should state the purpose along with the summarized meaning, the meaning of the words along with the connection and the objections and rebuttals.[17]

The five elements of the five-fold method are:

1. 'purpose' (Skt. *prayojana*, Tib. *dgos-pa*)
2. 'summarized meaning' (Skt. *piṇḍārtha*, Tib. *bsdus-pa'i-don*)
3. 'meaning of the words' (Skt. *padārtha*, Tib. *tshig-don*)
4. 'connection' (Skt. *anusaṃdhi*, Tib. *mtshams-sbyar-ba*)

---

rtogs-pa-zhes | *bya-ba-rtsom-pa'i-dgos-pa-yin* || (Rgyan-snang, p. 66, Tib. 5b, ll. 4-5).

"The purpose of my undertaking (in composing the present treatise) is to enable the wise to behold the way to the knowledge of all modes, demonstrated here (in the Prajñāpāramitā) by the Teacher, though others cannot experience it. And when they have in their memory arranged the sense of the Sutra, they will be able to make quick progress in the tenfold practice of the Dharma." (Conze 1954: 4.)

[17] Skt. *Prayojanaṃ sapiṇḍārthaṃ padārthaḥ sānusaṃdhikaḥ* | *sacodyaparihāraś ca vācyaḥ sūtrārthavādibhiḥ* || (Ālokā, p. 15, ll. 24-25).

Tib. *De-la-mdo-don-smra-bar-'dod-pa-yis* | *dgos-pa-bsdus-pa'i-don-bcas-dang* | *tshig-don-bcas-dang-mtshams-sbyar-bcas* | *brgal-lan-bcas-pas-bsnyad-par-bya* | *zhes-rnam-par-bshad-pa'i-rigs-pa-las-rnam-pa-lngas-mdo-sde-bshad-par- bya'o* | (Rgyan-snang, p. 70, Tib. 15b, ll. 2-3).

5. 'objections and (their) rebuttals' (Skt. *codya-parihāra*, Tib. *brgal-ba-dang-lan-gnyis*).

As the 'purpose' was already stated by Haribhadra earlier, when he discussed the four *anubandha*s, he does not explain it again at this point and simply points out that the 'purpose' has already been discussed.[18] Thus he identifies the 'purpose' from the list of four introductory terms with the 'purpose' from the five categories of Vasubandhu.[19]

Haribhadra proceeds to the second element, *piṇḍārtha*, and introduces the topics of the AA first by mentioning briefly the eight principal subjects and subsequently by giving a more elaborate list

---

[18] Ālokā, p. 15, ll. 26-27: *iti pañcabhir ākāraiḥ sūtraṃ vyākhyātavyam iti Vyākhyāyuktau nirṇītam ity abhihitam eva prayojanam* |

[19] The fact that Harbhadra in his *Ālokā* used both systems may suggest that these two systems were compatible. See also Jamgon Kongtrul, p. 166, line 1 – p. 167, line 5: *Gsum-pa-dam-bca'-ba-la-gnyis* | *dngos-dang-**zhar-byung-dgos-sogs-chos-bzhi-bshad-pa'o*** | ... (line 6) *Gnyis-pa-ni* | *Slob-dpon-dbyig-gnyen-zhabs-kyis* | ***dgos-pa-bsdus-pa'i-don-bcas-dang*** | ***tshig-don-bcas-dang-mtshams-sbyar-bcas*** | ***brgal-lan-bcas-te-bsnyad-par-bya*** | *zhes-bstan-bcos-bshad-thabs-kyi-yan-lag-lnga-man-ngag-tu-stsal-ba-las* | *thog-mar-bstan-par-bya-ba-ni-dgos-pa'i-don-yin-la* | *de-yis-grub-don-bsdus-do-gyis-mdor-bstan* | *de'i-don-tshig-don-gyi-cha-rgyas-par-bshad* | *go-rim-dang-mi-'gal-bar-mtshams-sbyor-dang-rigs-pa-dang-mi-'gal-bar-brgal-len-ni-snga-phyi-ci-rigs-su-'chang-pa'i-thog-ma-la-dgos-'brel-bzhi-gsum-bcu-gnyis-kyi-rnam-gzhag-rgyas-par-byar-yod-kyang* | *skabs-'dir-bstun-bzhi-ste* | *gdul-bya'i-zhing-khams-'dul-byed-kyi-ston-pa-dang-bstan-pa* | *de-la-'jug-pa'i-rim-pas-tshul-khrims-dang-thos-pas-ma-sgom-gsum-gyi-gnas* | *de-las-lam-bgrod-cing-'bras-bu-yongs-su-rdzogs-par-'gyur-ba-thar-pa-sgrub-pa'i-rnam-gzhag-shin-tu-cha-tshang-ba-ni-bstan-bcos-'di'-brjod-bya* | *de-la-'chad-nyan-gyis-blo-sbyangs-pas-sde-snod-dang-theg-pa'i-rim-pa-la-'jug-rung-gi-thos-pa-las-byung-ba'i-shes-rab-skye-zhing-rim-gyis-bsam-sgom-gyi-shes-rab-phyin-cim-log-pa-skye-rung-du-'gyur-ba-ni-dgos-pa* | *de-las-thar-pa-dang-thams-cad-mkhyen-pa'i-go-'phang-bde-blag-tu-'grub-bar-'gyur-ba-ni-nying-dgos* | *nying-dgos-dgos-pa-dang-'brel* | *dgospa-brjod-bya-dang-'brel* | *brjod-bya-sogs-kyang-phyi-ma-phyi-mar-ltos-pa-ni-'di'i-'brel-bar-grub-bo* |

The third part of the introduction, devoted to the author's resolve to complete the treatise, consists of two subsections. In the second subsection the four components such as purpose etc. are explained. In the same subsection there is a quotation from Vasubandhu, which introduces the five-fold explanatory method. It seems that Kongtrul, like Haribhadra, uses both methods and does not clearly distinguish them from one another.

of seventy topics. The eight principal subjects and seventy topics are closely related to each other, since the principal subjects introduce the major structure while the seventy topics, being incorporated in the major structure, offer a more detailed outline of the contents. It is noteworthy that the *piṇḍārtha* procedure is twofold, consisting of *samāsa-nirdeśa,* 'brief statement', and *vyāsa-nirdeśa,* 'detailed statement'.

1. *Samāsa-nirdeśa*[20], which introduces eight principal subjects, strongly resembles *uddeśa* from the *tantrayukti* list. Haribhadra says that *piṇḍārtha* procedure first outlines *śāstra* briefly to help listeners to grasp the meaning of *śāstra* and commentators to elucidate it.[21] After that he introduces one by one the eight subjects of the AA and after this enumeration quotes the third and fourth *ślokas* from the AA, in which these eight subjects are also listed.

2. *Vyāsa-nirdeśa*[22], which further elaborates the list of eight subjects introduced by *samāsa-nirdeśa*, corresponds to the *tantrayukti nirdeśa.* Haribhadra says that a brief outline of *śāstra* will now be elaborated because good explanation requires both 'brief' (*samāsa*) and 'detailed' (*vyāsataḥ*) expositions.[23] After that he introduces all seventy topics of the AA in accordance with the AA's eight subjects and supplies quotations from *śloka*s five to seventeen after appropriate passages.

After having discussed *piṇḍārtha* Haribhadra proceeds to the *padārtha,* 'the meaning of the words'. At this point he stresses that the *sūtra* will be explained now by means of explanation of the

---

[20] Ālokā, p. 15, l. 28 – p. 16, l. 11.

[21] Ālokā, p. 15, l. 28 – p. 16, l. 1: *ataḥ śrotṛ-jana-sukha-pratipattaye kṛta-vibhāgārthasya ca śāstrasya sukaraṃ vyākhyānam iti* ***samāsa-nirdeśena*** *piṇḍārthas tāvad abhidhīyate.* Compare this to the definition of *tantrayukti uddeśa,* which is described as *samāsa-vākya* by Kauṭilya and *samāsa-vacanam* in Suśruta. See also Appendix II.

[22] Ālokā, p. 16, l. 17 – p. 21, l. 14.

[23] Ālokā, p. 16, ll. 17-18: *samāsa-nirdiṣṭasya vyāsataś cākhyānāt sv-ākhyātatvam iti punar api vyāsataḥ piṇḍārtho 'bhidhīyate.*

meaning of the words etc.'[24] An example of *padārtha* procedure may be found in Appendix III.

III. Along with the four introductory terms and the five categories from the *Vyākhyā-yukti* Haribhadra also uses *tantrayukti*s. Indeed, Haribhadra uses *adhyāhāra* (= *vākyaśeṣa* = *śeṣa*) – 'completion of a sentence', *samāsa-nirdeśa,* which is similar to *tantrayukti uddeśa* – 'brief mention'[25], *vyāsa-nirdeśa,* which seems to correspond to *tantrayukti nirdeśa* – 'detailed explanation'[26], *arthāpatti* – 'implication', *saṃjñā* – 'technical term', and some others. It should be noted that I mention only *tantrayukti*s which are explicitly referred to by Haribhadra.[27]

Haribhadra applies heterogeneous techniques to compose his commentary. On the one hand, he uses *tantrayukti*s; on the other hand, he also employs new means: the four introductory terms and the five categories of Vasubandhu. *Tantrayukti*s, which determine the clarity and logical structure of a text, deal with compositional problems of the *Ālokā* as a text irrespective of its genre. The four introductory terms and the five categories consider that the *Ālokā* is a commentary. In the second part of the paper I will argue that a similar combination of different methods is also used in the *Nyāyabhāṣya* and *Yuktidīpikā.*

YUKTIDĪPIKĀ AND *NYĀYABHĀṢYA*

It is interesting to note that a similar combination of several techniques and methods is also found in other texts, for example the *Nyāyabhāṣya* and *Yuktidīpikā.*

---

[24] Ālokā, p. 21, l. 24: *idānīṃ **padārtha**ādivyākhyānena sūtrārtho vidhīyate* I

[25] See the definition by Kauṭilya: *samāsa-vākyam uddeśaḥ*, and in Suśruta: *samāsa-vacanam uddeśaḥ.*

[26] See Kauṭilya: *vyāsa-vākyaṃ nirdeśaḥ*, and Suśruta: *vistaravacanaṃ nirdeśaḥ.*

[27] For examples see Appendix IV.

I. The *Yuktidīpikā* (c. 7th century CE) is one of the most significant treatises in the *Sāṅkhya* tradition. At its beginning the author first lists and later also defines eleven *tantraguṇa*s which according to him are important for the composition of a *śāstra.*[28] These eleven terms are listed in a separate section so they are distinct from the 'old'[29] *tantrayukti*s mentioned later in the text. According to Oberhammer[30] eleven *tantraguṇa*s result from the development of certain 'old' *tantrayukti*s[31]. Some of the eleven *tantraguṇa*s are indeed very close to the 'old' *tantrayukti*s in both definition and application; for instance, compare *uddeśa*[32], *nirdeśa*[33] and *upadeśa*[34].

II. The *Nyāyabhāṣya* (c. 5th century CE) by Vātsyāyana Pakṣilasvāmin is the earliest known commentary on the *Nyāyasūtra*s. At the beginning of his commentary on *sūtra* I.1.3. Vātsyāyana sets out the three-fold procedure for *śāstra*:

> The system will follow a three-fold procedure (viz.), 'naming (the topic)' (*uddeśa*), 'defining' (*lakṣaṇa*) and 'critically examining' (*parīkṣā*). Of these, *uddeśa* means the act of referring to an object by name, *lakṣaṇa* means the distinguishing characteristic (*tattva-vyavacchedaka-dharma*, lit. the characteristic which differentiates an object from all other objects) of the object named; *parīkṣā* means ascertainment, with the help of the *pramāṇas*, of the appropriateness of the distinguishing characteristic of the object defined.[35]

---

[28] YD, p. 3, l. 8 – p. 8, l. 1. See also Appendix V for the list of *tantraguṇas*.

[29] Here the term "old" *tantrayukti*s refers to *tantrayukti* lists found in the *Arthaśāstra* and *Suśruta-saṃhitā*.

[30] Oberhammer 1967-68: 605.

[31] Oberhammer 1967-68: 606-614.

[32] YD, p. 7, l. 8.

[33] YD, p. 7, l. 10.

[34] YD, p. 7, l. 28.

[35] Nyāya (1967), p. 181: *trividhā cāsya śāstrasya pravṛttiḥ – uddeśo lakṣaṇaṃ parīkṣā ceti* | *tatra nāmadheyena padārtha-mātrasya abhidhānam uddeśaḥ* | *tatra uddiṣṭasya tattva-vyavacchedako dharmo lakṣaṇam* | *lakṣitasya yathālakṣaṇam upapadyate na vā iti pramāṇair avadhāraṇaṃ parīkṣā* | (Translated into English by Gangopadhyaya 1982: 11).

Vātsyāyana was probably the first to introduce this three-fold procedure and later it became generally used in *nyāya-vaiśeṣika.*[36] Oberhammer in his paper also linked these three terms to *tantrayukti.*[37] Along with this three-fold procedure Vātsyāyana uses *tantrayukti*s: *nidarśana*[38], *anumata*[39], *arthāpatti*[40], *viparyaya*[41], not to mention such *tantrayukti*s as *uddeśa*, *nirdeśa*, *apadeśa* and others dealt with by Oberhammer (1967).[42]

CONCLUSION

All the three texts discussed above show a similar pattern in the use of two techniques for their composition. I will tentatively consider *tantrayukti*s to constitute the first technique, which governs the

---

[36] The three-fold procedure is also used in Vaiśeṣika. For instance, Śrīdhara, in *Nyāyakandalī* (commentary on *Padarthasamgraha*, 10th century CE), gives, with some slight changes, the same definition of the three-fold procedure as Vātsyāyana. Skr. *nāmadheyena padārthānām abhidhānam uddeśaḥ uddiṣṭasya svaparajātīyavyāvartako dharmo lakṣaṇaṃ lakṣitasya yathālakṣaṇaṃ vicāraḥ parīkṣā* I (Praśastapādabhāṣya, p. 26). Madhvācārya in Vaiśeṣika section of his *Sarvadarśanasaṅgraha* (c. 15th century CE) also gives a definition similar to the one by Vātsyāyana.

[37] "No doubt, these three terms must have developed out of the pair *uddeśa-nirdeśa* by differentiating the *vistaravacanam* of the *nirdeśa* in *lakṣaṇam* and *parīkṣā* according to its content." (Oberhammer: 1967-68: 611.) On the role of *padārtha* "category" in Nyāya and its relation to the eleven *tantraguṇa*s and the three-fold procedure see Manevskaia & Olenev 2004. It goes beyond the scope of the present paper to discuss these questions here.

[38] Nyāya (1925), p. 898, l. 8: *nidarśanam – ekaprakṛti idaṃ vyaktam iti pratijñā* I See also Nyāya (1925), p. 909, l. 2 ff.

[39] Nyāya (1925), p. 70, l. 3: *paramatam apratiṣiddham* ***anumatam*** *iti hi tantrayuktiḥ* I

[40] Nyāya (1925), p. 909, ll. 5-6: *artha-sampratyaya-arthe śabdaprayoge pratītaḥ so 'rtho* ***'rthāpattyā*** *iti* I

[41] Nyāya (1925), p. 49, l. 1: *tattvajñānaṃ tu khalu mithyājñāna-****viparyayeṇa*** *vyākhyātam* I

[42] This paper was prepared while I was a fellow at the International Institute of Asian Studies in Leiden. The financial support was provided by the Gonda Foundation.

clear and logical composition of any text. The four introductory terms and the five categories of Vasubandhu in the *Ālokā*, the eleven *tantraguṇa*s in the *Yuktidīpikā*, and the three-fold procedure for *śāstra* from the *Nyāyabhāṣya* belong to the second compositional technique, which takes into account the genre of the text and its doctrinal purpose within a particular tradition.

Further research is needed to support and clarify these preliminary observations.

REFERENCES

Ālokā = *Abhisamayālaṃkārāloka Prajñāpāramitāvyākhyā (Commentary on the Aṣṭasāhasrikā-Prajñāpāramitā) by Haribhadra.* Ed. by U. Wogihara (Toyo Bunko Publications, D.2.) Tokyo: Toyo Bunko, 1973.

BROIDO. M. 1983. A note on Dgos-'brel. *Journal of the Tibet Society* 1983: 5-19.

CABEZON, J. 1992. Vasubandhu's Vyākhyāyukti on the authencity of the Mahāyāna Sūtras. In: J. R. Timm (ed.), *Texts in Context: Traditional Hermeneutics in South Asia*, 221-243. Albany: State University of New York Press.

CONZE, E. 1954. *Abhisamayālamkāra. Introduction and Translation from Original Text with Sanskrit – Tibetan Index.* (Serie Orientale Roma, 6.). Roma: Istituto Italiano per il Medio ed Estremo Oriente.

FUNAYAMA, T. 1995. Arcata, Śāntarakṣita, Jinendrabuddhi, and Kamalaśīla on the aim of a treatise (*prayojana*). *Wiener Zeitschrift für die Kunde Südasiens* 39: 181-201.

GANGOPADHYAYA, Mrinalkanti (transl.) 1982. *Nyaya: Gautama's Nyaya-Sutra, with Vatsyayana's commentary.* (Indian Philosophy in its Sources.) Calcutta: Indian Studies.

HINÜBER, O. 1996. *A Handbook of Pāli Literature.* Berlin: de Gruyter.

Jamgon Kongtrul = *Kongtrul's Encyclopaedia of Indo-Tibetan culture.* Ed. by Lokesh Chandra. New Delhi: International Academy of Indian Culture, 1970.

JHA, Ganganatha (transl.) 1937. *The Tattvasaṃgraha of Śāntarakṣita with the Commentary of Kamalaśīla.* Baroda: Oriental Institute.

Kauṭilya = *The Kauṭilīya Arthaśāstra*, I: *A Critical Edition with a Glossary.* Ed. by R. P. Kangle. Bombay: University of Bombay, 1960.

LELE, W. K. 1981. *The Doctrine of the Tantrayukti-s. Methodology of Theoretico-Scientific Treatises in Sanskrit.* (The Chaukhamba Surbharati Studies, 3.) Varanasi: Chaukhamba.

MANEVSKAIA, I. & D. OLENEV 2004. On the role of *tantrayukti* in Indian intellectual tradition. *Istorija Filosofii* 11: 8-35.

NAKAMURA, H. 1980. *Indian Buddhism: A Survey with Bibliographical Notes*. Osaka: KUFS Publication.

Nyāya (1925) = *The Nyāyadarśana. The Nyāyasūtras of Gautama and Bhāṣya of Vātsyāyana with Two Commentaries*: 1) The Khadyota by Ganganatha Jha; 2) The Bhāṣyacandra by Raghūttama. Ed. by G. Jha & D. Sh. Nyayopadhyaya. (Chowkhamba Sanskrit Series, 55.) Benares: Chowkhamba, 1925.

Nyāya (1967) = *Nyāyadarśana of Gautama. With the Bhāṣya of Vātsyāyana, the Vārttika of Uddyotakara, the Tātparyaṭīkā of Vācaspati and the Pariśuddhi of Udayana*, I: Ch. 1. (Mithila Institute Series, 20.) Muzaffarpur: Mithila Institute, 1967.

OBERHAMMER, G. 1967-68. Notes on the Tantrayukti-s. *The Adyar Library Bulletin* 31-32: 600-616.

OBERHAMMER, G., E. PRETS & J. PRANDSTETTER 1991-96. *Terminologie der frühen philosophischen Scholastik in Indien. Ein Begriffswörterbuch zur altindischen Dialektik, Erkenntnislehre und Methodologie.* Band 1: A-I (1991); Band 2: U-Pū (1996). (Denkschriften der philosophisch-historischen Klasse der Österreichischen Akademie der Wissenschaften, 223 & 248.) Wien: Österreichischen Akademie der Wissenschaften.

Praśastapādabhāṣya = *The Bhāshya of Praśastapāda. Together with the Nyāyakandalī of Śrīdhara.* Ed. by Vindhyeśvarīprasāda Dvivedin. (Vizianagaram Sanskrit Series, 6.) Benares: Lazarus, 1895.

SCHOENING, J. 1995. *The Śālistamba Sūtra and its Tibetan Commentaries.* Wien: Wiener Studien zur Tibetologie und Buddhismuskunde.

SKILLING, P. 2000. Vasubandhu and the Vyākhyāyukti literature. *Journal of International Association for Buddhist Studies* 23.2: 297-350.

Suśruta = *Suśruta-saṃhitā. Chātra-subodhinī ṭīkā sahitā.* Ed. by Śambhunāth Pāṇḍeya Śāstrī. Kanapur, 1952.

VERHAGEN, P., this volume. Studies in Indo-Tibetan Buddhist hermeneutics (6): validity and valid interpretation of scripture according to Vasubandhu's Vyākhyāyukti.

YD = *Yuktidīpikā*, I. Ed. & transl. by Sh. Kumar & D. N. Bhargava. Delhi: Bharatiya Book Corporation, 1990.

APPENDIX I:

The list of the "old" *tantrayukti*
(Borrowed from Oberhammer 1967-68)

A = *Arthaśāstra*, S = *Suśruta-saṃhitā*, C = *Caraka-saṃhitā*

Tantrayukti	**Translation**	**Source**		
1. *adhikaraṇam*	Topic	A(1)	S(1)	C(1)
2. *vidhānam*	Statement (of contents)	A(2)	S(21)	C(21)
3. *yogaḥ*	Employment	A(3)	S(2)	C(2)
4. *padārthaḥ*	Meaning of words	A(4)	S(3)	C(4)
5. *hetvarthaḥ*	Reason	A(5)	S(4)	C(3)
6. *uddeśaḥ*	Mention	A(6)	S(5)	C(6)
7. *nirdeśaḥ*	Exposition	A(7)	S(6)	C(7)
8. *upadeśaḥ*	Advice	A(8)	S(7)	C(10)
9. *apadeśaḥ*	Reference	A(9)	S(8)	C(11)
10. *atideśaḥ*	Application	A(10)	S(10)	C(12)
11. *pradeśaḥ*	Indication	A(11)	S(9)	C(5)
12. *upamānam*	Analogy	A(12)	—	—
13. *arthāpattiḥ*	Implication	A(13)	S(13)	C(13)
14. *saṃśayaḥ*	Doubt	A(14)	S(24)	C(24)
15. *prasaṅgaḥ*	(Similar) consequence	A(15)	S(15)	C(15)
16. *viparyayaḥ*	Contrary	A(16)	S(14)	C(19)
17. *vākyaśeṣaḥ*	Completion of a sentence	A(17)	S(12)	—
18. *anumatam*	Agreement	A(18)	S(20)	C(22)
19. *vyākhyānam*	Explication	A(19)	S(25)	C(23)
20. *nirvacanam*	Derivation of a word	A(20)	S(27)	C(31)
21. *nidarśanam*	Illustration	A(21)	S(28)	C(30)
22. *apavargaḥ*	Exception	A(22)	S(11)	C(18)

23. *svasaṃjñā*	One's own technical term	A(23)	S(26)	C(27)
24. *pūrvapakṣaḥ*	Provisional view	A(24)	S(18)	C(20)
25. *uttarapakṣaḥ*	Final view	A(25)	— —	
26. *ekāntaḥ*	Generally valid sentence	A(26)	S(16)	C(16)
27. *anāgatāvekṣaṇam*	Reference to a future statement	A(27)	S(22)	C(26)
28. *atikrāntāvekṣaṇam*	Reference to a past statement	A(28)	S(23)	C(25)
29. *niyogaḥ*	Restriction	A(29)	S(29)	C(32)
30. *vikalpaḥ*	Option	A(30)	S(30)	C(33)
31. *samuccayaḥ*	Combination	A(31)	S(31)	C(29)
32. *ūhyam*	What is understood	A(32)	S(32)	C(28)
33. *anaikāntaḥ*	Not generally valid sentence	—	S(17)	C(17)
34. *pratyutsāraḥ*	Opposition	—	—	C(34)
35. *uddhāraḥ*	Refutation	—	—	C(35)
36. *saṃbhavaḥ*	Union	—	—	C(36)
37. *vākyadoṣaḥ*	Fault of argumentation	—	—	C(8)
38. *prayojanam*	Purpose	—	—	C(9)
39. *nirṇayaḥ*	Decision	—	S(19)	C(14)

APPENDIX II:

Definitions of the *tantrayukti*s provided by the *Arthaśāstra* and *Suśruta-saṃhitā*

(*Caraka-saṃhitā* confines itself to a mere listing of the *tantrayukti*s, without defining them; sandhis have been undone.)

Tantrayukti	Definition in the *Arthaśāstra*	Definition in the *Suśruta-saṃhitā*
1. *adhikaraṇam*	*yam artham adhikṛtya ucyate tad* ***adhikaraṇam***	*yam artham adhikṛtya ucyate tad* ***adhikaraṇam***
2. *vidhānam*	*śāstrasya prakaraṇa-ānupūrvī* ***vidhānam***	*prakaraṇa-ānupūrvyā abhihitaṃ vidhānam*
3. *yogaḥ*	*vākya-yojanā* ***yogaḥ***	*yena vākyaṃ yujyate sa* ***yogaḥ***
4. *padārthaḥ*	*pada-avadhikaḥ* ***padārthaḥ***	*yaḥ arthaḥ abhihitaḥ sūtre pade vā sa* ***padārthaḥ***
5. *hetvarthaḥ*	*hetuḥ artha-sādhako* ***hetvarthaḥ***	*yad anyad uktam anya-artha-sādhakaṃ bhavati sa* ***hetvarthaḥ***
6. *uddeśaḥ*	*samāsa-vākyam* ***uddeśaḥ***	*samāsa-vacanam* ***uddeśaḥ***
7. *nirdeśaḥ*	*vyāsa-vākyaṃ* ***nirdeśaḥ***	*vistara-vacanaṃ* ***nirdeśaḥ***
8. *upadeśaḥ*	*evaṃ vartitavyam iti* ***upadeśaḥ***	*evam iti* ***upadeśaḥ***
9. *apadeśaḥ*	*evam asau āha iti* ***apadeśaḥ***	*anena kāraṇena iti* ***apadeśaḥ***
10. *atideśaḥ*	*uktena sādhanam* ***atideśaḥ***	*prakṛtasya-anāgatasya sādhanaṃ* ***pradeśaḥ***
11. *pradeśaḥ*	*vaktavyena sādhanaṃ* ***pradeśaḥ***	*prakṛtasya-atikrāntena sādhanaṃ* ***pradeśaḥ***
12. *upamānam*	*dṛṣṭena adṛṣṭasya sādhanam* ***upamānam***	N/A
13. *arthāpattiḥ*	*yad anuktam arthād āpadyate sā* ***arthāpattiḥ***	*yad akīrtitam arthād āpadyate sā* ***arthāpattiḥ***

14. *saṃśayaḥ*	*ubhayataḥ hetumān arthaḥ* ***saṃśayaḥ***	*ubhaya-hetu-darśanaṃ* ***saṃśayaḥ***
15. *prasaṅgaḥ*	*prakaraṇa-antareṇa samānaḥ arthaḥ* ***prasaṅgaḥ***	*prakaraṇa-antareṇa samāpanaṃ* ***prasaṅgaḥ***
16. *viparyayaḥ*	*pratilomena sādhanaṃ* ***viparyayaḥ***	*yad yatra abhihitaṃ tasya prātilomyaṃ* ***viparyayaḥ***
17. *vākyaśeṣaḥ*	*yena vākyaṃ samāpyate sa* ***vākyaśeṣaḥ***	*yena padena anuktena vākyam samāpyate sā* ***vākyśeṣaḥ***
18. *anumatam*	*para-vākyam apratiṣiddham* ***anumatam***	*para-matam apratiṣiddham* ***anumatam***
19. *vyākhyānam*	*atiśaya-varṇanā* ***vyākhyānam***	*tantre atiśaya-upavarṇanaṃ* ***vyākhyānam***
20. *nirvacanam*	*guṇataḥ śabda-niṣpattiḥ* ***nirvacanam***	*niścitaṃ vacanaṃ* ***nirvacanam***
21. *nidarśanam*	*dṛṣṭāntaḥ dṛṣṭānta-yuktaḥ* ***nidarśanam***	*dṛśṭānta-vyaktiḥ* ***nidarśanam***
22. *apavargaḥ*	*abhipluta-vyapakarṣaṇam* ***apavargaḥ***	*abhivyāpya-apakarṣaṇam* ***apavargaḥ***
23. *svasaṃjñā*	*paraiḥ asamitaḥ śabdaḥ* ***svasaṃjñā***	*anya-śāstra-asāmānyā* ***svasaṃjñā***
24. *pūrvapakṣaḥ*	*pratiṣeddhavyaṃ vākyaṃ* ***pūrvapakṣaḥ***	*ākṣepa-pūrvakaḥ praśnaḥ* ***pūrvapakṣaḥ***
25. *uttarapakṣaḥ*	*tasya nirṇayana-vākyam* ***uttarapakṣaḥ***	N/A
26. *ekāntaḥ*	*sarvatra āyattam* ***ekāntaḥ***	*yad avadhāraṇena ucyate sa* ***ekāntaḥ***
27. *anāgatāvekṣa-ṇam*	*paścād evaṃ vihitam iti* ***anāgatāvekṣaṇam***	*evaṃ vakṣyatīti* ***anāgatāvekṣaṇam***
28. *atikrāntā-vekṣaṇam*	*purastād evaṃ vihitam iti* ***atikrāntāvekṣaṇam***	*yat pūrvam uktaṃ tad* ***atikrāntāvekṣaṇam***
29. *niyogaḥ*	*evaṃ na anyathā iti* ***niyogaḥ***	*idam eva kartavyam iti* ***niyogaḥ***
30. *vikalpaḥ*	*anena vā anena vā iti* ***vikalpaḥ***	*idaṃ vā idaṃ vā iti* ***vikalpaḥ***

31. *samuccayaḥ*	*anena ca anena ca iti* ***samuccayaḥ***	*idaṃ ca idaṃ ca iti* ***samuccayaḥ***
32. *ūhyam*	*anukta-karaṇam* ***ūhyam***	*yad anirdiṣṭaṃ buddhyā avagamyate tad* ***ūhyam***
33. *anaikāntaḥ*	N/A	*kvacit tathā kvacit anyathā iti yaḥ saḥ* ***anekāntaḥ***
34. *nirṇayaḥ*	N/A	*tasya* [= *pūrvapakṣaḥ*, this word added by IM] *uttaraṃ* ***nirṇayaḥ***

APPENDIX III:
Example of *padārtha* procedure

Ālokā, p. 21, ll. 22-27

tatra khalu Bhagavān āyuṣmantam Subhūtim sthaviram āmantrayate sma **|** **:**
idānīṃ padārthādivyākhyānena sūtrārtho vidhīyate. tatretyādi. ***tatra*** *iti vākya-upanyāse.* ***Khalu****-śabdo vākya-alaṃkāre. Śobhanā 'raṇa-vihāriṇāṃ madhye 'grā bhūtiś cetasaḥ sampattir yasya sa* ***Subhūtiḥ****. Sa-devake loke pūjādibhiḥ sthāvirya-prāptatvāt* ***sthaviraḥ****.*

APPENDIX IV:

Some examples of the application of the *tantrayuktis* in the *Ālokā*

1. *samāsa-nirdeśa:*

Ālokā, p.15, l. 29 – p. 16, l. 1
samāsanirdeśena *piṇḍārthas tāvad abhidhīyate*

Ālokā, p.25, l. 5
tatrāyaṃ parārthasya ***samāsanirdeśo*** *yad āha:*

2. *vyāsa-nirdeśa:*

Ālokā, p.25, ll. 2-4
tatrāyaṃ tasyā ***vyāsanirdeśo*** *yad āha: iha Śāriputra bodhisattvenāsthānayogena prajñāpāramitāyāṃ sthitvā dānapāramitā paripūrayitavyā deyadāyakapratigrāhakānupalabdhim upādāyetyādi.*

Ālokā, p. 25, ll. 8-10
tatrāyaṃ tasya ***vyāsanirdeśo*** *yad āha: matsariṇaḥ sattvān dāne duḥśīlān śīle vyāpādabahulān kṣāntau pratiṣṭhāpayitukāmena bodhisattvena prajñāpāramitāyāṃ śikṣitavyam ityādi.*

3. *adhyāhāryaṃ:*

Ālokā, p. 87, ll. 7-9
atas tāṃ pratipādayituṃ praśnayann āha: mahāsaṃnāhasaṃnaddha ityādi. Kiyateti kiyatsaṃkhyāvacchinnenārthāntareṇa dharmeṇa yukta ity ***adhyāhāryaṃ***.

4. *arthāpatti:*

Ālokā, p. 87, ll. 21-22
etad uktam: kṛpayā vihīnasyānupāyavataḥ pareṣāṃ kvacid apratiṣṭhāpanena nirvāpaṇāsambhavād idam ***arthād ākṣiptaṃ*** *bhavati:*

5. *nigamanam:*

Ālokā, p. 112, ll. 20-21
prasādhitam arthaṃ ***nigamayann*** *āha: tad ityādi.*

6. *śeṣaḥ:*

Ālokā, p. 68, ll. 8-9
vyatirekamukhena viparītapratipattim evāha na khalu punar ityādinā. Kaṃcid dharmaṃ vaiyavadānikaṃ. Grāhyavikalpaneti śeṣaḥ.

7. *upasaṃhāraḥ:*

Ālokā, p. 59, ll. 3-5
evaṃ carann ityādy ***upasaṃhāraḥ****. svasāmānyalakṣaṇānupapattyā sarvadharmāṇām animittatvaviśiṣṭaṃ rūpādyālambanam ity evaṃ caran bodhisattvaś carati prajñāpāramitāyām adhimātrakṣāntisvabhāvāyāṃ.*

APPENDIX V:

Definitions of the *tantrayuktis* in the *Yuktidīpikā*
(Cited from YD, ed. Kumar & Bhargava 1990)

1. *sūtra*: "*ucyate – sūcanāt sūtram | sūcayati tāṃs tān artha-viśeṣān iti sūtram*", p. 6
2. *pramāṇa*: "*pramāṇāni ca pratyakṣa-ādīni, tāni uttaratra vakṣyati 'dṛṣṭam anumānam āptavacanaṃ ca* (kā. 4), *'prativiṣaya-adhyavasāyo dṛṣṭam iti ādi'* (kā. 5)", p. 8
3. *avayava*: "*avayavāḥ punaḥ jijñāsādayaḥ, pratijñādayaḥ ca | tatra jijñāsādayaḥ vyākhyā-aṅgam | pratijñādayaḥ parapratyāyanāṅgaṃ tān uttaratra vakṣyāmaḥ*", p. 8
4. *anyūnatā*: "*anyūnatā | padārtha-kārtsnyam aśeṣatā 'nyūnatā iti abhidhīyate*", p. 15, l. 1
5. *saṃśaya*: "*sāmānya-abhidhānaṃ saṃśayaḥ*", p. 16
6. *nirṇaya*: "*viśeṣa-abhidhānaṃ nirṇayaḥ*", p. 16
7. *uddeśa*: "*saṅkṣepa-vacanam uddeśaḥ*", p. 17
8. *nirdeśa*: "*vistara-vacanaṃ nirdeśaḥ*", p. 17
9. *anukrama*: "*padārthānām ānupūrvyā sanniveśa-upadeśo 'nukramaḥ*", p. 17
10. *saṃjñā*: "*saṃjñi-pratyāyana-arthaṃ śabdaḥ saṃjñā*", p. 17
11. *upadeśa*: "*itikartavyatā-phala-samākhyānam upadeśaḥ*", p. 19

Vasubandhu's *Abhidharmakośa* in non-Buddhist philosophical treatises

MAREK MEJOR

0. The *Abhidharmakośa* or the 'Treasure-store of Higher Doctrine' or the 'Treasury of Scholastics' (La Vallée Poussin) by Vasubandhu (400-480 AD, Frauwallner) is one of the foremost works in the history of Buddhist and, in general, Indian philosophy.[1] The *Abhidharmakośa* has been an authoritative textbook for many Buddhist schools. Its overall importance has been attested in the philosophical literature of India over the centuries, and the text became a standard handbook, a kind of Summa of the Doctrine, for the students of Buddhism also outside India: in China and Japan, in Tibet and Mongolia, until the present.

Interestingly, the *Abhidharmakośa* was also highly regarded by non-Buddhist, i.e. Brahmanic and Jaina, thinkers in their discussions of various questions relating to ontology, epistemology, ethics, etc. It has been referred to by non-Buddhist authors for more than six hundred years after its conception (ca. 450 AD). Although from the 7th century onwards it was Dharmakīrti and his followers who dominated the scene of philosophical debate between the Buddhist schools and non-Buddhist thinkers, the *Abhidharmakośa* still preserved its high position as a reference textbook. The passages quoted come from various parts of the AKBh: I.17, 32;

[1] Cf. La Vallée Poussin 1936-37; see also Glasenapp 1954; Kher 1992 (not seen).

II.22, 50, 52; III.18, 19, 50; IV.1, 73; V.7; IX. The occurrence of so many different passages from AKBh in various non-Buddhist treatises is a proof of the popularity of Vasubandhu's *magnum opus* and its great authority.

In the present paper I have attempted to collect from various non-Buddhist philosophical texts the passages which explicitly refer to the *Abhidharmakośa* as well as those references which indicate direct dependence on or close relation to the *Abhidharmakośa* formulations. So far as I can see, the *Abhidharmakośa* was referred to explicitly in Sāṃkhya, Nyāya and Jaina texts. I have tried also to take into consideration the context in which the quoted passages from AKBh appear. However, an exhaustive discussion of all the passages is not possible within the limits of this paper, and the number of such references may still increase due to further investigation by scholars more competent in the history of Indian philosophy.

1. SĀṂKHYA

The basic text of Sāṃkhya, the *Sāṃkhyakārikā* by Īśvarakṛṣṇa (before 500 AD, Frauwallner) has been commented upon very often. Among many commentaries on it preserved, the anonymous *Yuktidīpikā* has been regarded by modern scholars as the most ancient and most important. Its unknown author, the Yuktidīpikākāra, was active probably about the middle of the 6th century (ca. 550 AD, Frauwallner), or perhaps about 600 AD (cf. Mejor 2000). YD contains several explicit quotations from the AKBh (identified by the recent editors, Wezler and Motegi) and also a clear reference to the Buddhist criticism of the notion of the existence of *ātman* in AKBh III.18 f. (identified and discussed in Mejor 1999).[2] In the following

---

[2] According to the Buddhist tradition Vasubandhu composed a treatise (not preserved) against the Sāṃkhya, the *Paramārthasaptati* (Mejor 1999: 107 ff.); see also below 3.3.1.2.

I comment upon those passages from the YD which refer to AKBh (the text of the YD is reproduced according to Wezler and Motegi's edition)

1.1. YD 111.16-22 = AKBh 159.19

The following passage from YD on SK 9 concerns the problem of causality. As we know, the Sāṃkhyas held the doctrine of the real (pre)existence of effect in cause (*satkāryavāda*). SK 9 defends that thesis against the criticism of other schools and rejects the opinions of the Buddhists as well as of the followers of Nyāya, Vaiśeṣika and Vedānta (according to Vācaspati Miśra's explanation in his *Sāṃkhyatattvakaumudī*) by means of the following five arguments:

> Effect subsists even prior to the operation of the cause: for that which does not exist cannot be by any means brought into existence; further, only appropriate materials are selected; every thing is not by every means possible; capable causes produce only that which they are competent to produce; and the effect is not different from the cause.[3]

The proper commentary on SK 9 is in YD preceded by a kind of long polemical introduction in which are presented objections of Sāṃkhya's opponents, claiming that the effect does not exist (*asat kāryam*). It seems that one should take this introduction as a *pūrvapakṣa*, because in the following comments on the arguments listed in SK 9 the Yuktidīpikākāra introduces his answers to the objections.

In his answer to one of these objection the YD-kāra introduces a definition of transformation (*pariṇāma*) which is similar to the one found in AKBh ad III.50a (AKBh 159.20 f.):

---

[3] SK 9: *asadakaraṇād upādānagrahaṇāt sarvasambhavābhāvāt* I *śaktasya śakyakaraṇāt kāraṇabhāvāc ca sat kāryam* II Transl. Mainkar 1972: 65; cf. Jha 1934: 32.

mārgāntarānupapatteḥ | [4] parināmo hi nāmāvasthitasya dravyasya dharmāntaranivṛttir dharmāntarapravṛttiś ca (cf. AKBh 159.19, YBh on YS III.13) | [5] *tatra sato dharmāntarasya nirodhābhyupagamād asataś cotpattipratijñānān nedaṃ mārgāntaram ārabhyate | evaṃ vyūhādayo 'py upasaṃhartavyāḥ | tasmāt pariṇāmādibhir abhibhavāc [ca] kartrādīnām arthavattvād asat kāryam iti* | **tathā coktam –*

jahad dharmāntaraṃ pūrvam upādatte yadā param |
tattvād apracyuto dharmī pariṇāmaḥ sa ucyate ||*
(YD 111.16-22)

Because another way is impossible. For transformation is the disappearance of one quality and the appearance of another quality in an unchanging substance. In that, because of admission of the disappearance of one existing quality, and because of acceptance of the appearance of non-existent [quality], this cannot begin another way. So also arrangement and the rest should be brought near [in that case]. Therefore, because it is dominated by transformation and the rest and because the agent and the rest possess a purpose, the effect does not exist.

*Accordingly, it was said[6] –

"When the possessor of a quality abandons a former quality and takes on another one while not deviating from its essence, this is called transformation."*

The question of transformation was also raised by Vasubandhu in AKBh ad III.50a, where he described the structure of Mount Meru: its four sides – from the north to the west – are made of gold, silver, lapis lazuli and crystal, respectively; the waters, which contain germs of various potentialities, under the influence of wind are transformed into different substances; causes and effects are different, do not arise simultaneously.[7] On this occasion Vasubandhu

[4] See also YD 120.17 ff.

[5] Edition reads: *parimāṇo*. Underlining is mine, M.M.

[6] *--* Mss K, P and D omit this stanza (YD 111, n. 15; but see YD(P) 49, n. 3). It seems that the stanza has been added later, because here it does not fit the stream of the argument but is an explanation of the term *pariṇāma*. The stanza is quoted by the Yuktidīpikākāra once more ad SK 16c (YD 163.12-13) in his answer to the question "What is transformation (*pariṇāma*)?". There there is also the answer to the above mentioned objections and rejection of the thesis of non-existence of effect.

cited the Sāṃkhya definition of transformation and criticised the position of its followers (AKBh 159.21-25):

> *katham ca* ***sāṃkhyānāṃ*** *pariṇāmaḥ* | *avasthitasya dravyasya dharmāntaranivṛttau dharmāntaraprādurbhāva iti* | *kaś cātra doṣaḥ* | *sa eva hi dharmī na saṃvidyate yasyāvasthitasya dharmāṇāṃ pariṇāmaḥ kalpyeta* | *kaś caivam āha dharmebhyo 'nyo dharmīti* | *tasyaiva tu dravyasyānyathābhāvamātraṃ pariṇāmaḥ* | *evam apy ayuktam* | *kim atrāyuktam* | *tad eva cedaṃ na cedaṃ tatheti apūrvaiṣā vācoyuktiḥ*[8] |

> How do the Sāṃkhya followers [define] transformation? – As an appearance of a different quality in an unchanged substance when another quality has been destroyed. – What is the fault? – That one cannot discern such a substrate which would have remained unchanged while it could be conceived of being subject to modification. – And who says that the possessor of qualities is different from the qualities? Transformation is but an alteration of that substance. – Such [a statement] is wrong too. – And what is wrong with it? – It is quite a new use of words to say that the same thing both is that and [at the same time] is not that.[9]

---

[7] "What is the origin of the different substances that make up Meru? – The waters which have fallen on the sphere of gold are rich in different potentialities; under the action of the winds which possess different efficacies, they disappear and make room for different jewels. It is thus that the waters are transformed into jewels: the water is the cause, the jewels are a result different from the cause, and there is no simultaneity. This is quite different from the concept of transformation (*pariṇāma*) that the Sāṃkhyas imagine. – What do the Sāṃkhyas understand by *pariṇāma*? – They admit that *dharmas* arise and disappear within a permanent substance (a *dharmin* or *dravya*). – How is this incorrect? – One cannot admit the simultaneous existence of a permanent *dharmin*, and of *dharmas* arising and disappearing. – But the Sāṃkhyas do not hold that there is a *dharmin* separate from the *dharmas*; they say that a *dharma*, when it is transformed (*pariṇam*), becomes the support of different characteristics: this *dharma* they call *dharmin*. In other words, transformation (*pariṇāma*) is only the modification (*anyathābhāvamātra*) of a substance (*dravya*). – This thesis is not correct. – Why is it not correct? – Because there is a contradiction in terms: you admit that that (the cause) is identical to this (the result), but that this is not like that." (Pruden, Kośa II, 453.)

[8] AKBh 159.22; 298.19 reads: *vāyo yuktiḥ*. Recte: *vācoyuktiḥ* = AKBh(S) 509.7; reading confirmed by Yaśomitra (AKVy 325.3 and its Tibetan translation: *tshig gi lugs*).

1.1.1. Interestingly, the definition of *pariṇāma* with almost the same wording is found in other texts too:

(i) At the end of Vyāsa's commentary on the YS III.13 (YBh ad YS III.13 132.11-12; cf. YSBhV 255.23-24): *avasthitasya dravyasya pūrvadharmanivṛttau dharmāntarotpattiḥ pariṇāma iti* | – "The coming into being of another characteristic of a substance when the earlier characteristic has ceased to be is 'change'." (Rukmani 2000, II: 19)

(ii) In Dharmakīrti's *Vādanyāya* (VN I: 13.11-13; cf. I: 66.3-5; cf. II: 32, n. 155) in wording almost identical with that of the AKBh: *avasthitasya dravyasya dharmāntaranivṛttir dharmāntaraprādurbhāvaś ca pariṇāmaḥ* |

[9] Bronkhorst 1997: 393 f.: "(a) How do the Sāṃkhyas [define] modification? (b) [As follows:] The appearance of a new property in a substance which remains the same, while another property is destroyed. (c) What is wrong with that? (d) For there is no such substrate (*dharmin*) which remains the same and whose properties could undergo modification. (e) Who says that the substrate is different from the property? Modification is merely the becoming otherwise of that very substance. (f) This, too, is incorrect. (g) What is incorrect about it? (h) This is a new way of speaking, to say that this is that, but [at the same time that] it is not like that."

In the following (p. 396 f.) Bronkhorst's argument is based on the reading **na hy avasthitasya ... sa eva* (so reads AKBh(S), p. 509.3, 4; Yaśomitra AKVy 324.31, 33, but see p. 325, n. 1-1; Peking Tanjur, Cu 154a5-8), instead of *avasthitasya ... sa eva hi* – so reads AKBh manuscript (photo 9A, leaf 8, fol. 44a3; Pradhan ed. 159.19, 20), which is corroborated by the Tibetan translation of the *Abhidharmakośa* (Peking Tanjur, Gu 167b7-167a1: ***grangs can pa rnams kyi*** *'gyur ba ji lta bu zhe na | rdzas gnas pa la chos gzhan log na chos gzhan 'byung ba'o || 'di la nyes pa ci zhig yod ce na | gnas pa gang gi chos rnams kyi bye brag brteg par bya ba'i chos can nyid (8) med do || chos rnams las chos can gzhan no zhes de skad du zor | chos de nyid gzhan du 'gyur ba tsam ni 'gyur ba yin no zhe na | de ltar na yang rigs pa ma yin no || 'di la mi rigs ci zhig yod ce na | de nyid 'di yin la | 'di [167a1] de lta bu yang ma yin no zhes bya ba'i tshig gi lugs 'di ni sngon ma byung ba yin no ||*) and the commentaries by Pūrṇavardhana (Peking Tanjur, Ju 389b1-390a4) and Sthiramati (Peking Tanjur, Tho 99a7-99b7).

1.2. YD 154.24 = cf. AK, p. 192.5

SK 15 presents five arguments in favour of the thesis that the unmanifest matter (*avyakta*) exists as a main cause (*kāraṇa*) of the manifest (*vyakta*):

> A general cause, the Unevolved is to be regarded as existing because specific objects are finite; since there is homogeneity; since effects exist through energy; since there is an issuing forth of effect from the cause and since there is a reunion of the universe.[10]

In the extensive commentary on SK 15, the Yuktidīpikākāra mentioned the expression *jagadvaicitrya* – 'variety of the world'. A similar characteristic expression – *lokavaicitrya* – is found in Vasubandhu's AK IV.1, which is often cited both by Buddhist and non-Buddhist authors (see below).[11]

In YD, following the opponent's argument concerning the notion of causal connection (*anvaya*)

> As it was said by the venerable sir that the Principal foundation is the cause which has the capacity to produce the world, so the other schools [of thought] declare the atoms, spirit, god, actions and destiny, own nature, time, free will (accident), non-existence [etc.] to be causation.[12]

we find the passage: *karmadaivānvayo jagadvaicitryopalambhāt* (cf. AK, p. 192.5) | – "[There is] causal connection of actions and

---

[10] SK 15: *bhedānāṃ parimāṇāt samanvayāt śaktitaḥ pravṛtteś ca | kāraṇakāryavibhāgād avibhāgād vaiśvarūpasya* || Transl. Mainkar 1972: 87; cf. Jha 1934: 54.

[11] In AK IV.1 Vasubandhu claims that all variety in the world originates from deeds (*karmajaṃ lokavaicitryam*), i.e. from acts of will and that which is their result (*cetanā tatkṛtaṃ ca tat*). The deeds are of three kinds, viz. bodily, verbal, and mental. An act of will is of mental character (*cetanā mānasaṃ karma*); from it result bodily and verbal deeds.

[12] (YD 154.14-16) *yathā bhavān āha pradhānaṃ jagadutpattisamarthaṃ kāraṇam asti, evaṃ tantrāntarīyāḥ paramāṇupuruṣeśvarakarmadaivasvabhāvakālayadṛcchābhāvān kāraṇatvenâbhidadhat* | Cf. also AK II.64cd and AKVy 237.13: *īśvarapuruṣapradhāṇādikam iti* | *ādiśabdena kālasvabhāvaparamāṇvādi gṛhyate* |

destiny[13], because of ascertainment of the variety of world." However, from the long discussion in YD (160.31–161.23) it does not follow that the expression *jagadvaicitrya* was used in direct relation to the AKBh.

1.3. YD 163.27-29 = AKBh 159.24

The following passage concerns the discussion of the notion of transformation (*pariṇāma*) (see above fragment 1); here the Yuktidīpikākāra quotes a formula found in Vasubandhu's AKBh ad III.50 (AKBh 159.24):

> *āha:* ***dharmadharminor ananyatvābhyupagamād dharmotpattivināśe dharmyutpattivināśaprasaṅgaḥ** (cf. AKBh 159.24)* । *na hi vo dharmebhyo 'nyo dharmī* ।[14] *tatra yadi dharmasya nivṛttir abhyupagamyate dharmiṇo 'pi nivṛttir ananyatvāt prāptā dharmotpattau tadutpatt<eḥ>* । *tatra yad uktaṃ* (163.14) *dharmotpattivi<nāśe> dharmisvarūpāvasthānam ity etad ayuktam* ।
>
> [The opponent] says: From accepting the identity of the possessor of properties and the properties there follows the consequence that when the occurrence of a property is annihilated the arising of the possessor of properties is annihilated [too], since – according to you – the possessor of properties is no different from the properties. In that case, if the annihilation of a property is admitted, then the annihilation of the possessor of properties follows, because it is no different; because the properties arise when it [= the possessor of properties] arises. In that it was said that the possessor of properties remains unchanged in its own form when there is annihilation of the arising of properties. This [we find] unreasonable.

---

[13] According to the explanation in YD 161.21 f., *daiva* is just a different name for actions which have attained maturity (*karmaṇām eva prāptaparipākāṇām abhidhānam*).

[14] *--* The *vārttika* (underlined bold type) has no true counterpart in the AKBh, whereas it is the next sentence (underlined italics mine) which we find in the AKBh *verbatim*.

1.4. YD 167.4-20 = AKBh 466.5-13
1.5. YD 167.21-23 = AKBh 468.20-22

These two fragments make a unit. They contain a polemic against Vasubandhu's refutation of the existence of *ātman* (AKBh ad III. 18 f.: *nātmāsti* 'there is no self') and are indisputable proof of the Yuktidīpikākāra's acquaintance with the *Abhidharmakośa* (translated and discussed in Mejor 1999: 110-111; cf. Mejor 2000: 261 = 2004: 405).

1.6. YD 170.13-20 = AK II.34ab, AK II.24

The following passage again corroborates the thesis of the Yuktidīpikākāra's acquaintance with the *Abhidharmakośa*. Here we find the reference to the definition of the mind (AK II.34ab: *cittaṃ mano 'tha vijñānam ekārtham* | = AKBh 61.22 f.; cf. also Vasubandhu's *Viṃśatikāvṛtti*) and the mental factors (AK II.24: *vedanā cetanā saṃjñā cchandaḥ sparśo matiḥ smṛtiḥ* | *manaskāro 'dhimokṣaś ca samādhiḥ sarvacetasi* || = AKBh 54.17-18).[15]

> What then is that "consciousness"? –
>
> It is said: thought, mind, and consciousness [designate the same thing]. It is sixfold cognition, [viz.] eye consciousness, ear consciousness, nose consciousness, tongue consciousness, body consciousness, and mind consciousness. In that, in dependence on visible form and the eye arises eye consciousness; and similarly, sound and the ear, odour and the nose, taste and the tongue, [the tangible and the body,] mental factors and the mind, produce [the appropriate type of] consciousness. There are [ten] mental factors[16]: sensation, perception, volition, contact, act of attention and the rest [which coexist in every mind].[17]

---

[15] Mejor 1999: 106; cf. also Mejor 2000: 281 f. = 2004: 425 f.

[16] The order given by the YD-kāra is that of the Sarvāstivāda Abhidharma (*Prakaraṇapāda*), cf. Pruden, Kośa I, 333 f., n. 109B.

[17] YD 170.13-20: *ucyate: kiṃ punar idaṃ vijñānaṃ nāmeti* | *āha: cittaṃ mano vijñānam iti* (Viṃś., p. 3.3; AKBh 62.1-2) | *tac ca ṣaḍvidhaṃ jñānaṃ cakṣurvijñānaṃ śrotravijñānaṃ ghrāṇavijñānaṃ jihvāvijñānaṃ kāyavijñānaṃ manovijñānam iti* | *tatra rūpaṃ pratītya cakṣuś cotpadyate cakṣurvijñānam* | *evaṃ śrotraśabdaghrāṇagandhajihvārasamanodharmāś cittam ut-*

1.7. YD 259.1-10 = AKBh III.19

The last fragment of the YD refers to the SK 55ab:

> The intelligent being, the dweller in the body, experiences pain arising from decay and death, until his deliverance from the subtle body. Pain, therefore, is of the nature of things.[18]

1.7.1. Here the Yuktidīpikākāra introduced a very interesting description of the development of a human being as an embryo and its painful birth.

> [The opponent] says: One should add [the suffering which is] produced by birth. Just as old age and death cause one extreme distress, so also birth [is to be regarded as the cause of suffering]. For instance, this person has his body covered with a membrane in his mother's womb, is drenched in filth in that embryo container which is nothing but a wound, has his limbs squeezed due to the impossibility of a comfortable position under pressure from the mother's eating etc., and after suffering pain in the womb, then emerges through the tight opening between two bones, his limbs wet with lots of urine and blood, being struck as if by swords by the rush of air outside and [people's] hands; unable to tell of the suffering he has to experience which is going on within him, tortured by thoughts of the happiness and misery which he conceives of in others because of their similarity to his own, and by the accumulated afflictions, with stiff limbs, he experiences the suffering of birth. Therefore that should be said too.[19]

---

pādayanti | tasya dharmā vedanā saṃjñā cetanā sparśo <manaskāra> evamādayaḥ (cf. AK. II.24) | *tasmād vijñānaskandhasyaivopabhogasāmarthyān nāsty ātmeti* |

[18] SK 55: *atra jarāmaraṇakṛtaṃ prāpnoti cetanaḥ puruṣaḥ | liṅgasyāvinivṛttes tasmād duḥkhaṃ samāsena* || Transl. Mainkar 1972: 181; cf. Jha 1934: 116.

[19] YD 259.1-10: *āha:* ***janmakṛtasyopasaṃkhyānam*** | *yathaiva hi jarā maraṇaṃ cātmanaḥ prakṛṣṭodvegakārakam evaṃ janmāpi | tathā hy ayaṃ mātur udare jarāyupariveṣṭitaśarīro 'medhyaparipluto vraṇamātrāyāṃ garbhadhānyāṃ yathāsukham asambhavāt paripīḍitagātro mātur aśanādibhiḥ pīḍyamāno garbhavāse duḥkham anubhūya paścāt saṃvṛtenāsthidvayavivareṇa nissṛto mūtrarudhirakalilaiḥ pariṣiktagātro bāhyena vāyunā karaiś ca saṃsparśād asibhir iva tudyamānaḥ svasaṃvedyaṃ duḥkham ātmani vartamānam ākhyātum asamarthaḥ svasukhaduḥkhasāmānyāt paratra parikalpitasukhaduḥkhabuddhibhir dṛḍhagātrair uc<c>itakleśaiś ca yātyamāno janmaduḥkham anubhavati | tasmāt tad api vaktavyam iti* |

1.7.2. A parallel description of the development of a human embryo we find in the AKBh ad III.19:

Kalala, *arbuda*, *peśin*, *ghana*, and *praśākha* are the names of the five successive stages of the embryo. When the embryo becomes ripe, the winds blowing from the interior of the mother's womb turn it towards the 'exit gate'. An unfavourable development results in removal of dead foetus by the 'expert women' who pull out the embryo after having cut its limbs with a knife, and a favourable one results in coming into the painful world –

> (...) Or else the birth is fortunate. The mother and the servants take the newborn baby into their hands which are like knives and acids for this body now as sensitive as an open wound. One washes the child; one nourishes it with milk and fresh butter, and later with solid foods: thus does he grow.(...)[20]

2. YOGA

It was Louis de La Vallée Poussin who observed a long time ago that there are surprising parallels, both terminological and doctrinal, between Patañjali's *Yogasūtras* and Buddhism, and especially the *Abhidharmakośa* and Vyāsa's *Yogasūtrabhāṣya* (perhaps ca. 500 AD, Frauwallner) and put together parallel passages from both texts.[21]

---

[20] AKBh 130.5-22; Pruden, Kośa II, 400. Full translation of the passage with additional materials in Kritzer 2004.

[21] La Vallée Poussin 1936-37: 239: "Que Vyāsa dépende de la Vibhāṣā ou de Vasubandhu, ce point est acquis. Son interprétation des Sūtras, iii, 13, iv, 12, ne laisse place à aucun doute." List of parallel passages with the Buddhist texts in the *Yogasūtra* put together by La Vallée Poussin: YS I.13 (*īśvarapraṇidhāna*, cf. Aṅguttara Nikāya I, 173; Majjhima Nikāya II, 227; cf. Bodhicaryāvatāra IX.120); YS I.20 (5 *upāya*: *śraddhā*, *vīrya*, *smṛti*, *samādhi*, *prajñā*; cf. LVP, Kośa II, 105); YS I.17, 43, 52, II.33 (4 *dhyāna*); YS I.24, II.4, 12 (theory of germs – *bīja*; *āśaya*, cf. LVP, Kośa V, 4-5, 7, 87; II, 5; IV, 172); YS I.25 (definition of *īśvara*, cf. LVP, Kośa II, 64cd); YS I.33 (4 *brahmavihāra*, cf. LVP VIII, 196-203); YS I.48-49 (*prajñā* called *ṛtambharā*); YS II.5 (*avidyā*, cf. LVP V, 21); YS IV.7 (doctrine of action); YS IV.7 (4 kinds of action, cf. LVP, Kośa IV, 128); YS II.12-13 (different kinds of action; Vyāsa gives the same compa-

2.1. La Vallée Poussin's list of parallel passages can be extended, e.g. with the following one:

> *kecit tu sattvamātram api parikalpya, asti sa sattvo ya etān pañcaskandhān nikṣipya anyāṃś ca pratisandadhāti – ity uktvā tata eva punas tapyanti** | *tathā skandhānāṃ mahānirvedāya virāgāyānutpādāya praśāntaye guror antike brahmacaryaṃ cariṣyāmīty uktvā sattvasya punaḥ sattvam evāpahnuvate* | (YBh ad YS IV.21)
>
> *YSBhV 353.6: *trasyanti.*
>
> There are some who assume 'being' as such and say that this 'being' is the one that discards those five 'skandhas' (divisions of being) and takes on (puts together) other (skandhas). Then having said this they are afraid of this 'being'. Similarly, they say that in order to feel total disgust towards the said five skandhas and for the sake of their non-production and calmness they would go to a teacher (guru) and lead the life of a brahmacārī (disciple); having said that they deny, after all, the existence of the being. (Rukmani 2000, II: 181.)

2.1.1. This refers to the passage ad AK III.18a in which Vasubandhu quoted a canonical text, the *Paramārthaśūnyatādharmaparyāya*[22], saying that actions and results exist, but no agent can be

---

rison as LVP, Kośa III, 116); YS II.31 (4 great vows *mahāvrata*, cf. LVP, Kośa IV, 89); YS II.34 (Vyāsa discusses different results, 'fruits' of killing, cf. LVP, Kośa IV, 85); YS II.15 (suffering, *duḥkhatā*, cf. LVP, Kośa VI, 125); YS II.25, III.50, 55, IV.26-34 (problem of *kaivalya*); YS II.27 (7 kinds of *prajñā*); YS II.26 (*dṛśyaparityāga*, cf. LVP, Kośa VII, 64); YS II.39 (Vyāsa, *janmakathaṃtā*, cf. LVP, Kośa III, 67); YS II.42 (*saṃtoṣa*); YS II.47 (*ānantyasamāpatti*); YS III.13, IV.12 (*sarvāstivāda*: III.13, Vyāsa – Saṅghabhadra; III.13, LVP, Kośa V, 52; see conclusion La Vallée Poussin 1936-37: 239: "no doubt, Vyāsa relied on the [Great] Commentary *Vibhāṣā* or on Vasubandhu"); YS III.20-21 (*paracittajñāna*, cf. LVP, Kośa VII, 99; LVP, Kośa VII, 7-9, 26; cf. Bhoja – *praṇidhāna*, cf. *praṇidhi-jñāna*, LVP, Kośa VII, 88); YS III.26 (*bhuvanajñāna*, 'cognition of the world', Vyāsa – cosmological description, cf. Buddhist description); YS III.48 (*manojavita*, 'rapid transfer like thought', LVP, Kośa VIII, 113); YS III.46 (4 kinds of *sampad*, or 'perfections' of yogin – cf. LVP, Kośa VII, 84; cf. also Vyāsa ad YS III.24 and LVP, Kośa VII, 73, simile of elephant); YS III.51, IV.28-29 (stages of yoga, *bhūmi*; cf. LVP, Kośa VI, 150, 151, VII, 95); YS IV.1 (5 kinds of *siddhi*, 'powers', cf. LVP, Kośa VII, 122, *ṛddhi*); YS IV.16 & notes (theory of cognition).

discerned which abandons these aggregates of the elements of existence and takes on others:

> ***nātmāsti*** | *kīdṛśātmā* [|] *ya imān nikṣipaty anyāṃś ca skandhān pratisaṃdadhātīti parikalpyate* | *sa tādṛśo nāsty antarvyāpārapuruṣaḥ* | *evaṃ tūktaṃ bhagavatā "asti karmāsti vipākaḥ kārakas tu nopalabhyate ya imāṃś ca skandhān nikṣipaty anyāṃś ca skandhān pratisaṃdadhāty anyatra dharmasaṃketāt* | *tatrāyaṃ dharmasaṃketo yadutāsmin satīdaṃ bhavatīti vistareṇa pratītyasamutpādaḥ"* | (AKBh 129.7-12)

> The *ātman* does not exist. – The *ātman* in which you believe, an entity that abandons the *skandhas* of one existence and takes up the *skandhas* of another existence, an internal agent of action, a Puruṣa, – this *ātman* does not exist. In fact the Blessed One said, 'Actions exist, and results exist, but there is no agent who abandons these *skandhas* here and takes up those *skandhas* there, independent of the causal relationship of the *dharmas*. What is this causal relationship? Namely, if this exists, then that exists; through the arising of this, there is the arising of that; *pratītya-samutpāda*. (Pruden, Kośa II, 399.)

2.2. Another example of relationship between the *Yogaśāstra* and the *Abhidharma(kośa)* was brought forward by A. Wezler (1984: 317 ff.) He called attention to the passage found in the *Yogabhāṣya* and in the *Yogasūtrabhāṣyavivaraṇa* ad YS II.15 and analysed the similarity between the quadruple division of the *Yogaśāstra* and the Buddha's teaching of the Four Noble Truths in the context of medical science.[23] In that he discussed the Buddhist *Vyādhyādisūtra* or

---

[22] Cf. Mejor 1999: 99.

[23] YBh 80.2-6: *yathā cikitsāśāstraṃ caturvyūham* | *rogo rogahetur ārogyaṃ bhaiṣajyam iti, evam idam api śāstraṃ caturvyūham eva* | *tadyathā saṃsāraḥ saṃsārahetur mokṣo mokṣopāya iti* | *tatra duḥkhabahulaḥ saṃsāro heyaḥ* | *pradhānapuruṣayoḥ saṃyogo heyahetuḥ* | *saṃyogasyātyantikī nivṛttir hānam* | *hānopāyaḥ samyagdarśanam* |

"Just as the science of medicine has four parts – disease, the cause of disease, absence of disease, remedy – this science also has four parts. They are as follows – the round of births and deaths (saṃsāra), the cause of saṃsāra, liberation and the means of liberation. Of these, saṃsāra, which is filled with pain, is to be got rid of. The cause for saṃsāra is the association between pradhāna and puruṣa; the

'The Sūtra [dealing with] disease, etc.' which was referred to by Vasubandhu and explained by the commentator Yaśomitra in his *Abhidharmakośavyākhyā* (ad AK VI.2).[24] According to Wezler (1984: 320), "it is here that the Four Noble Truths are expressly compared to the corresponding systematic parts of the science of medicine". The passage is another proof of great affinity between Vyāsa's *Bhāṣya* and Vasubandhu's *Abhidharmakośa*.

3. NYĀYA

3.1. The fundamental text of the Nyāya school, Akṣapāda Gautama's *Nyāyasūtra* (ca. 4th century), together with its commentary *Nyāyasūtrabhāṣya* by Pakṣilasvāmin Vātsyāyana (first half of the 5th century, Frauwallner), was commented upon by Uddyotakara Bhāradvāja (ca. 650 AD, Frauwallner) in his *Nyāyabhāṣyavārttika.*[25] Uddyotakara twice quoted AK II.22ab.[26]

3.1.1. First, AK II.22ab is quoted in the section on the definition of the objects of valid knowledge (*prameyalakṣaṇaprakaraṇam*), in connection with the discussion on qualities of the five great elements, which at the same time function as the sense objects (NS I.1.14):[27]

---

total cessation of this association is liberation; the means to liberation is true insight (knowledge)." (Rukmani 2000, I: 266 f.; cf. I: 280)

[24] AKBh 328.6 ff. (translated in Wezler 1984: 324); AKVy 514.24-34; cf. Pruden, Kośa III, 897 & n. 9.

[25] Bronkhorst 1996; Frauwallner 1933.

[26] AK II.22: (*rūpiṇāṃ sahotpādaniyamaḥ*) *kāme 'ṣṭadravyako 'śabdaḥ paramāṇur anindriyaḥ* | *kāyendriyī navadravyaḥ, daśadravyo 'parendriyaḥ* ||

"In Kāmadhātu, an atom into which there is no entry of sound, and into which there is no entry of any organ, is made of eight substances. When the organ of touch enters into it, it is made up of nine substances. When any other organ enters into it, it is made up of ten substances." (Pruden, Kośa I, 185.)

[27] NS I.1.14: *gandharasarūpasparśaśabdāḥ pṛthivyādiguṇās tadarthāḥ* ||

"Smell, taste, colour, touch, and sound, which are respectively the qualities of earth, etc., are the objects of the senses." (Gangopadhyaya 1982: 24.)

nāyaṃ hetur anekāntāt, ye ghaṭādibhāvam āpannāḥ pṛthivyādayas teṣāṃ pṛthivyāṃ saṃgṛhyamāṇāyām arthāntarabhūtānām abādīnām agrahaṇam | *atha cārthāntarabhūtā abādayo na darśanaviṣayabhājo bhavanti, tasmād anekāntaḥ* | *atha na catvāri mahābhūtāni tathā sanniviṣṭānīti pakṣas tathāpi rūpaṃ catvāri mahābhūtānīti vacanaṃ vyāhanyate* | *atha brūṣe, naiva no rūpādivyatiriktāḥ pṛthivyādaya iti ? tathāpy asya vākyasyāyam artho bhavati rūpādayo rūpam iti, tathā ca kāme 'ṣṭadravyako 'ṇur iti vyāhanyeta* | *atha pṛthivyādīnāṃ saṃghātamātre rūpādivyavahāraḥ ? tathāpi na rūpaṃ pṛthivyādayo vastutaḥ santi* | *katham iti* | *pṛthivyādīnāṃ saṃghāto rūpaṃ pṛthivyādayaś ca rūpādisaṃghāta iti saṃhanyamānasyābhāvāt na saṃghāto 'sti* | *sarvaḥ saṃghātaḥ saṃhanyamānatantro dṛṣṭa iti sarvathā na vyāghātān mucyase* | (NBhV 71.4-13)

This is not the reason, because it is not certain. The [elements of] earth, etc. which have become a pot, etc. are not grasped as different things – water, etc. – in the inclusive [elements of] earth. Now, the water and other [elements], which are different things, do not form part of visible objects, therefore it [= the reason] is not certain.

Now if the thesis is that the four great elements are not assembled in such a way, then it contradicts the statement that matter is made of four great elements [cf. AK I.9, 12].

Now if you say – 'For us the earth and other [elements] are not different from visible form, etc.', then the meaning of that statement is that the visible form, etc. is matter and thus it contradicts [the statement that] in the Kāmadhātu an atom is made of eight substances [AK II.22ab].

Now if visible form and other [elements] are active only in the aggregate of earth and other [elements], then the earth and other [elements] do not exist in reality as visible form. – How? The visible form is aggregate of the earth and other [elements], and the earth and other are the aggregate of visible form and other, thus because of non-existence of anything to be put together an aggregate does not exist. Every aggregate is perceived as depending on what is to be put together. Therefore you cannot escape defeat in any way.

3.1.2. Secondly, AK II.22 is quoted in the section on the refutation of the view that no object is a single entity (*sarvapṛthaktvanirākaraṇaprakaraṇam*), in connection with the discussion on NS IV.1.36: *lakṣaṇavyavasthānād evāpratiṣedhaḥ* || – "(The view that an object is a single entity) is not refuted due to the very fact that a term indicative of an object refers specifically to (a single entity)." (Gangopadhyaya 1982: 301.)

athānantaṃ samudāyaṃ pratipadyase 'aṣṭau dravyāṇi samuditāni paramāṇur' iti śāstraṃ vyāhataṃ bhavati, 'kāme 'ṣṭadravyako 'ṇur aśabdaḥ' iti || *ekānupapattau cānekopapattir ity etad vyāhatam* | *yaś cāyaṃ hetuḥ samūhe bhāvaśabdaprayogād iti, ayam ubhayato vyāghātān na kiñcit* | *katham ubhayataḥ* | *na kaścid eko bhāvaḥ* | *samūhe bhāvaśabdaprayogād iti pratijñāhetvor vyāghātaḥ* | (NBhV 450.18-451.1)

Now, [when] you admit an infinite collection (aggregate) saying that an atom is made of eight assembled substances, it contradicts the śāstra-statement that in the 'realm of desire' (*kāmadhātu*) an atom deprived of sound is made of eight substances. The occurrence of many [things] when a single entity is not logically tenable, this is contradicted. What concerns the reason [of the statement that there is no single entity but only a collection,] for the word 'entity' refers [only] to a collection, it is not at all [the reason] because it is contradicted in both ways. – How in both ways? There is no single entity, for the word 'entity' refers [only] to a collection, [and] both the thesis and the reason are contradicted.

3.2. The *Nyāyabhūṣaṇa* (NBhū), or "Ornament of logic", is a large autocommentary on the *Nyāyasāra*, or "Essence of logic". Its author, Bhāsarvajña (860-920 AD), introduced significant changes into the hitherto prevailing interpretation of the basic Nyāya text.[28]

3.2.1. Bhāsarvajña quoted AK IV.1[29] in his commentary on the third chapter of his *Nyāyasāra*, in the section on 'uncertainty about the volitional character of action and its refutation' (*karmaṇaś caitanyasandehas tannirāsaś ca*).

nanu ca 'karmajalokavaicitryam' icchadbhiḥ saugataiḥ na kartṛmātrasyādhikṣepaḥ kriyate | *na ca karmaṇo 'cetanatvāt tena siddhasādhyatānutpattiḥ, 'cetanā mānasaṃ karma' iti vacanāt tadanyasya cetanatvāsiddheḥ* |

[28] On Bhāsarvajña's explanation of the doctrine of liberation in the context of the quadruple division of the Yogaśāstra (and its relevance for the Buddha's teaching of the Four Noble Truths) see Wezler 1984: 326-335.

[29] AK IV.1: *karmajaṃ lokavaicitryaṃ cetanā tatkṛtaṃ ca tat* | *cetanā mānasaṃ karma tajjaṃ vākkāyakarmaṇī* ||
"The variety of the world arises from action. It is volition and that which is produced through volition. Volition is mental action: it gives rise to two actions, bodily and vocal action." (Pruden, Kośa II, 551-552.)

Surely, the Buddhists who accept that the variety of the world arises from action(s) do not dismiss (do not manage to reject) the mere agent, and from the non-volitional character of action does not follow that it is impossible to prove what is to be proved. Because from the statement that volition is mental action cannot be proved the volitional character of [action] different from it.

3.3. The well-known passage from AK IV.1a is also referred to in Jayanta Bhaṭṭa's (840-900 AD) *Nyāyamañjarī*, or 'Cluster of flowers of logic', in the first part – on the means of valid knowledge (*pramāṇaprakaraṇa*), in the third chapter (*tṛtīyāhnika*), in the section on 'God's bodilessness' (*īśvarasyāśarīratvam*):

nanv evaṃ tarhi īśvarecchaiva bhavatu kartrī saṃhartrī ca kiṃ karmabhiḥ I *maivam* I *karmabhir vinā jagadvaicitryānupapatteḥ* I *karmanairapekṣyapakṣe 'pi trayo doṣā darśitā eveśvarasya nirdayakarmacodanānarthakyam anirmokṣaprasaṅgaś ceti, tasmāt karmaṇām eva niyojane svātantryam īśvarasya, na tan nirapekṣam, kiṃ tādṛśaiśvaryeṇa prayojanam iti cen na, na prayojanānuvartti pramāṇaṃ bhavitum arhati* (...) I (NM 187.18-19)

Is it not so then – let the will of God be creator and destroyer, what is the use of actions? That is impossible. Because without actions the variety of the world is not possible. Also in the thesis which declares independence from actions three faults have been shown, [it is] nonsensical [to admit that] God is prompting to pitiless actions and [there follows] the consequence of non-liberation. Therefore the freedom of will (independence) of God is only when applied to actions, [and] not regardless of them. If it is said what is the purpose of such sovereignty like that, [we say] none, because the valid means of cognition cannot follow any purpose. (...)

3.3.1. Cakradhara (ca. 1050 AD, Potter) in his commentary *Granthibhaṅgavyākhyā* on Jayanta Bhaṭṭa's *Nyāyamañjarī* several times quoted the stanzas of the *Abhidharmakośa* in the sections on the refutation of the views of the Buddhist schools – twice in the first chapter, in the section *nirākārajñānavādivaibhāṣikamatam*, and in the seventh chapter, in the section *anityajñānātiriktātmavādibauddhamatam*, and in the section *kṣaṇikajñānātmavāde doṣapradarśanam*. The quotations, however, have a few different readings.

3.3.1.1. In the passage from the first chapter of Jayanta Bhaṭṭa's NM it was said:

> Some others, again, accept that knowledge and object of which depend upon the same assemblage [*sāmagrī*], (means) are mutually related as *grāhya* (which is to be known, the object) and *grāhaka* (which is the means of knowledge) and therefore, knowledge itself is the means (of valid knowledge). (...) When knowledge is produced, knowledge is the material cause and the object is the auxiliary cause; when object is produced (in the next moment) object is the material cause, knowledge is the auxiliary one. Knowledge, again, is produced by both knowledge as well as object. Similarly, object is produced by both object as well as knowledge. Therefore, knowledge alone is *pramāṇa* there because it is always with the object since it depends on the same assemblage (i.e. means such as knowledge and object. (NM Jha, pp. 32-33)[30]

Cakradhara in his commentary explained that this is the opinion of the Vaibhāṣikas who follow the theory of cognition without form and claim that also the non-produced object is seized by knowledge which is the auxiliary cause.[31] In that connection Cakradhara quoted definitions of the *sabhāgahetu* ('similar cause') from

---

[30] NM 14.27-32: *anye tulyasāmagryadhīnayor jñānārthayor grāhyagrāhakabhāva vadanto bodhaṃ pramāṇam abhyupāgaman, kṣaṇabhaṅgiṣu padārtheṣu sahakāryupādānakāraṇāpekṣakṣaṇāntarasantatijananena ca lokayātrām udvahatsu jñānajanmani jñānam upādānakāraṇam arthaḥ sahakārikāraṇam arthajanmani cārtha upādānakāraṇaṃ jñānaṃ sahakāri kāraṇam iti, jñānaṃ ca jñānārthajanyam arthaś cārthajñānajanyo bhavatīty evam ekasāmagryadhīnatayā tam artham avyabhicarato jñānasya tatra prāmāṇyam iti* I

[31] NMGBh 24.17 ff.: ***anye tulyasāmagryadhīnayor**** *iti* I *ajanako 'py arthaḥ* [8A] *sahabhāvijñānena gṛhyata iti nirākārajñānavādināṃ vaibhāṣikāṇāṃ darśanam* I *ajanakasya ca grāhakatve 'nyasyāpi tatkālabhāvino 'rthakṣaṇasya tad jñānaṃ kim iti na grāhakam ity atiprasaṅganivāraṇāya tulyasāmagryadhīnayor ity uktam* I *ekasāmagryutpannatvena tasyaiva tad grāhakaṃ nānyasya; yathaitadgrahaṇe tulyasāmagryadhīnatvaṃ tasya niyāmakam asti tathā 'nyagrahaṇe na kiñcid astīty arthaḥ* I *pūrvabhāvī svasantānagatasadṛśakṣaṇa upādānakāraṇam* I *yad uktam* –

"*sabhāgahetuḥ sadṛśāḥ svasantānabhuvo kṣaṇāḥ*" [AK II.52ab] *iti* I
tadanyaḥ sahakārikāraṇam I *tathā cāhuḥ* –
"*tato 'nye kāraṇaṃ hetuḥ sahabhūr ye mithaḥphalāḥ*" [AK II.50ab] *iti* I (...)

* Cf. *Tattvasaṃgraha*, verse 2043.

AK II.52ab[32], and of the *kāraṇahetu* ('immediate cause') and the *sahabhūhetu* ('coexistent cause') from AK II.50ab[33].

3.3.1.2. In the seventh chapter of NM is quoted a well-known stanza:

> *varṣātapābhyāṃ kiṃ vyomnaś carmaṇy asti tayoḥ phalam* ।
> *carmopamaś cet so 'nityaḥ khatulyaś ced asatsamaḥ* ॥
> (NM, part 2: 16.17-18)
>
> What is [the efficacy] of rain and sunshine with regard to the air? Their effect is [seen only] on the skin. If it [i.e. ātman] were similar to the skin, it would be temporal; if it were similar to the air, it would be inefficient.

It has been suggested that the stanza may come from the *Paramārthasaptati*, Vasubandhu's lost work refuting the Sāṃkhya doctrine (Mejor 1999: 107 ff.).

In that connection Cakradhara quoted stanza AK V.7:

> *ātmātmīyadhruvocchedanāstihīnoccadṛṣṭayaḥ* ।
> *ahetvamārgataddṛṣṭir etā hi pañca dṛṣṭayaḥ* ॥[34] (AK V.7)
>
> The view of self and things pertaining to self, the view of eternity and annihilation, the view of negation, the view that holds as high that which is low, and that which holds for cause and Path that which is not cause and Path: these are the five views. (Pruden, Kośa III, 776.)

---

[32] AK II.52ab: *sabhāgahetuḥ sadṛśāḥ svanikāyabhuvo 'grajāḥ* । – "Similar dharmas are *sabhāgahetu* or similar causes. [Similar causes are the similar dharmas which] belong to the same category (*nikāya*) and the same stage (*bhū*), [and which have] arisen previously." (Pruden, Kośa II, 262 f.)

[33] AK II.50ab: *svato 'nye kāraṇaṃ hetuḥ sahabhūr ye mithaḥphalāḥ* । – "All dharmas are *kāraṇahetu* with regard to all, with the exception of themselves. *Sahabhūhetu*, coexistent causes, (...) are the dharmas that are causes one of the other." (Pruden, Kośa II, 255.)

[34] So reads edition NMGBh 223.22-23; AKBh 281.18-19 (also AKBh(S) 772.4-5) reads in pāda b: *-hināgradṛṣṭayaḥ*, in pāda cd: *ahetvamārge taddṛṣṭir etās tāḥ pañca dṛṣṭayaḥ*.

3.3.1.3. Finally Cakradhara (NMGBh 254.25-26) quotes the stanza AK III.18 which says:

> *nātmāsti skandhamātraṃ tu kleśakarmābhisuṃskṛtam* |
> *antarābhavasaṃtatyā kukṣim eti* pradīpavat* || (AK III.18)
>
> *NMGBh reads: *yāti kukṣiṃ*.
>
> There is no self and it is only [the continuum of] the aggregates formed by the [previously accumulated] afflictions and actions which, by means of a stream of intermediate being, enters [a mother's] womb, like the light.[35]

4. VAIŚEṢIKA

4.1. The fundamental text of the Vaiśeṣika school, Kaṇāda's *Vaiśeṣikasūtra*, together with the available commentaries – the *Praśastapādabhāṣya* (= *Padārthadharmasaṃgraha*) by Praśastapāda (second half of the 6th century), and the *Vaiśeṣikasūtravṛtti* by Candrānanda – do not contain references to the *Abhidharmakośa*. Frauwallner (1982: 205) pointed out that Candramati (5th century) in his *Daśapadārthaśāstra* commentary[36], which was preserved in the Chinese translation only (Taisho 2138 = Nanjio 1295, transl. by Xuanzang in 648 AD), used a classification of the categories different from Praśastapāda's pattern and very similar to that which was used by Vasubandhu in the first chapter of the *Abhidharmakośa*.

4.1.1. On the other hand one should observe many references to the Vaiśeṣika in the *Abhidharmakośa*, and especially in its ninth chapter *Pudgalaviniścaya*, where is found sharp criticism of the Vaiśeṣika tenets[37]. It is difficult to say whether that criticism has been refuted by the later Vaiśeṣika authors.

---

[35] See Mejor 1999: 98.

[36] Ui 1917.

[37] Cf. LVP, Kośa IX, 227-302; Stcherbatsky 1988; Duerlinger 1989a; 1989b.

However, in reference to the discussion on the question of 'variegated colour' (*citrarūpa*), which was not mentioned by the earlier Vaiśeṣika authors (and who, seemingly, were not unknown to Praśastapāda), Bronkhorst[38] has called attention to the passage at the AKBh ad III.100a-b[39]. Here Vasubandhu attacked the opinion that a whole is an entity different from its parts. Vasubandhu mentioned the notion of 'variegated colour'[40].

Now Vyomaśiva (second half of the 7th century, Gaurinath Shastri; 9th century, Frauwallner) in his *Vyomavatī* commentary on the *Padārthadharmasaṃgraha*, while discussing the *citrarūpa* referred to a sūtra which is otherwise unknown[41]. It seems that it was that sūtra which justified the notion of variegated colour as a quality.

Vyomaśiva often criticized Buddhist opinions[42], and above all Dharmakīrti's *Pramāṇavārttika*.

---

[38] Bronkhorst 1993: 76-77 & n. 3, with reference to Grohma 1975: 151 f.

[39] AKBh 189.24-26: *saṃvartanyaḥ punas tisro bhavanty agnyambuvāyubhiḥ* I – "There are three destructions: through fire, water, and wind." (Pruden, Kośa II, 490.)

[40] Bronkhorst 1993: 76-77: "Vasubandhu mentions here the variegated colour in the following lines (p. 189 l. 24-26): 'In case the threads have different colours ... the cloth could not have a colour ... If [you accept] 'variegated' as its colour ... there would be production of [a colour] belonging to a different universal (from the colours in the threads).' (*bhinnarūpajātikriyeṣu tantuṣu paṭasya rūpādyasaṃbhavāt* I *citrarūpāditve vijātīyārambho 'pi syāt*). It must be admitted that the variegated colour in this passage from the *Abhidharmakośa Bhāṣya* is rather hypothetical, and does not prove beyond doubt that anyone known to Vasubandhu believed in it.

Vyomaśiva's commentary on the *Padārthadharmasaṃgraha*, called *Vyomavatī*, cites a sūtra in its discussion of the variegated colour. The sūtra reads: 'Because there cannot be, in one-omnipresent substance, [several] specific qualities (*viśeṣaguṇa*) that are perceived by the same sense-organ.' It is not impossible that this sūtra was indeed meant to justify variegated colour as a quality. Unfortunately it is only known through this passage of the *Vyomavatī*; it does not occur in the different versions of the *Vaiśeṣika Sūtra* that have been preserved, nor does it appear to be cited by any other commentator."

[41] Bronkhorst 1993: 76-77 (*Vyomavatī* I.63.20: *avibhuni dravye samānendriyagrāhyāṇāṃ viśeṣaguṇānām asambhavāt, iti vyāhanyeteti* I).

5. MĪMĀṂSĀ

In the Mīmāṃsā texts, so far as I can see, there are no explicit references to the *Abhidharmakośa*. Vijaya Rani (1982) in her study of Kumārila's *Ślokavārttika* (first half of the 7th century) gave in the footnotes multiple references to the *Abhidharmakośa*, but I am unable to trace any explicit parallel passages in the two texts. Dharmakīrti is the main target of Kumārila's criticism.

6. VEDĀNTA

The *Brahmasūtras* do not contain explicit references to the *Abhidharmakośa*, however, it is evident from the analysis of the Buddhist tenets presented in the second chapter of Śaṅkara's *Brahmasūtrabhāṣya* that the opinions of three Buddhist schools: Sarvāstivādins, Vijñānavādins, and Śūnyatāvādins were referred to.[43] Śaṅkara (788-820 AD) well knew the doctrines of the Abhidharma. Murakami in his study of Vedāntic interpretation and criticism of the Buddhist doctrine of dependent origination (*pratītyasamutpāda*), analysed the *Brahmasūtras* 2.2.18-32 and its major commentaries, with references to the AKBh (Murakami 2002: 271, 289, etc.).

6.1. The *Brahmasūtra* II.2.22: *pratisaṃkhyāpratisaṃkhyānirodhāprāptir avicchedāt* ||[44] may refer to the *Abhidharmakośa* I.5cd-6:

---

[42] In his *Vyomavatī* one can find, among others, discussion on the notion of 'insufficiency of cause' (*kāraṇavaikalya*); in II.126.22-25 Vyomaśiva gives the opinions of the Buddhists; in the AKBh ad I.6 occurs the notion of *pratyayavaikalya* or "insufficiency of the causes [of arising]".

[43] BSBh 450.2-3: *tatraite trayo vādino bhavanti – kecitsarvāstitvavādinaḥ, kecidvijñānāstitvamātravādinaḥ, anye punaḥ sarvaśūnyatvavādina iti* |

[44] "Cessation dependent on a sublative act of the mind, and cessation not so dependent cannot be established, there being no (complete) interruption." (Thibaut 1890: 410.)

ākāśaṃ dvau nirodhau ca tatrākāśam anāvṛtiḥ ||
pratisaṃkhyānirodho yo visaṃyogaḥ pṛthak pṛthak |
utpādātyantavighno 'nyo nirodho 'pratisaṃkhyayā ||

Space and the two types of extinctions. (...) Space is 'that which does not hinder'. (...)

Pratisaṃkhyānirodha is disjunction. (...) Each [disjunction occurs] separately. (...) A different type of extinction, which consists of the absolute hindering of arising, is called *apratisaṃkhyānirodha*. (Pruden, Kośa I, 59, 60.)

6.1.1. Vasubandhu explains:

anāvaraṇasvabhāvam ākāśaṃ yatra rūpasya gatiḥ | (...) *yaḥ sāsravair dharmair visaṃyogaḥ sa pratisaṃkhyānirodhaḥ* | (...) *anāgatānāṃ dharmāṇām utpādasyātyantavighnabhūto visaṃyogād yo 'nyo nirodhaḥ so 'pratisaṃkhyānirodhaḥ* | (AKBh 3.23; 4.1; 4.13-14)

Cf. Śaṅkara's explanations in his BSBh 459.7-8:

buddhipūrvakaḥ kila vināśo bhāvānāṃ pratisaṃkhyānirodho nāma bhāṣyate, tadviparīto 'pratisaṃkhyānirodhaḥ, āvaraṇābhāvamātram ākāśam iti |

By 'cessation dependent on a sublative act of the mind', we have to understand such destruction of entities as is preceded by an act of thought; by 'cessation not so dependent' is meant destruction of the opposite kind; by 'space' is meant absence in general of something covering (or occupying space). (Thibaut 1890: 410.)

6.2. The commentators on the *Brahmasūtra*s refer also to AK I.4cd, which contains a definition of defilement(s) with characteristic elements of "etymology" – it is called *āśaya* because impurities are deposited (*āśerate*) on it: *sāsravā āsravās teṣu yasmāt samanuśerate* || – "They are impure because the defilements adhere to them." (Pruden, Kośa I, 58.)

See Govindānanda's *Bhāṣyaratnaprabhā* (ad Śaṅkara's BSBh 452.1) (BSBh 452.10): *āśayasyeti* | *āśerate 'smin rāgādaya ityāśayaḥ saṃtānaḥ* | cf. AKVy 13.1 ff.

Cf. Vācaspatimiśra's *Bhāmatī* (BSBh 452.18): *āśerate 'smin karmānubhavavāsanā ityāśaya ālayavijñānaṃ tasya* | cf. Ānandagiri's *Nyāyanirṇaya* (BSBh 452.37): *āśayasyeti* | *āśerate 'smin karmānubhavavāsanā ityāśayaḥ saṃtānaḥ* |

7. JAINA

Two basic commentaries on the fundamental Jaina doctrinal text, the *Tattvārthādhigamasūtra* or 'Mnemonic Rules on the Meaning of the Reals' composed by Umāsvāti (4th or 5th century)[45] – contain clear references to the *Abhidharmakośa*.

7.1. Siddhasenasūri Gaṇi (*floruit* before Akalaṅka, 650-750 AD, but rather ca. 750 AD, after Yaśomitra – see below), the author of the first of these commentaries, the *Tattvārthaṭīkā*, sharply criticised Vasubandhu for his formulation in AK IV.73a-b of the thesis: *prāṇātipātaḥ saṃcintya parasyābhrāntimāraṇam*, i.e. "Murder is to kill another, consciously, without making an error."[46] In his AKBh Vasubandhu criticised the Nirgranthas, i.e. Jainas for their too formalistic – according to Vasubandhu – definition of murder[47], which lacks the essential factor of intention:

> According to the Nirgranthas, a transgression (*adharma*) results for the doer from killing, even committed without knowing it, or without desiring it, in the way that contact with fire results in burning.[48]

Siddhasena Gaṇi sharply attacked Vasubandhu.[49] First he quoted almost *verbatim* the text of the *Abhidharmakośa* ad IV.73 as a *pūrvapakṣa*; it is evident that he used also Yaśomitra's *Sphuṭārthā Abhidharmakośavyākhyā*. Then he criticised Vasubandhu's argu-

---

[45] Dundas 2002: 86 f.

[46] Pruden, Kośa II, 649.

[47] TS VII.8. [= TSRV VII.13: *-vyāparopaṇam*] *pramattayogād prāṇavyāropaṇam hiṃsā* |

[48] AKBh 243.27: *abuddhipūrvād api prāṇivadhāt kartur adharmaḥ, yathā agnisaṃyogād dāhaḥ – iti nirgranthāḥ* | Pruden, Kośa II, 650.

[49] Interestingly, he mentioned Vasubandhu by name. See Kapadia 1932-33.

ments, not sparing Vasubandhu abusive epithets[50]. The above controversy was also critically treated in the anonymous Buddhist text *Abhidharmadīpa*[51]. The topic will be dealt in detail elsewhere (Mejor, forthcoming).

7.2. Akalaṅkadeva (720-780),[52] the author of the *Tattvārthavārtika* (*Rājavārtika*), quoted passages from the *Abhidharmakośa* concerning his critical approach to the definition of perception (*pratyakṣa*). He also briefly commented upon the question of 'taking life' (*prāṇātipāta*), which was treated so thoroughly by Siddhasena (see above).

In his comment on the TS I.12: *pratyakṣam anyat* Akalaṅka criticised Dignāga's definition of *pratyakṣa* from his *Pramāṇasamuccaya*[53]. Here, in that connection Akalaṅka quoted the following passages from the *Abhidharmakośa*: AK I.32a-b, AK I.33a-b, and AK I.17.[54]

> *atha matam – nāsmākam ekāntaḥ 'kalpanāpoḍham eva' iti | kim arthaṃ tarhi viśeṣaṇam | paramatāpekṣaṃ viśeṣaṇam | paramate hi nāmajātyādi-*

---

[50] TSSG II: 68.1, 28-29: *tasmād enaḥpadam etad* ***vasubandhor*** *āmiṣagṛddhasya gṛdhrasyevāprekṣākāriṇaḥ | vikalpasamā ceyaṃ jātirūpanyastā* ***vasubandhu****vaidheyena svāśrayadāhitvam agner viśeṣadharmo 'sti |*

[51] See AD(V), p. 157 f. & nn. 2, 3; p. 158, n. 3.

[52] Cf. Shah 1967.

[53] Dignāga, *Pramāṇasamuccaya* 3c-d: *pratyakṣaṃ kalpanāpoḍhaṃ nāmajātyādiyojanā |*

"Among these [two means of cognition] – *k. 3c.* perception is free from conceptual construction (*kalpanā*);

The cognition in which there is no conceptual construction is perception. What, then, is this conceptual construction? – *k. 3d.* the association of name (*nāman*), genus (*jāti*), etc. [with a thing perceived, which results in verbal designation of the thing]." (Hattori 1968: 25.)

[54] Besides cf. TSRV, pp. 45, 55: *ṣaṇṇām* = AK I.17; TSRV p. 55: *savitarka* = AK I.32. Cf. also TSRV, p. 440, n. 2 = AKVy 78; TSRV, p. 467, n. 7 = AK I.5; TSRV, p. 45, n. 6 = AKVy ad I.17; TSRV, p. 55, n. 10 = AKVy ad II.32; TSRV, p. 67, n. 11 = AKVy 84; TSRV, p. 68, n. 15 = AKBh I.43; TSRV, p. 15, n. 4 = *kṣaṇikāḥ sarvasaṃskārāḥ sthirāṇāṃ kutaḥ kriyā.*

bhedopacārakalpanā proktā, tato'poḍhaṃ na svavikalpād iti I *uktaṃ ca –*
savitarkavicārā hi pañca vijñānadhātavaḥ I
nirūpaṇānusmaraṇavikalpenāvikalpakāḥ II [AK I.32] *iti* I (...)
atrocyate – tathā mānasam api pratyakṣaṃ nopapadyate I *api ca, 'ṣaṇṇām anantarātītaṃ vijñānaṃ yaddhi tan manaḥ'* [AK I.17] *iti – atītam asat kathaṃ vijñānasya kāraṇaṃ syāt* I (...) (TSRV 55.14-19])

Now, there is the opinion: – We do not hold to the one-sided [thesis] 'free of conceptualization'. What is the purpose of distinction? Distinction is with regard to the other opinion. For in the opinion of others conceptualization was metaphorically expressed by division into name, genus, etc. Free of that [conceptualization], not of one's own conceptualization. – It was said [in AK I.32-33]: "Five kinds of consciousness are always connected with ratiocination (*vitarka*) and investigation (*vicāra*). They are free of conceptualization which is consisting of examination (*nirūpaṇa*) and of remembering (*anusmaraṇa*)." (...)

Here it is said: – Thus also mental perception does not arise. Moreover, [it was said in AK I.17:] "of the six kinds of consciousness, that one which passes immediately is [called] the mind (*manas*)". – How can a non-existent [entity] which is past (*atīta*) be the cause of consciousness? (...)

7.3. The *Dvādaśāranayacakra* of Mallavādin together with its commentary *Nyāyāgamānusāriṇī* of Siṃhasūrigaṇi (probably 6th century) contains many references to the *Abhidharmakośa*[55], mainly in the sections on refutation of Vasubandhu's and Dignāga's definitions of *pratyakṣa*. Here we refer only to a few of the most conspicuous passages.[56]

7.3.1. DNC I: 78.2 (& DNCN 78.9-79.20):

yac cāpy abhihitam ***abhidharmakośe*** *– yad etad anekaprakārabhinnaṃ rūpāyatanaṃ tatra kadācid ekena* (79.1) *dravyeṇa cakṣurvijñānam utpadyate yadā nīlāditatprakāravyavacchedo bhavati, kadācid anekena yadā na tatprakāravyavacchedaḥ, tadyathā dūrān maṇisamūham anekavarṇasaṃsthānaṃ paśyataḥ* I

[55] See also Mejor 2004: 416-418 for the references to YD.

[56] Other references include: DNCN I: 60.16 (AK II.64); DNCN I: 67.7-8 (AK VI.4); DNCN I: 77.13 (AK VI.4); DNC I: 93.3-4 & DNCN I: 93.25-28 (AKBh ad I.10).

The parallel passage is AKBh ad I.10 (AKBh 7.18-20):

yad etad bahuvidhaṃ rūpam uktaṃ tatra kadācid ekena dravyeṇa cakṣur-vijñānam utpadyate yadā tatprakāravyavacchedo bhavati I *kadācid bahubhir yadā na vyavacchedaḥ* I *tadyathā senāvyūham anekavarṇasaṃsthānaṃ maṇisamūhaṃ ca dūrāt paśyataḥ* I

The manifold visible form was described. In that, sometimes visual consciousness arises [prompted] by one substance, when its kind is separated, and sometimes by many, when there is no separation. For example, when one sees from a distance an army formation or a heap of jewels having multiple colours and forms.

7.3.2. DNC I: 86.2-3 (& DNCN 86.16-18):

āyatanasvalakṣaṇaṃ pratyete svalakṣaṇaviṣayāḥ na dravyasvalakṣaṇaṃ prati, ity etat tu prāk coditam eva doṣaṃ pratiṣṭhāpitavān asi I

The parallel passage is AKBh ad I.10 (AKBh 7.23-24):

āyatanasvalakṣaṇaṃ pratyete svalakṣaṇaviṣayā iṣyante na dravyasvalakṣaṇam ity adoṣaḥ I

By the 'objects with specific characteristic' is meant specific characteristic of a domain (*āyatana*), and not specific characteristic of a substance (*dravya*).

7.3.3. DNC I: 92.6-8 (& DNCN 92.22–93.16):

yathoktam –
yasmin bhinne na tadbuddhir anyāpohe dhiyā ca tat I
ghaṭāmbuvat saṃvṛtisat paramārthasad anyathā II

The parallel passage is AK VI.4 (AKBh 334.1-2):

yatra bhinnena tadbuddhir anyāpohe dhiyā ca tat I
ghaṭāmbuvat saṃvṛtisat paramārthasad anyathā* II

*AKBh, ed. Pradhan: *ghaṭārthavat*; AKBh(S) 889.12: *ghaṭāmbuvat*; AKVy 524.9: *ghaṭāmbuvat*.

The idea of a jug ends when the jug is broken; the idea of water ends when, in the mind, one analyzes the water. The jug and the water, and all that resembles them, exist relatively. The rest exist absolutely. (Pruden, Kośa III, 910.)

ACKNOWLEDGMENTS

I would like to thank Professor Richard Gombrich for his corrections and improvements of my paper. My thanks are also due to Dr. Piotr Balcerowicz and Dr. Monika Nowakowska for their comments. The sole responsibility for the final version of the paper is, of course, mine.

REFERENCES

AD(V) = *Abhidharmadīpa with Vibhāṣāpravṛitti*. Ed. by P. S. Jaini. (Tibetan Sanskrit Works Series, 4.) 2nd edition. Patna: K. P. Jayaswal Research Institute, 1977.

AK = Abhidharmakośa(-kārikā)

AKBh = *Abhidharmakośabhāṣya*. Ed. by P. Pradhan. (Tibetan Sanskrit Works Series, 8.) 2nd edition. Patna: K. P. Jayaswal Research Institute, 1975.

AKBh(S) = *Abhidharmakośabhāṣya* (with Yaśomitra's *Sphuṭārthā Abhidharmakośavyākhyā*), I-IV. Ed. by Swami Dwarikadas Shastri. 3rd ed. (Bauddha Bharati Series, 5-8.) Varanasi: Bauddha Bharati 1987.

AKVy = *Abhidharmakośavyākhyā*, I-II. Ed. by U. Wogihara. Tokyo: Publishing Association of Abhidharmakośavyākhyā, 1932-36. (Reprint: 1989.)

BSBh = (Brahmasūtrabhāṣya). *Brahmasūtra-Śaṅkarabhāṣyam with the commentaries Bhāṣyaratnaprabhā of Govindānanda, Bhāmatī of Vācaspatimiśra, Nyāyanirṇaya of Ānandagiri*. Ed. by J. L. Shastri. Delhi: Motilal Banarsidass, 1980.

BRONKHORST, Johannes 1993. Studies on Bhartṛhari, 5: Bhartṛhari and Vaiśeṣika. *Asiatische Studien/Études Asiatiques* 47.1: 75-94.

—— 1996. L'Inde classique et le dialogue des religions. *Asiatische Studien/ Études Asiatiques* 50.4: 779-796.

—— 1997. Sāṃkhya in the Abhidharmakośa Bhāṣya. *Journal of Indian Philosophy* 25: 393-400.

DNC = *Dvādaśāraṃ Nayacakraṃ of Ācārya Śrī Mallavādi Kṣamāśramaṇa. With the Commentary Nyāyāgāmānusāriṇī of Śrī Siṃhasūri Gaṇi Vādi Kṣamāśramaṇa*, I-III. Ed. by Muni Jambūvijayajī. Bhavnagar: Śrī Jaina Ātmanand Sabhā 1966-88.

DNCN = The *Nyāyāgāmānusāriṇī* commentary. See DNC.

DUERLINGER, James 1989a. Vasubandhu's "refutation of the theory of selfhood" (*ātmavādapratiṣedha*) *Journal of Indian Philosophy* 17: 129-135.

DUERLINGER, James 1989b. Acharya Vasubandhu, refutation of the theory of selfhood: A resolution of questions about persons. *Journal of Indian Philosophy* 17: 137-187.

DUNDAS, Paul 2002. *The Jains*. 2nd edition. London: Routledge.

FRAUWALLNER, Erich 1933. Zu den Fragmenten buddhistischer Logiker im Nyāya-vārttikam, *Wiener Zeitschrift für die Kunde des Morgenlandes* 40: 281-304. [= Frauwallner 1982: 460-483]

—— 1953. *Geschichte der indischen Philosophie*, I. Salzburg: O. Müller.

—— 1982. *Kleine Schriften*. Hrsg. von G. Oberhammer & E. Steinkellner. Wiesbaden 1982.

GANGOPADHYAYA, Mrinalkanti (transl.) 1982. *Nyāya. Gautama's Nyāya-sūtra with Vātsyāyana's Commentary*. Calcutta: Indian Studies.

GLASENAPP, Helmut von 1954. Der Buddhismus in der Vorstellungswelt der Hindus. In: J. Schubert & U. Schneider (eds.), *Asiatica. Festschrift Friedrich Weller*: 174-183. Leipzig: Otto Harrassowitz.

GROHMA, Otto 1975. Theorie zur bunten Farbe im älteren Nyāya und Vaiśeṣika bis Udayana. *Wiener Zeitschrift für die Kunde Südasiens* 19: 147-182.

HATTORI, Masaaki 1968. *Dignāga, On Perception. Being the Pratyakṣapariccheda of Dignāga's Pramāṇasamuccaya*. (Harvard Oriental Series, 47.) Cambridge, Mass.: Harvard University Press.

JHA, Ganganatha (transl.) 1934. *The Tattva-Kaumudī. Vācaspati Miśra's Commentary on the Sāṃkhya-Kārikā*. 2nd edition. Poona: Oriental Book Agency, 1934.

KAPADIA, Hiralal Rasikdas 1932-33. References to the Bauddhas and their philosophy in Umāsvāti's Tattvārthabhāṣya and Siddhasena Gaṇi's commentary to it. *Annals of the Bhandarkar Oriental Research Institute* 14: 142-144, 273.

KHER, Chitrarekha 1992. *Buddhism as Presented by the Brahmanical Systems*. Delhi: Sri Satguru Publications.

KRITZER, Robert 2004. Childbirth and the mother's body in the Abhidharmakośabhāṣya and related texts. In: *Indo tetsugaku bukkyō shisō ronshū: Mikogami Eshō kyōju shōju kinen ronshū*: 1085-1109. Kyoto: Nagata Bunshōdo.

LA VALLÉE POUSSIN, Louis de 1901-02. Le Bouddhisme d'après les sources brahmaniques. *Le Muséon*, N.S. 2: 52-73, 171-207; 3: 40-54, 391-412.

—— 1936-37. Le bouddhisme et le yoga de Patañjali. *Mélanges chinois et bouddhiques* 5: 223-242.

LVP, Kośa = La Vallée Poussin, Louis de, *L'Abhidharmakośa de Vasubandhu. Traduction et annotations*. Nouvelle édition anastatique présentée par Étienne Lamotte. (Mélanges chinois et bouddhiques, 16.) Tome I:

Introduction, Chapitres 1 et 2; Tome II: Chapitre 3; Tome III: Chapitre 4; Tome IV: Chapitres 5 et 6; Tome V: Chapitres 7, 8 et 9; Tome VI: Fragments des kārikās. Index. Additions. Bruxelles: Institut Belge des Hautes Études Chinoises, 1980.

MAINKAR, T. G. (transl.) 1972. *Sāṃkhya-kārikā of Īśvarakṛṣṇa with the Commentary of Gauḍapāda*. 2nd revised & enlarged edition. Poona: Oriental Book Agency.

MEJOR, Marek 1999. "There is no self" (*nātmāsti*) – Some observations from Vasubandhu's *Abhidharmakośa* and the *Yuktidīpikā*. In: Bart Dessein (ed.), *The Notion of 'Self' in Buddhism* (Communication & Cognition, [Ghent], 32.1-2): 97-126.

—— 2000. Some observations on the date of the Yukti-dīpikā (apropos of a new edition). In: P. Balcerowicz & M. Mejor (eds.), *On the Understanding of Other Cultures. Proceedings of the International Conference on Sanskrit and Related Studies to Commemorate the Centenary of the Birth of Stanislaw Schayer (1899-1941), Warsaw University, Poland, October 7-10, 1999.* (Studia Indologiczne, 7): 255-289. [= Mejor 2004]

—— 2004. Some observations on the date of the *Yukti-dīpikā* (apropos of a new edition). In: P. Balcerowicz & M. Mejor (eds.), *Essays in Indian Philosophy, Religion and Literature*: 399-433. Delhi: Motilal Banarsidass. [= Mejor 2000]

—— , forthcoming. Buddhist-Jaina controversy about the question of "taking life" (*prāṇātipāta*) [provisional title].

MURAKAMI, Shinkan 2002. Vedāntic interpretation and criticism of the Buddhist dependent oigination (*pratītya-samutpāda*). *Zeitschrift der Deutschen Morgenländischen Gesellschaft* 152.2: 269-294.

NBhū = *Śrīmadācāryabhāsarvajñapraṇītasya nyāyasārasya svopajñaṃ vyākhyānaṃ nyāyabhūṣaṇam*. Ed. by Svāmī Yogīndrānanda. Vārāṇasī: Ṣaḍdarśana Prakāśana Pratiṣṭhānam, 1968.

NM = *The Nyāyamañjarī of Jayanta Bhaṭṭa*, Ed. by Pandit Śri Sūrya Nārāyana Śukla. Benares City: Jaya Krishna Das Haridas Gupta, 1936.

NMGBh = *Nyāyamañjarī of Jayanta Bhaṭṭa. With the Commentary of "Granthibhaṅga" by Cakradhara*, I-III. Ed. by Gaurinath Sastri. Varanasi: Sampurnanand Sanskrit Vishvavidyalaya, 1982-84.

NM Jha = *Nyāyamañjarī of Jayantabhaṭṭa. Āhnika–I.* English Translation by V. N. Jha. Delhi: Sri Satguru, 1995.

NBhV = *Nyāyabhāṣyavārttika of Bhāradvāja Uddyotakara*. Ed. by Anantalal Thakur. New Delhi: Indian Council of Philosophical Research, 1997.

Pruden, Kośa = *Abhidharmakośabhāṣyam by Louis de La Vallée Poussin*, I-IV. English translation by Leo M. Pruden. Berkeley, Calif.: Asian Humanities Press, 1988-90.

RANI, Vijaya 1982. *The Buddhist Philosophy as Presented in Mīmāṃsā-ślokavārttika*. Delhi: Parimal Publications 1982.

RUKMANI, T. S. (transl.) 2000. *Yogasūtrabhāṣyavivaraṇa of Śaṅkara*. Vivaraṇa text with English translation, and critical notes along with text and English translation of Patañjali's Yogasūtras and Vyāsabhāṣya. Vol. I: *Samādhipādaḥ* and *Sādhanapādaḥ*. Vol. II: *Vibhūtipādaḥ* and *Kaivalyapādaḥ*. Delhi: Munshiram Manoharlal. See also YSBhV.

SHAH, Nagin J. 1967. *Akalaṅka's Criticism of Dharmakīrti's Philosophy. A Study*. Ahmedabad: L.D. Institute of Indology.

SK = *Sāṃkhyakārikā*. See Jha 1934; Mainkar 1972.

STCHERBATSKY, Theodore 1988. *The Soul Theory of the Buddhist. With Sanskrit text*. 3rd edition revised and enlarged. Delhi: Bharatiya Vidya Prakashan. [1st edition: Bulletin de l'Académie des Sciences de Russie, 1919.]

Tattvasaṅgraha = *The Tattvasaṅgraha of Ācārya Śāntarakṣita with the "Pañjikā" Commentary of Śrī Kamalaśīla*, I-II. Ed. by Swami Dwarikadas Shastri. (Bauddha Bharati Series, 1-2.) Varanasi: Bauddha Bharati, 1968.

THIBAUT, George (transl.) 1890. *Vedânta-Sûtras with the Commentary by Śaṅkarācārya*, I. (The Sacred Books of the East, 34.) Oxford: Clarendon Press. (Reprint: Delhi: Motilal Banarsidass, 1973.)

TS = (*Tattvārthādhigamasūtra, & -bhāṣya*). *Tattvārthādhigama by Umāsvāti*, I-III. Ed. by Keshavlal Premchand Mody. Calcutta: Asiatic Society, 1903-05.

TSRV = *Tattvārthavārtika (Rājavārttika) of Śri Akalaṅkadeva*, I-II. Ed. & transl. [into Hindi] by Mahendra Kumar Jain. 6th edition. New Delhi: Bharatiya Jnanapeeth, 2001.

TSSG = *Tattvārthādhigamasūtra. A Treatise on the Fundamental Principles of Jainism*, I-II. Elucidated by Śrī Siddhasenagaṇi. Ed. by Hiralal Rasikdas Kapadia. Surat: Jivanchand Sakerchand Javeri, 1926-30.

UI, Hakuju 1917. *The Vaiśeṣika Philosophy According to the Daśapādārthaśāstra. Chinese Text with Introduction, Translation, and Notes*. Ed. by F. W. Thomas. London: Paul Geuthner, 1917.

Viṃś. = *Viṃśatikāvṛtti*. In: *Vijñaptimātratāsiddhi. Deux traités de Vasubandhu: Viṃśatikā (La Vingtaine) et Triṃśatikā (La Trentaine)*, I: texte. Ed. by Sylvain Lévi. Paris: Libraire Ancienne Honoré Champion, 1925.

VN = *Dharmakīrti's Vādanyāyaḥ*, I-II. Ed, & transl. by Michael Torsten Much. Wien: Österreichischen Akademie der Wissenschaften, 1991.

Vyomavatī = *Vyomavatī of Vyomaśivācārya*, I-II. Ed. by Gaurinath Sasıri. Varanasi: Sampumanand Sanskrit Vishvavidyalaya, 1983-84.

WEZLER, Albrecht 1984. On the quadruple division of the Yogaśāstra, the caturvyūhatva of the Cikitsāśāstra and the 'four noble truths' of the Buddha. *Indologica Taurinensia* 12: 289-337.

WOODS, James Haughton (transl.) 1914. *The Yoga-System of Patañjali. Or the Ancient Hindu Doctrine of Concentration of Mind.* Embracing the Mnemonic rules, called Yoga-sūtras, of Patañjali and the comment, called Yoga-bhāṣya, attributed to Veda-Vyāsa and the explanation, called Tattva-vaiçāradī, of Vāchaspati-miçra. (Harvard Oriental Series 17.) Cambridge, Mass.: Harvard University Press. (Reprint: Delhi: Motilal Banarsidass, 1992.)

YD = *Yuktidīpikā. The Most Significant Commentary on the Sāṃkhyakārikā*, I. Critically edited by Albrecht Wezler & Shujun Motegi. (Alt- und Neu-Indische Studien, 44.) Stuttgart: Franz Steiner Verlag, 1998.

YD(P) = *Yuktidīpikā. An Ancient Commentary on the Sāṃkhyakārikā of Īśvarakṛṣṇa.* Ed. by R. Ch. Pandeya. Delhi: Motilal Banarsidass, 1967.

YS = (Patañjali, *Yogasūtra*). *Patañjalasūtrāṇi with the Scholium of Vyāsa and the Commentary of Vāchaspati.* Ed. by Rājārām Shāstrī Bodas. (Bombay Sanskrit and Prakrit Series.) Bombay: Government Central Book Depot, 1892.

YBh = *Yogabhāṣya.* See YS, YSBhV.

YSBhV = *Pātañjala-Yogasūtra-bhāṣya-vivaraṇa of Śaṅkara-Bhagavatpāda.* Ed. by Polakam Sri Rama Sastri & Krishnamurthi Sastri. Madras: Government Oriental Manuscripts Library, 1952. See also Rukmani 2000.

Historical and Geographical Contexts for Avadānas in Kharoṣṭhī Manuscripts

JASON NEELIS

1. INTRODUCTION

Several brief summaries of avadānas in the British Library collection of Kharoṣṭhī manuscripts supply unique literary evidence for the localization of Buddhism in ancient Gandhāra during the 1st century of the Common Era. The avadāna genre is very well represented in this collection of twenty-nine fragments of birch-bark scrolls, with approximately forty avadānas written in separate groups on five different scrolls.[1] The avadānas were apparently secondary texts written below primary texts (including sūtras, verse texts and commentaries) in the remaining spaces on the recto and continuing on the verso.

Previous-birth stories labeled pūrvayogas (Gāndhārī *provayoge/ pruvayoge*) are closely linked with avadānas in the British Library

[1] Groups of avadānas are preserved in British Library (BL) fragments 1, 2, 4, 12 + 14, and 21 (Salomon 1999: 35). Nine avadānas belong to BL fragment 1, a relatively long scroll with a Gāndhārī version of the *Anavataptagāthā* as the primary text (two avadānas of Zadamitra in this group are published by Salomon 1999: 145-149 and Lenz 2003: 203-208). A few avadānas appear in BL fragment 2 (the avadāna of Jihonika is described in Salomon 1999: 141-145). The largest collection of at least sixteen avadānas belongs to BL fragment 4 following a commentary on verses with correspondences in the Dharmapada and Pali texts (Salomon 1999: 45). Nine avadānas belong to BL fragments 12 + 14, which formed a single scroll with three Ekottarikāgama-type sūtras (the avadāna of Puniga is published in Allon 2001: 303-306 and an edition of the remaining avadānas is being prepared by Neelis).

collection of Kharoṣṭhī manuscripts, since almost all examples of abbreviated narratives were written by the same scribe.[2] Lenz (2003: 108) and Salomon (1999: 35-36) view this scribe as a specialist who scavenged leftover writing surfaces for story summaries. They have also observed that these secondary texts were original compositions (rather than copies of source texts) written in a more colloquial linguistic register closer to spoken Gāndhārī than the primary texts in "translationese" and scholastic styles of Gāndhārī.[3]

Although both types of prose summaries share stylistic, structural and formulaic elements, avadānas are distinguished from pūrvayogas by "orientation in time" (Lenz 2003: 92). Avadānas in Kharoṣṭhī manuscripts generally concern actions in the characters' present lives, while pūrvayogas relate actions in previous lives. Unlike avadānas in Buddhist Sanskrit, jātakas in Pali, or Gāndhārī pūrvayogas, the avadānas in these fragments narrate the "story of the present" (Skt. *pratyutpannavastu* / Pali *paccuppannavatthu*) without reference to the "story of the past" (Skt. *atītavastu* / Pali *atītavatthu*) or an "identification" (Skt. *samavadhāna* / Pali *samodhāna*). As Salomon (1999: 37) observes, these avadānas are often more akin to edifying narratives (corresponding with the broad use of the term *avadāna* in Sanskrit literature) than to Buddhist records

[2] A collection of previous-birth stories written below a Gāndhārī version of the *Bhikṣuvarga* of the *Dharmapada* is edited by Lenz (2003). Avadānas and pūrvayogas are written by BL scribe 2 except for the first five avadānas in BL fragment 4, which are written by BL scribe 7 (Salomon 1999: 35-36). Lenz (2004) makes additional comments about the writing habits of BL scribe 2 ("Big Hand").

[3] According to Salomon (1999: 140; 2002: 124, 130), present tense narration of past events, constructions with active and passive participles, omission of the quotative particle *iti*, and use of the unprefixed verb *matredi* in dialogues indicate that the informal language of the avadānas (and pūrvayogas) is closer to the spoken language of Gandhāra than registers of Gāndhārī preserved in other types of texts, inscriptions and administrative documents. However, Lenz (2003: 107) cites hiatus bridging consonants, Buddhist Hybrid Sanskrit preterite forms, and common Sanskrit/Buddhist Sanskrit stock phrases as evidence for the influence of classical Sanskrit and Buddhist languages other than Gāndhārī.

of the karmic results of past actions. Nevertheless, ripening of karma (*karmavipāka*) is a major theme in avadāna narratives, since the actions of various characters function as examples of proper conduct, while stories about types of misconduct leading to pain or suffering provide counterexamples of improper actions resulting in demerit.

Avadānas in Kharoṣṭhī manuscripts include narratives about early followers and patrons of Śākyamuni Buddha in northeastern India and contemporary local figures from the northwestern borderlands between modern northwestern Pakistan and eastern Afghanistan (ancient Gandhāra). Toponyms, proper names and titles of characters in avadānas place the British Library Kharoṣṭhī manuscript fragments in specific geographical and historical contexts. Avadānas in Kharoṣṭhī manuscripts also provide a brief glimpse into an early stage in the written transmission of this important genre of Buddhist narrative literature.

2. AVADĀNAS IN BRITISH LIBRARY FRAGMENTS 12 + 14

This paper focuses on geographical and historical contexts for nine avadānas written at the bottom of the recto and on the verso of British Library fragments 12 + 14 (see the synopsis given in Figure 1). The reconstruction of the manuscript follows the edition of the primary text of three Ekottarikāgama-type sūtras in the first 73 lines on the recto (Allon 2001). The first avadāna is written in the last five lines of the recto, following a large punctuation mark. The next eight avadānas are written on the verso in 43 lines, but the text is incomplete at the end of each line due to deterioration of the left margin of the scroll.

The skeletal prose summaries of avadānas share similar introductory and concluding formulae. The avadānas typically begin with a variant of *evo ṣuyadi* (corresponding to Sanskrit *evaṃ śrūyate*), "thus it is heard". The avadānas of Puniga (no. 1) and the avadāna of Sarpadaṣa (no. 7) begin with titles explicitly labeling the stories as avadānas. The story summaries follow general patterns. In some cases, toponyms at the beginning of the summary refer to particular cities. In lieu of specific toponyms, names and titles of rulers provide more general information about areas and time frames. Sometimes the time frame for the story is expressed with reference to the lifespan of Śākyamuni Buddha or to the reign of a king. The main characters are typically introduced with titles indicating their names and social positions. The most important actions or dialogues are briefly summarized in terse sentences referring only to the most important details. Sometimes the lesson to be drawn is indicated at the end of the story summary. Like the pūrvayogas, most of the avadānas conclude with some version of a final abbreviation formula meaning "expansion should be according to the model" (*vistare yaṣayupamano siyadi*), usually followed by a circular punctuation mark and a numeral (Lenz 2003: 91). Lenz (2003: 87) concludes that abbreviation formulae in avadānas and pūrvayogas signal the readers to fill in the remaining details in the stories (with which they would no doubt be familiar) rather than copying or reciting verbatim.

3. HISTORICAL AND GEOGRAPHICAL CONTEXTS

The writer of avadāna summaries employs various narrative techniques to establish historical and geographical contexts for the stories. Toponyms, titles, proper names, style of dialogue, and significant details in the plot of the story provide mnemonic clues to identify specific contexts of time and place. Among the nine avadānas in this group, five (nos. 1, 4, 7, 8, 9) are localized in the Buddhist homeland of northeastern India between approximately the 5th to 3rd centuries BCE, three stories (avadāna nos. 2, 3, 6) are probably set in the northwestern borderlands of the Indian subcontinent, and one (no. 5) is indeterminate (but likely to belong to the former group). This distribution shows that avadānas set in northeastern India are freely interspersed with narratives localized in the Northwest during the 1st century CE. Variation between avadānas set in northeastern India while Śākyamuni Buddha was teaching and those set in the Gandhāran milieu during the 1st century suggests that standards for the written redaction and transmission of avadānas had not been firmly established.[4] Thus, Gāndhārī avadānas illustrate an early stage in the development of the avadāna literary tradition.

3.1. Buddhist homeland

Avadānas set in northeastern India during Śākyamuni's lifetime demonstrate that certain Indian Buddhist narratives were transmitted to Gandhāra with their settings intact. The avadānas of Puniga (no. 1) and Sarpadasa (no. 7) have parallel versions in other Buddhist literary traditions and can be securely located in the Buddhist homeland of northeastern India.

The Gāndhārī avadāna of Puniga (Sanskrit Pūrṇikā / Pali Puṇṇikā or Puṇṇā) has been securely identified with a story about a maidservant of the prosperous householder Anāthapiṇḍada (Allon 2001: 303-306). The avadāna also refers to King Prasenajit, the ruler of Kosala who was contemporary with Śākyamuni Buddha. Along with Anāthapiṇḍada and other wealthy householders, he petitioned the Buddha to stay longer during the rainy season retreat, but the Buddha did not agree to their requests. Ultimately, as indicated in similar stories in Pali, Sanskrit and Chinese literature, Puniga persuaded the Buddha to stay by promising to take the three refuges and to observe the five precepts.[5] Although Śrāvastī is not explicitly mentioned as the setting for the Puniga avadāna, the

---

[4] Unlike Pali jātakas and suttas, Gāndhārī avadānas do not reflect systematic localization. Schopen (1997: 575-578) points out that the *Kṣudrakavastu* of the *Mūlasarvāstivāda-vinaya* calls for jātaka stories of the past to be set in Vārāṇasī when the original circumstances were forgotten. According to Schopen's calculations, in 547 Pali Jātakas, more than 400 stories of the past are set in Banaras (Vārāṇasī).

[5] Stories about Puniga are found in Pali (*Manorathapūraṇī* 34-35), Central Asian Sanskrit fragments of the *Kalpanāmaṇḍitikā* (Lüders 1926: 178), and Kumārajīva's Chinese translation (Huber 1908: 313-321).

audience would have recognized when and where the story took place from the Buddha's denial of the requests of Anāthapiṇḍada and King Prasenajit.[6]

The avadāna of Sarpadasa (Sanskrit Sarpadāsa / Pali Sappadāsa) is also set in northeastern India during the lifetime of Śākyamuni.[7] *Theragāthā* verses 405-410 are attributed to Sappadāsa, a contemporary follower of Śākyamuni from Kapilavastu who received this name after attempting suicide by causing a poisonous snake to bite him, according to the commentary on *Dhammapada* verse 112.[8] The beginning of the Gāndhārī avadāna resembles *Theragāthā* 405, in that he wandered for twenty-five years without attaining success.[9] Surprisingly, the Gāndhārī avadāna of Sarpadasa does not seem to refer to stories about his suicide attempts, either by snake or by razorblade, as related in other versions.[10] Instead, the Gāndhārī version of the Sarpadasa avadāna reports a dialogue between Sarpadasa and the Buddha in which Sarpadasa asks: "what is the root of merit" (*sarpadaso budhasa prucha[d]i ki kuśalamulo*) and the Buddha answers, "among the four Buddhas, chaste conduct in all circumstances" (*caduhi bu[dh.]h[i] sarvatro bramacaryo*). Although this alternative version of the Sarpadasa avadāna is not identical with stories about this character in Pali and other Buddhist

[6] It is interesting to note that this is the only Gāndhārī avadāna among those preserved in the British Library collection to be set in Śrāvastī, whereas *nidānas* in Kharoṣṭhī manuscripts belonging to the Senior collection localize many Gāndhārī sūtras there (see Salomon 2003: 88 for a typical example).

[7] This name was previously read as Sarthadasa (Salomon 1999: 36, 48), but Sarpadasa is clear in improved digital images and in the original.

[8] Burlingame 1921, II: 247-249; Norman 1970, II: 256-258; Malalasekera 1937-38, II: 1030

[9] Compare BL fragment 12 v, ll. 102-103: ... *p.[caviś.]////(*-varṣa) cakramido na kici ??[n]o a[sigadi]* ·... "he wandered [twenty-five](*years). He did not attain any ?" to *Theragāthā* 405: *paṇṇavīsati-vassāni yato pabbajito ahaṃ accharā-sanghāta-mattam pi ceto-santim anajjhagaṃ.*

[10] The avadāna of Sarpadāsa in the *Anavataptagāthā* in the *Mūlasarvāstivāda-vinaya* (Hofinger 1982: 107-111, 250-253) is partially preserved in a Gilgit manuscript (Wille 1990: 105-107, 209r8-209v10), but unfortunately not in the extant Gāndhārī *Anavataptagāthā*.

literary traditions, the dialogue indicates that Sarpadas̱a and the Buddha were contemporaries in northeastern India.

The fourth avadāna, about a courtesan (Gāndhārī *ganiga* / Sanskrit *gaṇikā*) and a wealthy householder from Ujjayinī (*ujani[ge] graha[vadi]*), is explicitly located in the city of Pāṭaliputra (*nagare palaḍipu[_trami]*). This story probably took place sometime after Ajātaśatru renamed the city Pāṭaliputra, which continued to be the capital of the Nanda and Maurya dynasties.[11] Unfortunately, the name of the courtesan is missing in the damaged left margin of the text. Although Sanskrit and Pali Buddhist texts retell many stories about famous courtesans, none of these characters are from Pāṭaliputra.[12] What transpires between the courtesan and the character from Ujjayinī is not entirely clear, but someone (probably the wealthy householder) faints and rolls on the ground (*muchido bh<*u>mi parivartadi*)[13] and attains Āryadharma (*aryadharma praü[ṇad]i*).[14] While details in the narrative remain uncertain, the prosperous cosmopolitan milieu of long-distance contacts between

---

[11] Pāṭaliputra was an important setting for other avadānas in BL Kharoṣṭhī manuscripts. Attestations include *nagare palaḍiputr[e]* in the 17th avadāna of BL fragment 4.2v, line 3 and *nagare palaḍipu(*tr)e* in Story A of BL fragments 16 + 25, line 16 (Lenz 2003: 145). *nagare palaḍiputre* may be conjecturally restored in two other BL Kharoṣṭhī avadānas: *nagare pa ///(*laḍi)putre* in the 6th avadāna of BL fragment 1, lines 161-162 and *nagare pa[l.](*ḍiputre)* in the 2nd avadāna of BL fragment 4.

[12] Famous courtesans in Buddhist literature (particularly *Therīgāthā* and its commentary by Dhammapāla) include Sirimā from Rājagṛha, Vāsavadattā from Mathurā, Padumavatī from Ujjayinī, and Vimalā and Amrapālī from Vaiśālī (see Wilson 1996 for several stories about courtesans).

[13] I am grateful to Mark Allon and Timothy Lenz for providing numerous references to the motif of fainting and falling to the ground following major disasters or immediate realizations in Sanskrit and Pali literature. This motif also occurs in the 16th avadāna of BL fragment 4.2v, line 1: *muchito pras̱avi pravadido*.

[14] Lenz (2003: 184-185) observes that *aryadharma* in the 5th pūrvayoga in BL fragments 16 + 25 and *saddharma* in the avadāna of Zadamitra in BL fragment 1 are "more or less synonymous" in two stories dealing with the disappearance of the Buddha's teachings. *Aryadharma* is also attested in the 17th avadāna of BL fragment 4: *sa bhaga[pado] ladho aryadharma prat[ista?] ///*

Pāṭaliputra and Ujjayinī in northern India underlies the primary message. The following avadāna (no. 5), about a courtesan and a Yakṣa, does not provide information about place or time, but may also belong to a milieu like that of the previous avadāna about a courtesan, since the two stories are in sequence.

The eighth avadāna, about the Buddha's four great disciples, is set during the reign of Ajātaśatru. Ajātaśatru's role is not very clear, and an enigmatic character named Yola Arutega is introduced immediately after Ajātaśatru. Yola, the first element in this compound Iranian name, is found in names of Kṣatrapas and other governing officials in Kharoṣṭhī inscriptions.[15] Perhaps Yola Arutega is inserted into the story as an official of Ajātaśatru. The names of the Four Mahāśrāvakas (*catvari mahaṣavaga*) are listed as Śāriputra (*Śariputra*), Mahākāśyapa (*Mahakaśapa*), and Aniruddha (*Anar[u]dha*), with Maudgalyāyana (**Mogalana*) reconstructed in the deteriorated final lines. While this avadāna is clearly situated in the geographical and historical context of ancient Magadha, the appearance of a character with an Iranian name recognized in Kharoṣṭhī inscriptions provides evidence for local innovation in the transmission of the narrative.

The poorly preserved incomplete final avadāna (no. 9) in the scroll (BL fragments 12 + 14) takes place during the Buddha's time, since the Buddha is introduced right after the opening formula (*ev[o] ṣuyadi budh[o] u[v]o ///*). The narrative seems to involve a dialogue between a woman and a monk (*/// striga ṣamanasa anava ? ///*), but the content of the dialogue remains uncertain due to the condition of the surface of the scroll.

---

[15] Examples include *Ṣahi Yola-mira* in Tor Ḍherai potsherds (Konow 1929: 173-176), *Yola-moṇalatra* in a copper seal from Taxila (Konow 1929: 101), and *Kṣatrapasa Yola[sa]* in a dedication of Ramaka (Fussman 1980: 5-8, 19-20, pl. III). *Yola* is derived from the Iranian root *yud* (Sanskrit *yudh*) meaning "fight" and *arutega* may be related to Iranian *'rwt* meaning "swift", attested as naming components in Sogdian graffiti from Shatial (*ywδk'n*, *'rwδ'ync*, *'rwt'kk*) and Hunza-Haldeikish (*'spyw[δ?]*) (Sims-Williams 1992: 25, 42-43, 82). I wish to thank Hassan Rezai Baghbidi for discussing these Iranian etymologies with me during the 12th World Sanskrit Conference in Helsinki.

3.2. Northwestern borderlands

Three avadānas in BL fragments 12 + 14 are localized in geographical and historical contexts of the Northwest around the 1st century CE. Local toponyms (Puṣkalāvatī), Indo-Iranian titles (Kṣatrapa and Mahākṣatrapa), and proper names of characters indicate that these avadānas take place in the northwestern frontiers of the Indian subcontinent. Avadānas that incorporated local rulers and other officials were probably intended to acknowledge and encourage patronage by extolling the generosity of supporters and by criticizing the shortcomings of opponents of their supporters. Stories with contemporary regional settings were also likely to have been composed for local audiences in order to convey the relevance of the main points of the narrative more directly. Literary parallels for avadānas localized in Gandhāra and other areas of the northwestern borderlands are generally more difficult to identify in Buddhist textual traditions than narratives set in northeastern India at the time of Śākyamuni Buddha (although many of these stories lack direct parallels as well).

The second avadāna, beginning at the top of the verso of BL fragment 14, concerns two characters from Puṣkalāvatī (*pokhaladige*/*pokhaladago*). Puṣkalāvatī (located near Chārsada in northwestern Pakistan) was the primary urban center of Gandhāra until the capital shifted across the Kabul River to Puruṣapura (modern Peshawar) in the Kuṣāṇa period.[16] One of the characters from Puṣkalāvatī is a previously unattested *kṣatrapa* named Spaduka. Spaduka's name is derived from Iranian *spāda* ("army"), which appears as Spala or Spāla in coins and inscriptions from the Northwest and Upper Indus regions.[17] The other character from Puṣkalā-

[16] For brief historical summaries of Puṣkalāvatī, see Marshall & Vogel 1902-03: 143; Konow 1929: 117; Foucher 1931: 341-348; 1942: 41-45.

[17] For coins of Spalirises, Spalahora, and Spalagadama, see Mitchener 1976: 439-444; Rapson 1897: 8; Raychaudhuri 1923: 228-229. For hybrid Indo-Iranian names ending in *-spāla* in Brāhmī graffiti from the Upper Indus, see Bandini-König & Hinüber 2001: 376; Hinüber 1986: 150-151.

vatī was probably a generous donor, a deduction based on the phrase "money was given by me" (*dhana mi dite*). Stories about an artist from Puṣkalāvatī (or a painter from Gandhāra) who donated all of his money to the Saṃgha appear in two Chinese Buddhist collections: Kumārajīva's translation of the *Kalpanāmaṇḍitikā* and *Za pao zang jing*.[18] In the Gāndhārī avadāna, a Kṣatrapa (presumably Spaduka) falls down at the feet of a Mahārāja (*maharayasa pade païdo*). This episode is missing in the Chinese stories, which emphasize other important features that do not seem to be included in the Gāndhārī. While links between the Gāndhārī and Chinese stories are tenuous, the geographical and cultural context for the story is contemporary Gandhāra.

The third Gāndhārī avadāna in the group is about the father of King Kardamaga, who was reborn as a pig because he was selfish (Gāndhārī *maca[ri]* / Sanskrit *matsarin*). Since the story's outline is extremely brief, it is not clear what the father of King Kardamaga did to deserve rebirth as a pig. An avadāna in BL fragment 4, referring to a king with a name ending in *-maga* reborn as a pig, is probably a parallel version of the story.[19] Kardamaga can be related to the dynastic name of the Kārddamaka lineage of Western Kṣatrapa rulers of western India between the 1st and 4th centuries CE. A single reference to the Kārddamaka lineage is found in a 2nd century CE Sanskrit inscription from Kāṅherī, north of Mumbai.[20] The inscription records a donation on behalf of a Sātavāhana queen who was the daughter of Mahākṣatrapa Ru- (probably identifiable with Rudradāman) and "a descendant of the Kārddamaka royal

[18] Huber (1908: 117-119) translates the story of the artist from Puṣkalāvatī in Kumārajīva's translation of the *Kalpanāmaṇḍitikā* into French. The story of the painter from Gandhāra in *Za pao zang jing* is translated into French by Chavannes (1910-11: 3.40) and into English by Willemen (1994: 103-104).

[19] BL fragment 4.1v: */// [ma]go rayo suarayoṇiṣu upavarṇo* ... "King (**karda-*) *[ma]ga* was reborn (*upavarṇo*) as a pig (literally 'in pig-wombs')".

[20] References include Bühler 1883a: 78, pl. LI, no. 11; Bühler 1883b: 272-273; Gokhale 1991: 62; Lüders 1912: 103, no. 994; Mirashi 1981, II: 68-69, no. 25; Raychaudhuri 1933: 36-39.

lineage" (*kārddamakarājavaṃśa-pra[bha]v[ā]y[ā]*). The Kārddamaka line of Western Kṣatrapas continued to employ Kharoṣṭhī script on coins after coming to western India from the Iranian borderlands sometime during the 1st century. This reference to a "Kardamaga King" in a Gāndhārī avadāna provides additional evidence for links between the Western Kṣatrapas and Indo-Scythians or Sakas in the Northwest.

The primary character in the sixth avadāna is a Mahākṣatrapa whose name is illegible. In this avadāna, the Mahākṣatrapa asks another character, "Why is [this] the result?" (*ki ?[ṣo] vivage*) and the other character replies that someone "was presented with a single alms-meal" (*ekapiḍa[vada]no paḍiva[ï]do*). The avadāna might illustrate a lesson that even a small donation given with pure intention can result in great rewards. Perhaps this story involving a Mahākṣatrapa is similar in thematic content to the episode of the "gift of dirt" in the *Aśokāvadāna*, in which a young boy's small act of generosity leads to the Buddha's prediction that he will become the Mauryan emperor Aśoka in a future rebirth.[21] Kṣatrapas and Mahākṣatrapas whose proper names are either unknown (such as Spaduka) or not clearly preserved (as in this story) seem to belong to pre-Kuṣāṇa (or more precisely, pre-Kaniṣka) historical contexts, since coins and inscriptions of Mahākṣatrapa Jihonika and Stratega Aśpavarman who appear in other avadānas in BL Kharoṣṭhī manuscripts, belong to the early decades of the 1st century CE (Salomon 1999: 141-151).[22]

---

[21] Cowell & Neil 1886: 364-366; Strong 1983: 198-201.

[22] Falk (2000: 211) questions Salomon's dating of the manuscripts in the 1st century, a *terminus post quem* date based on synchronisms between Kharoṣṭhī inscriptions of Aśpavarman and Jihonika and a Kharoṣṭhī inscription on a pot recording a donation of Suhasoma and Vāsavadattā, who are also known from 1st century Kharoṣṭhī inscriptions of the Oḍis and Apracas. The historical characters and titles referred to in other avadānas in BL Kharoṣṭhī manuscripts seem to belong to 1st century CE contexts before Kaniṣka, since he and other Kuṣāṇa rulers are not mentioned.

FIGURE 1: Synopsis of Avadānas in British Library Fragments 12 + 14

#	Frag-ment & line nos.	Title and/or introductory formula	Time/Place *(Sanskrit equivalent)* {hypothesis}	Proper names	Titles	Action/Topic/Theme	Abbreviation formula
1	14 r 73-77	*puniga avadano vistara ka ? ? ? /// evo śuyadi*	Buddha's time {Śrāvastī}	Puniga *(Pūrṇikā)* Anas̱apiḍiga *(Anāthapiṇḍada)* Pras̱eniga *(Prasenajit)*	Grahavadi *(gṛhapati)* Rayeno *(rājñā)*	Puniga convinces the Buddha to stay when requests by Anāthapiṇḍada and Prasenajit fail	*vistare avadano ° 1*
2	14 v 78-86	*evo ṣuyadi*	Pokhaladige *(Puṣkalāvatī)*	Spadu[k]a	Maharayo *(mahārāja)* Kṣatrapa	Wealth given away; Kṣatrapa falls at the feet of a Mahārāja	*vistare sarve yas̱a-yupamano s.[ya](*di)* ○ 2
3	14v 86-89	*evo śruyadi*	{Northwest}	Kardamaga *(Kārddamaka)*	Raya *(rājan)*	Kardamaga king's father is reborn as a pig; selfishness	*[° tri] sarvo yas̱a-yu[p.](*mano)* ○ 3
4	14v 89-93	*evo ṣuyadi*	Palaḍipu[_trami] *(Pāṭaliputra)* Ujani[ge] *(Ujjayinī)*		Ganiga *(gaṇikā)* Grah[vadi] *(gṛhapati)*	Householder from Ujjayinī faints and rolls on the ground; Āryadharma attained	*vi[stare y.] ///* ○ 4
5	12v 93-95	*eva śruya[di]*			[Ga]niga *(gaṇikā)* Yakṣa	Dialogue between a Yakṣa and a courtesan; invitation	*vistar.?[+][y.](*u) /// (*pamano 5)*

6	12v 96-101	*evo ṣuyadi*	{Northwest}	?	Mahakṣa[.r.](*po) *(mahākṣatrapa)*	Mahākṣatrapa asks: "What is the result?" Answer: "A single alms-meal was given to ..."	○ *ṣo [6] ///*
7	12v 102-108	*(*sarpa-) da̱sasa avadano vistare karyam=ida di*	Buddha's time	Sarpada̱sa *(Sarpadāsa)*	Bhikṣu	Sarpada̱sa asks Buddha: "What is the *kuśalamūla*?" Buddha answers: "Chaste conduct in all regards"	*(*avada)no vistare ya̱sa[y]u sa 7* ○
8	12v 108-115	*e vo ṣu[ya] ///* *(*di)*	Buddha's time or shortly afterwards	Ajadaśatruno *(Ajātaśatru)* Yola Arutega [Śariputro] *(Śāriputra)* Mahakaśa[po] *(Mahākāśyapa)* Anar[u]dh[o] *(Aniruddha)* (*Mogalana) {*Maudgalyāyana*}	Mahaṣavaga *(mahāśrāvaka)*	Four Mahāśrāvakas	*vistara sar[v]o [4] ///*
9	12v 116-120	*evo ṣuyadi*	Buddha's time		Ṣamana	Dialogue between a woman and a monk?	

4. CONCLUSIONS

The avadānas in BL fragments 12 + 14 show that many Indian Buddhist narratives were transmitted to the Northwest without significant modifications, but other story summaries incorporated places and characters specific to northwestern geographical and historical contexts. The majority of the avadānas in the British Library collection of Kharoṣṭhī manuscripts are stories about characters from northeastern India at or around the time of Śākyamuni. However, a significant proportion of the avadāna narratives (and at least one pūrvayoga) take place in the geographical, political and cultural milieu of the northwestern frontier during the 1st century CE. Avadānas localized in the Northwest reflect the heterogenous cultural environment in which Gandhāran Buddhism flourished, as already apparent from the integration of Indian, Iranian, Central Asian, Hellenistic, and of course local elements in Gandhāran art and architecture. Abbreviated written versions of avadānas and pūrvayogas probably functioned as frameworks for oral expansion by storytellers. More formal genres of Buddhist narrative literature demonstrate that such stories were elaborated and incorporated into texts like the *Divyāvadāna*, *Avadānaśataka*, *Mahāvastu*, and *Mūlasarvāstivāda-vinaya*. Brief summaries of edifying narratives set in northeastern India around the time of Śākyamuni Buddha and in the northwestern frontiers of ancient Gandhāra are like tiny islands emerging from the wide ocean of early Buddhist birth stories.

REFERENCES

ALLON, Mark 2001. *Three Gāndhārī Ekottarikāgama-Type Sūtras. British Library Kharoṣṭhī Fragments 12 and 14.* (Gandhāran Buddhist Texts, 2.) Seattle: University of Washington Press.

BANDINI-KÖNIG, Ditte & Oskar von HINÜBER 2001. *Die Felsbildstationen Shing Nala und Gichi Nala.* (Materialien zur Archäologie der Nordgebiete Pakistans, 4.) Mainz: Philipp v. Zabern.

BÜHLER, Georg 1883a. Inscriptions. In: James Burgess, *Report on the Elura Cave Temples and the Brahmanical and Jaina Caves in Western India; Completing the Results of the Fifth, Sixth, and Seventh Seasons' Operations of the Archæological Survey, 1877-78, 1878-79, 1879-80* (Archaeological Survey of Western India, 5): 59-87. London: Trübner & Co. (Reprint: Varanasi: Indological Book House, 1970.)

—— 1883b. On the relationship between the Andhras and the Western Kshatrapas. *Indian Antiquary* 12: 272-274.

BURLINGAME, Eugene 1921. *Buddhist Legends*, I-III. (Harvard Oriental Series, 28-30.) Cambridge, Mass.: Harvard University Press.

CHAVANNES, Édouard 1910-11. *Cinq cents contes et apologues extraits du Tripitaka chinois*, I-IV. Paris: Ernest Leroux. (Reprint: Paris: Adrien-Maisonneuve, 1962.)

COWELL, Edward & Robert NEIL 1886. *Divyâvadâna. A Collection of Early Buddhist Legends.* Cambridge: The University Press. [Reprint, Amsterdam: Oriental Press, 1970.]

FALK, Harry 2000. Review of Salomon 1999. *Journal of Asian Studies* 59.1: 210-211.

FOUCHER, Alfred 1931. De Kāpiśi à Pushkarāvatī. *Bulletin of the School of Oriental Studies* 6.2: 341-348.

—— 1942. *La vieille Route de l'Inde de Bactres à Taxila*, I. Paris: Les éditions d'art et d'histoire.

FUSSMAN, Gérard 1980. Nouvelles inscriptions śaka: Ère d'Azès, ère Vikrama, ère de Kaniṣka. *Bulletin de l'École Française d'Extrême-Orient* 67: 1-43.

GOKHALE, Shobhana 1991. *Kanheri Inscriptions.* Pune: Deccan College Post Graduate and Research Institute.

HOFINGER, Marcel 1982. *Le congrès du lac Anavatapta (Vies de saints bouddhiques)*, I. (Publications de l'Institut Orientaliste de Louvain, 28.) 2nd edition. Louvain-la-Neuve: Université Catholique de Louvain.

HUBER, Édouard 1908. *Sūtrālaṃkāra traduit en français sur le version chinoise de Kumārajīva*. Paris: Ernest Leroux.

KONOW, Sten 1929. *Kharoshṭhī Inscriptions with the Exception of Those of Aśoka*. (Corpus Inscriptionum Indicarum, II.1.) Calcutta: Government of India.

LENZ, Timothy 2003. *A New Version of the Gāndhārī Dharmapada and a Collection of Previous-Birth Stories*. (Gandhāran Buddhist Texts, 3.) Seattle: University of Washington Press.

—— 2004. Once upon a present time: an Avadānist from Gandhāra. *Buddhist Studies Review* 21.2: 197-215.

LÜDERS, Heinrich 1912. A List of Brāhmī Inscriptions from the Earliest Times to About 400 A.D. with the Exception of Those of Aśoka. Appendix to *Epigraphia Indica* 10.

—— 1926. *Bruchstücke der Kalpanāmaṇḍitikā des Kumāralāta*. (Kleinere Sanskrit-texte, 2.) Leipzig: Deutsche Morgenländische Gesellschaft.

MALALASEKERA, G. P. 1937-38. *Dictionary of Pāli Proper Names*, I-II. London: J. Murray. (Reprint, London: Pali Text Society, 1974.)

MARSHALL, John Hubert & Jean Philippe VOGEL 1902-03. *Annual Report of the Archaeological Survey of India*, I. Calcutta: Superintendent of Government Printing.

MIRASHI, Vasudev Vishnu. 1981. *The History and Inscriptions of the Sātavāhanas and the Western Kshatrapas*. Bombay: Maharashtra State Board for Literature and Culture.

MITCHENER, Michael 1976. *Indo-Greek and Indo-Scythian Coinage*, V. London: Hawkins Publications.

NORMAN, H. C. 1970. *The Commentary on the Dhammapada (Dhammapadatthakathā)*, II. London: Pali Text Society.

RAPSON, E. J. 1897. *Indian Coins*. Strassburg: K.J. Trübner.

RAYCHAUDHURI, Hemchandra 1923. *Political History of Ancient India, from the Accession of Parikshit to the Extinction of the Gupta Dynasty*. Calcutta: University of Calcutta.

—— 1933. The Kārddamaka Kings. *Indian Historical Quarterly* 9.1: 36-39.

SALOMON, Richard 1999: *Ancient Buddhist Scrolls from Gandhāra. The British Library Kharoṣṭhī Fragments*. Seattle: University of Washington Press.

—— 2002. Gāndhārī and its relationships with other Indo-Aryan languages in light of newly discovered Kharoṣṭhī manuscripts. In: Nicholas Sims-Williams (ed.), *Indo-Iranian Languages and Peoples* (Proceedings of the British Academy, 116): 119-134. Oxford: Oxford University Press for the British Academy.

SALOMON, Richard 2003. The Senior manuscripts: another collection of Gandhāran Buddhist scrolls. *Journal of the American Oriental Society* 123.1: 73-92.

SCHOPEN, Gregory 1997. If you can't remember, how to make it up: some monastic rules for redacting canonical texts. In Petra Kieffer-Pülz & Jens-Uwe Hartmann (eds.), *Bauddhavidyāsudhākaraḥ. Studies in Honour of Heinz Bechert on the Occasion of His 65th Birthday* (Indica et Tibetica, 30): 571-582. Swisttal-Odendorf: Indica et Tibetica Verlag.

SIMS-WILLIAMS, Nicholas 1992. *Sogdian and other Iranian Inscriptions of the Upper Indus*, II. (Inscriptions of the Seleucid and Parthian Periods and of Eastern Iran and Central Asia, III: Sogdian.) London: Corpus Inscriptionum Indicarum by School of Oriental and African Studies.

STRONG, John 1983. *The Legend of King Aśoka. A Study and Translation of the Aśokāvadāna.* Princeton: Princeton University Press. (Reprint: Delhi: Motilal Banarsidass, 1989.)

WILLE, Klaus 1990. *Die handschriftliche Überlieferung des Vinayavastu der Mūlasarvāstivādin.* (Verzeichnis der orientalischen Handschriften in Deutschland, Supplementband 30.) Stuttgart: Franz Steiner.

WILLEMEN, Charles 1994. *The Storehouse of Sundry Valuables, Translated from the Chinese of Kikkāya and Liu Hsiao-piao.* Compiled by T'an-yao. (Taisho, vol. 4, no. 203.) (BDK English Tripiṭaka, 10-I.) Berkeley: Numata Center for Buddhist Translation and Research.

WILSON, Liz 1996. *Charming Cadavers. Horrific Configurations of the Feminine in Indian Buddhist Literature.* Chicago: University of Chicago.

The Psalm of Sundarī in the *Therīgāthā*

SUNDARI SIDDHARTHA

Of all the writings in the Pali language the *Therīgāthā* stand out as the only text in the Buddhist tradition of known female authorship. These *gāthā* (tales) of the *therī* (distinguished women) are similar to other famous stories in Buddhism viz. the *Jātakakathā* or the *Apadāna*. But unlike them, these are not concerned with the past lives of the authors and the karmic events that led to their attainment of *nibbāna* (salvation). These *Therīgāthā* are distinct because of their preoccupation with the experiences of the ascribed authors in a single lifetime.

The tale of the *bhikkhunī* (female mendicant) named Sundarī is one of the 522 tales associated with the *therī*. It contains 26 verses. The first sixteen verses are a preamble to the story of Sundarī, which is related in the last ten verses.

Sujāta is a well-to-do citizen of Varanasi, living with his wife and two children – Sundarī and her brother. The brother dies and the *gāthā* starts. Sujāta is grief-stricken on losing his son. He goes to the *bhikkhunī* named Vaseṭṭhī and wonders how she bore the loss of her children. Her answer suggests that we, as one humanity, have collectively lost not one but many children and relatives. Sujāta wants to know the Dhamma or Doctrine which has given her this forbearance. Answering him, she explains about the Buddha and his doctrine, knowing which all grief ceases, Thereupon Sujāta decides on renunciation. He masters the three lores. He sends his charioteer, along with the chariot, back to his family. Sujāta's wife accepts the situation in her stride. She wants to reward the charioteer. But he has decided to follow his master on the path of renunciation.

In the second part of the *gāthā*, Sujāta's wife says to her daughter Sundarī that since her father has renounced his worldly assets, the entire wealth of the family now accrues to her. So she should accept and enjoy it. But Sundarī is not ready to accept it. Her contention is that just as her father was struck by the grief of losing his son, she too is suffering at the loss of her brother. She too wants to embrace the path of renunciation and give up worldly possessions. Her mother agrees and allows her to do what she wants.

In the next part of the *gāthā*, Sundarī is described as standing in front of her teacher – a *bhikkhunī*. She informs her that she has acquired the three lores (*tissa vijjā anuppattā*), and requests the *bhikkhunī* to lead her into the presence of the Master, the Buddha, at Sāvatthī. The *bhikkhunī* takes her to the Buddha. She first describes His glory to Sundarī; then introduces her to the Buddha, suggesting to Him that she is ready for entry into the Order. Sundarī speaks, proclaiming Him as her one and only Master. Then the Master welcomes her into the Order with encouraging words. And there the *gāthā* ends.

In this one psalm, there are seven characters, with the events woven around them. Even while narrating the story, the *gāthā* is successful in disseminating the knowledge of the basic tenets of Buddhist thinking. How does the *gāthā* manage to do this?

1. *NISSARAṆAM* IS ESCAPE

In the *gāthā*, the head of the family, Sujāta, is drowned in sorrow because of his son's death. His redemption or his distraction from this sorrow could have been accomplished through any of the various means of diversion: he could have tried to father another child; he could have adopted a boy; he could have gone for a trip around the world. But all these were means providing temporary relief. What was needed was the removal of the very root of the cause of suffering. This in turn needed a change in the mindset of the person concerned. For that, proper guidance was needed. The guidance in the form of the teachings of Buddhism is put in the mouth of the *bhikkhunī* Vaseṭṭhī. She does not preach. She merely relates all that happened to her own self. She talks of *nissaraṇaṃ* (escape) (*sāhaṃ nissaraṇaṃ jñātvā jātiyā maraṇassa ca* | *na socāmi na rodāmi na cāhaṃ paritappāmi* ||). She says: "I have learnt a way to escape from both birth and death. And that is why I no more mourn, nor weep, nor make my bitter wail."

Vaseṭṭhī indicated that she had the formula for the escape (*nissaraṇaṃ*) from *dukkha*. Now it was for the seeker to show his inclination. Sujāta was so inclined. So he asked: "Which doctrine have you learnt, that you speak such words (*kassa tvaṃ dhammaṃ aññaya giraṃ bhāsasi edisaṃ*)"? And in the answer of Vasetthī we unobtrusively get the tenets of Buddhism. She says: "It is He, the Awakened (the Buddha) ... Who did teach the norm, whereby all that hath life may put off every ill. (*esa ... sambuddho ... sabba-dukkhappahānāya dhammaṃ desesi pāṇinaṃ*). Then she adds: "Having heard his doctrine of the non-substrate, I understood the Gospel (*nirupadhiṃ dhammaṃ sutvā ... viññātasaddhammā*) and dispelled my child-grief (*puttasokaṃ vyapānudiṃ*)".

This was no mere preaching. She had gone through the fire of suffering and had come out effulgent with Wisdom. So Sujāta decided that he too would go to the Buddha. Sujāta saw Him. What the Buddha preached to him then, reveals the basic principles of Buddhism.

The Buddha taught him the Truth (*dhammaṃ*) which takes one beyond suffering (*dukkhassa pāragu*). He explained the truth of dissatisfaction (*dukkhaṃ*); the origin of that ill (*dukkha samuppādaṃ*); the transcendence of that (*dukkhassa atikkamaṃ*); the noble eightfold path (*ariyaṭṭhangikaṃ maggaṃ*) that leads to the abating of all misery (*dukkhūpasamagāminaṃ*). Consequently Sujāta, having known the Gospel, chose renunciation (*pabbajjaṃ samarocayi*); and realized and attained the three lores (*tisso vijjā*, viz. Buddha, Dhamma and Saṅgha.

2. *DUKKHA*

The Buddha's message has one specific refrain: "freedom from *dukkha*". The meaning of *dukkha* is well revealed in this *gāthā*.

Very rightly have the various translators emphasized that *dukkha* is not just sorrow. Unpleasantness, discomfort, dissatisfaction, being badly off and disease are some of the terms in English used to explain it better, *sukha* and *dukkha* are a pair (*dvandva*), *su-* and *duḥ-* are the two prefixes respectively. *su-* conveys the sense of easy, nice, appealing, likeable; and *duḥ-* indicates the opposite – difficult, not nice, not appealing, not likeable.

It is also significant that when Buddhism talks of *dukkha pahāna* (removal of *dukkha*), it does not mean the destruction, or the finishing off, of something external, something outside of the person. It means only that "the attitude towards life is changed", from the difficult way of seeing life, to the easy way. And what makes it easy is renunciation. This "giving up" changes the viewpoint and the mindset of the person. The change being internal, it is something which cannot be imposed upon anyone. The individual himself has to bring it about. It is said that one can only take a horse to water; one can't make it drink. If the horse is thirsty enough, it will drink. Sujāta was. That is why he could acquire the *tisso vijjā*.

3. PEOPLE'S RELIGION

Though propagated by a royal prince, Buddhism was of the people, of the society. Not all lay people were *bhikkhus* (monks and nuns); but awareness amongst the masses was very high. In this *Sundarī-gāthā*, the charioteer was a worldly man, as also his master Sujāta, his wife and daughter. But by inclination they were adherents to the precepts of their faith. Hence the charioteer could take to renunciation soon after his master did, and Sundarī could give up her wealth. But the most evolved was the mother. She first said: "Sundarī, the family wealth is yours now. Enjoy it!" But once the intentions of Sundarī were revealed, there was no note of dissent from the mother. She just said: "May this, your intention and your wish, be crowned with success." (Khalil Gibran would have thoroughly approved of this mother.)

4. ANOTHER IMPORTANT POINT IN THIS *GĀTHĀ*

The attainment of *nibbāna* by Sundarī is not explicitly described. The narration mentions that Buddha welcomes her with these words: "For you it was but a little way to come" (*tato te adūrāgataṃ*). Probably the commentators have inferred from this alone that after many happy rebirths, her knowledge having matured, she was born as the beautiful daughter of Sujāta. The message conveyed is clear. Emancipation is a continuous process; at times, a long-drawn one. Different people attain *nibbāna* differently. Emotions, obsessions, awareness, previous impressions (*saṃskāra*), karmic and moral states – all these cumulatively determine the process of emancipation. Thus by not mentioning the final attainment of salvation by the aspirant, the point suggested is that it is an ongoing process, spanning numerous lives/births.

These and such other facets of the Buddhist thinking are culled from such *gāthā*, besides the story element.

Therīgāthā are not didactic fairy tales or stories based on birds and animals like the *Hitopadeśa* and the *Pañcatantra*. Yet they too have a message; they too inspire and guide, albeit obliquely. They do not give any specific exposition but nor are they not giving it. Their sedate style, incorporating dialogues, is similar to that of ancient Vedic literature. The *gāthā* of *therī* Sundarī is a good, easy and interesting way of disseminating religious knowledge.

Other points of note are that major calamities hasten the inclination for renunciation. People from all strata of society sought spiritual salvation in those days too. Women had the liberty to take over the responsibility of running the house. People strove for knowledge and wisdom, then as ever.

Prajñāvādāṃś ca bhāṣase: Polemics with Buddhism in the Early Parts of the *Bhagavadgītā*

PRZEMYSŁAW SZCZUREK

1.

aśocyān anvaśocas tvaṃ prajñāvādāṃś ca bhāṣase |
gatāsūn agatāsūṃś ca nānuśocanti paṇḍitāḥ ||
BhG 2.11

This stanza of the *Bhagavadgītā* seems to play a considerable role in the first part of the poem. Kṛṣṇa starts speaking after having listened to Arjuna, who in the first canto presents his qualms about the coming battle, which will involve the mutual massacre of relatives, friends and masters. He refuses to take part in it (2.9). Kṛṣṇa begins to explicate his teachings in stanza 2.11, starting by directly confronting Arjuna's words of despair. First, Kṛṣṇa encourages Arjuna to undertake the fight, putting forward arguments for Arjuna's participation in the battle (2.11-38). Later (from 2.39), he explains how one should fight but also how to act and so sustain the world order. He then gradually moves beyond the topic of the fight, hardly ever touching it, and passes on to present a series of teachings referring to the human condition in general. Moreover, the reader of the poem becomes a witness to a conversation between man and God, who is trying to solve the dilemmas of human life and show a way leading to liberation which will allow not only Arjuna but any man to identify with it. Stanza 2.11 begins the process of showing Arjuna this new vision of the world and human life. It is the actual starting point of the teachings included in the *Bhagavadgītā*.

Kṛṣṇa's words from 2.11 – as the commentators unanimously state – do not imply a lack of compassion towards the dying, or a simple contempt for life and death, but aim to raise Arjuna above the opposition between life and death. In his perception of the world, Arjuna should give priority to a vision in which the omnipresent, immortal Self is inherent, rather than a simple, human compassion. This vision of the world is held by perfected wise men, pandits, who transcend the oppositions of the manifested world. According to the text of the *Gītā*, true wisdom is embodied by Kṛṣṇa.

It must be admitted, however, that the interpretation of Kṛṣṇa's words addressed to Arjuna in 2.11 has troubled interpreters and commentators. The question concerns the expression in pāda b: *prajñāvādāṃś ca bhāṣase*. Despite his criticism of Arjuna's attitude and argument against taking part in the battle, Kṛṣṇa states that he utters words of wisdom. That he says this while trying to persuade him that his sorrow and compassion are unwise has been interpreted in different ways.

According to some[1], the passage should be understood as follows: you grieve wrongly, though [generally/otherwise] you speak words of wisdom; that means: your words are wise, your deeds are not. Śaṅkara notices Arjuna's inconsistency: he uses arguments of wisdom, but in grieving for those he should not grieve for (as they are really eternal) he shows foolishness.[2] Śrīdhara emphasizes the word *bhāṣase*: you only speak words of wisdom (but you do not understand them).[3]

[1] Garbe 1905: 73; Ghose 1938: 20-21; Bahm 1970: 19; Sinha 1995: 37; Yogananda 1995: 194-195.

[2] Ramachandra Aiyar 1988: 41.

A slightly different shade of meaning is conveyed by the following interpretation:[4] (you grieve for those not to be grieved for, and) you speak words which pretend to be wise, but the wisdom of the truly learned is different.

Another interpretation suggests that Arjuna uses the words of wisdom in vain[5] or that he uses tall-talk ("philosophises") while speaking words of wisdom.[6] Belvalkar considers irony on Kṛṣṇa's part as "the most effective method of meeting Arjuna's arrogation of superior wisdom to his own side ...".[7]

The expression is interpreted by some to be Kṛṣṇa's acknowledgement of Arjuna's words as wise in part.[8] It seems that the interpretation of Rāmānuja[9] (and also Ānandagiri and Nīlakantha) has left its mark here. Rāmānuja refers Arjuna's words of wisdom to his speech on family rites (*kuladharma*) and mixing castes, BhG 1.39-44.

At the beginning of the 20th century, J. S. Speyer noted the problem concerning the interpretation of this stanza and (also stating that the compound *prajñāvādān* conflicts with the correct use of compounds in Sanskrit) he proposed his own conjecture: *prajāvādān*; consequently, he understood the whole passage as: "you grieve for those who should not be grieved for and you speak just in the way people do".[10] F. O. Schrader demonstrated that the

---

3 See Schrader 1930: 13-14, where the interpretations of Madhusūdana, Ānandatīrtha, Jayatīrtha, Vedāntakeśika are also mentioned.

4 Senart 1922: 50; Edgerton 1932: 70-71; 1939: 17, 180; Riviere 1979: 90-91; Gotshalk 1993: 6, 177.

5 Herman 1973: 47, 113.

6 Deutsch 1968: 37-38.

7 Belvalkar 1947: lxxxii (see also: Belvalkar 1939: 220; 1943: 9-10).

8 Zaehner 1969: 124; Minor 1982: 34-35.

9 Sampatkumaran 1985: 19; Telang (1882: 43-44) refers to Nīlakantha's interpretation (words of wisdom refer to "family rites, &c., for ... they indicate knowledge of soul as distinct from body"); Minor supports the interpretation of Rāmānuja referring also to the similar one of Ānandagiri.

10 Speyer 1902: 123-125.

original reading of this passage was transmitted by the so-called Kashmir recension of the *Bhagavadgītā*, which reads: *prajñāvan nābhibhāṣase* – "you do not speak like a wise man".[11]

None of the above interpretations seems fully satisfactory, though it must be admitted that Rāmānuja's suggestion appears to be worth particular attention. Arjuna's reasoning against the battle (following the moving description, 1.29-31) can be divided into two parts: 1) 1.32-38 – stanzas expressing his general grief over killing relatives; 2) 1.39-44 – stanzas referring to the *kuladharma*, depicting, step by step, the consequences that extermination of the clan could bring about. Therefore, if Kṛṣṇa's words are a direct response to what Arjuna said, stanza 2.11 may be considered in the following way:

- pāda a (*aśocyān anvaśocas tvaṃ*) – may refer to the first part of Arjuna's argument (1.32-38);
- pāda b (*prajñāvādāṃś ca bhāṣase*) – to the second part (1.39-44);
- whereas pāda c and d (*gatāsūn agatāsūṃś ca nānuśocanti paṇḍitāḥ*) – may be recognized as an introduction to the teaching on the immortal Self (2.12-30).

And yet even this interpretation recedes into the background in relation to what can be said about the stanzas preceding and following 2.11. It seems that the *Bhagavadgītā*, commonly perceived as an eclectic composition, may also be analysed as a polemical one. If this hypothesis is followed, the comparison of ideas and thoughts presented by the *Gītā* with those of early Buddhism appears particularly rewarding. The most reasonable hypothesis for the poem's date is 3rd–1st century BC. Among the different heterodox religious and philosophical currents which are known or thought to have existed at that time, Buddhism is the most recognizable as a religion capable of threatening Brahminical orthodoxy. The successful development of Buddhism in the last centuries BC must have

[11] Schrader 1930: 13-14.

contributed considerably to the evolution of Brahminism, its reform from inside and the assimilation of new ideas. The *Bhagavadgītā* combines various thoughts and currents, which indicate an intention to compete with religions which rejected Vedic and Brahminic tradition, above all with Buddhism.

In this paper I would like to approach the passage up to 2.38 of the *Gītā* as a text containing elements of discussion and polemics with early Buddhism, i.e. the Buddhism represented in the Pāli canon. Stanza 2.11 seems to be fit perfectly into this polemical context.

2.

Before coming to the main point of the paper, some basic problems concerning the origin and development of the *Bhagavadgītā*'s text should be considered. This is important in order to explain what place the analysed parts have in the poem. The problem of the composition's genesis and wording has been discussed for nearly 200 years.[12] Among over 20 works which have been trying to present (sometimes quite contradictory) views on the history of the poem's text, Mislav Ježić's research has in my eyes been of the greatest importance.[13] Ježić presented his own concept of the poem's wording, basing his research on convincing philological arguments. In the poem's text he first noticed repetitions (which are a typical feature of the originally orally transmitted poetry), and then he classified those repetitions (continuity repetitions, duplication repetitions). This allowed him to distinguish several textual layers in the *Bhagavadgītā*. The layers were added (most probably gradually) to the short epic episode *sensu stricto*, developed it and enriched it thematically. The basic layers the *Gītā* is composed of are as follows:

---

[12] See: Minor 1982: xxxiii-xli; Ježić 1986: 628-629; Malinar 1996: 21-51; Brockington 1998: 267-277.

[13] Ježić 1979; 1986; 2002.

- BhG 1.1–2.1-4, 9-10, 31-37: the epic layer (the oldest form of the epic episode);
- 2.11-30, 38: the first *sāṃkhya* layer (inserted into the epic layer; first of the series of Upaniṣadic layers)
- chapters 2-6: Upaniṣadic (didactic) layers:
    - 2.39–4.42 (minus interpolations): the first *yoga* layer;
    - 5: the second *yoga* layer;
    - 6: the third *yoga* layer;
- 2.5-8, 11.15-50: the hymn (independent text inserted into the poem);
- chapters 7-12: the *bhakti* synthesis;
- chapters 13-15: Upaniṣadic layers (*kṣetra-kṣetrajña, mahad brahma-pitā, kṣara-akṣara-uttama puruṣa*);
- chapters 16-18: classifications (*daiva-asurasampad,* the three *guṇas*), glosses;
- 18 (from 41, 49, 54 or) 64ff. (or 72-73): conclusion.[14]

By this stratification, the poem in its original form could have been a short, 60-stanza epic episode on the *dharma* of the warrior, being just a *Kṛṣṇārjunasaṃvāda* (and not yet the Bhagavadgītā). It was probably inserted into the *Mahābhārata* at an early stage of development.[15] Arjuna expressed his doubts and deep sorrow about the battle to come. He put forward arguments (among others referring to *kuladharma* rules) against his participation in the battle. In this original version, Kṛṣṇa encourages Arjuna to take part in the battle only in 9 stanzas (2.2-3, 31-37), emphasizing *kṣatriyadharma*, i.e.

[14] Moreover, interpolations within the texts of particular layers were observed. The most important ones are combined in the so-called *bhakti*-layer, being chronologically the last layer in the *Gītā*. The bhakti stanzas are scattered throughout the poem and belong to the bhakti layer in the middle sextet of the poem (chapters 7-12). The purpose of the bhakti interpolations is to reinterpret particular issues from the earlier layers in the light of the *bhakti* concept and the cult of Kṛṣṇa.

[15] Cf. Ježić 1986; Szczurek 2002.

the fact that Arjuna is a warrior and that the main duty of his class (*svadharma*) is to fight during a war.[16] Stanza 2.37 ends the epic layer with an exhortation to Arjuna to fight.

To this short episode another part was first added, the so-called first *sāṃkhya* layer, 2.11-30, 38, by being embedded in the text of the epic layer. This enlargement introduced new reasoning, but above all enriched Kṛṣṇa's argument, providing new arguments why Arjuna should fight. This part aimed to show the opposition between what is imperishable and eternal, i.e. the absolute Self, *ātman* (here *dehin* or *śarīrin*), and the bodily "covering". Only the human body is mortal and inevitably undergoes destruction. The real Self immanently inherent in every living being is immortal and so cannot be destroyed. Recognition of this fact should assure Arjuna of the incorrectness of his grief and moral dilemma, and should encourage him to fight without selfish motives. Ježić (1986: 632) noticed repetitions framing this layer, beginning and ending markers (classified as continuity repetitions).[17]

Stanza 2.38 creates a common ending for the epic and the first *sāṃkhya* layers. It partly repeats (by means of duplication repetitions) the epic call to fight from stanza 2.37, but, at the same time, it reinterprets 2.37 by referring to the topic of the first *sāṃkhya* layer.[18] These two earliest layers of the poem create a composi-

[16] Kṛṣṇa while addressing Arjuna in stanzas 2.31-37, develops arguments presented in 2.2-3 in the same order (cf. Szczurek 2002: 63-64). Both parts of the text are closely connected. According to the assumed here original version of the poem, the short (2.2-3) and the longer (2.31-37) speech of Kṛṣṇa were separated only by three stanzas (2.4, 9-10). Later on, a new part of the text (2.11-30) was embedded, and stanzas 2.5-8 (belonging to the hymn layer, 11.15-50) were added, which drew apart both Kṛṣṇa's speeches from the epic layer.

[17] 2.11: *aśocyān anvaśocas tvaṃ ..., nānuśocanti paṇḍitāḥ* – 2.30: *na tvaṃ śocitum arhasi*; 2.15: *samaduḥkhasukhaṃ dhīraṃ* – 2.38: *sukhaduḥkhe same kṛtvā*.

[18] 2.37: *hato vā prāpsyasi svargaṃ*
jitvā vā bhokṣyase mahīm |
tasmād uttiṣṭha *kaunteya*
yuddhāya *kṛtaniścayaḥ* ||

2.38: *sukhaduḥkhe same kṛtvā*
lābhālābhau jayājayau |
tato yuddhāya yujyasva
naivaṃ pāpam avāpsyasi ||

tional whole (though a miniature), which is the main reason why this part of the text, up to stanza 2.38, is taken into consideration in this paper.[19]

Stanza 2.11 is of particular significance here. Being the first stanza of the *sāṃkhya* layer, it is a sort of link between the two oldest parts of the *Gītā*. On the one hand, it refers to Arjuna's words from the epic layer (expressing grief, depression and reluctance to fight) and on the other, it introduces a new subject along with the next layer. Therefore, to answer the question what meaning "words of wisdom" from 2.11 may convey, it is necessary to have a close look at: firstly, the epic layer of the *Gītā* (1.1–2.4; 2.9-10, 31-37) and secondly, the first *sāṃkhya* layer (2.11-30, 38). As stated above the proposed key to the interpretation is a comparison of those parts with the ideas of early Buddhism.

3.

Not many scholars have noticed references, echoes or allusions to Buddhism in the *Bhagavadgītā*. Among interpreters and commentators on the poem, R. C. Zaehner (1969) seems to pay attention more frequently to both similarities and dissimilarities with Buddhist ideas expressed in particular fragments of the Pāli canon.[20] Some aspects of ethics contained in the *Gītā* and Buddhist thought, such as the attitude towards war and the caste system, were analysed and compared by K. N. Jayatilleke (1955). He pointed out that as far as the two issues are considered, we have to do with two opposite approaches. In his detailed study *Early Buddhism*

[19] It is not unlikely that, at some early stage of the great epic's wording, the epic episode was of that short. Stanza 2.39 clearly "patches up" the preceding text with the new layer (the so-called first *yoga* layer). The call for fight from 2.37-38 allowed for a smooth transition to the subsequent part of the epic narration, i.e. to the first stanza following the end of the whole *Bhagavadgītā* (MBh 6.41.1).

[20] A. Malinar (1996), too, while analysing the contents of the *Gītā*, sometimes refers to the Buddhist ideas and passages in the Pāli canon.

and the Bhagavadgītā (1971), K. N. Upadhyaya showed in the most thorough way to date the relations between the poem and Buddhism. He analysed the texts of both the *Bhagavadgītā* and the Pāli canon and compared them. He points out both common and different elements in the two traditions, traces the places in the *Gītā* which reveal any sign of assimilating Buddhist thought, and draws attention to parts of the poem which oppose some Buddhist doctrines.[21]

Upadhyaya discusses the two attitudes towards war and fighting. He compares a fragment of the *Vepacitti* (or *Khanti*) *Sutta* of the *Saṃyutta Nikāya* (SN I 221-222) with a part of the *Gītā* which corresponds precisely to the epic layer as recognized in the above presented reconstruction (though Upadhyaya himself does not distinguish the textual layers of the poem).[22] Basing myself on Upadhyaya, I find it quite interesting and useful to compare the dialogue of Sakka (Skt. Śakra, i.e. Indra) and Mātali to the short dialogue between Kṛṣṇa and Arjuna from the epic layer.

In SN I 221-222[23] there is the Buddha's parable about the power of patience and forbearance of Sakka, the ruler of the gods. A long time ago a battle between devas and asuras took place in which the latter were defeated. The defeated and bound ruler of the asuras, Vepacitti, was brought before Sakka. Although defeated, Vepacitti

---

[21] It should be mentioned that Upadhyaya's attitude to the problem of the origin, rise and wording of the *Gītā* is considerably different from the one presented in the paper. The scholar inclines to the conviction that the poem is a homogenous piece of literature (and not a multi-layered composition), although he does not exclude some possible interpolations and modifications. Also, he claims that as a whole the *Gītā* was an integral part of the epic, the *Bhārata*, even before its extension to the size of the *Mahābhārata* (Upadhyaya 1983: 4-16).

Upadhyaya's book became a starting point for the present considerations. Moreover, I would like to remark that in this paper I occasionally pay more attention to the *Gītā*'s discussions and polemics. In Upadhyaya's book I have not found any remarks on the interpretation of 2.11.

[22] Upadhyaya 1983: 132-133.

[23] All the references, quotations and translations of the Pāli canon texts follow the Pali Text Society editions, unless stated otherwise.

insults Sakka with coarse words. Mātali, Sakka's charioteer, reacts by saying that ignoring Vepacitti's rude words is a sign of fear and weakness. The answer of the gods' ruler is that a person as wise as he is cannot equal a fool. Mātali responds that a wise man should reprimand a fool severely to prevent him from becoming angrier. Sakka replies that the best way to control a fool is to stay calm and aware yourself, to which Mātali responds that a patient and gentle attitude brings about a bad reputation. It makes a fool think that he is tolerated because others are afraid of him, and thus the fool swaggers in his blindness. Finally, Sakka persuades him that one's opponent's opinion is not important any more than the views of weak, foolish people ignorant of morality (*dhamma*). The true power and measure of morality is patience and forbearance towards others' anger. It is very sinful to return anger with anger. True victory and happiness are based on lack of anger, steadfastness, gentleness. After having quoted this story, the Buddha encourages monks to follow the path of Sakka, the way of forbearance and patience.

The same arguments can be found in the very next sutta, *Subhāsitam-jayaṃ Sutta* (SN I 222-224), where a dialogue between Vepacitti (presenting the earlier arguments of Mātali) and Sakka (repeating his own earlier arguments) takes place.

While comparing the dialogue of Mātali an Sakka to the one of Kṛṣṇa and Arjuna, Upadhyaya noticed that Mātali's arguments are used by Kṛṣṇa to overcome Arjuna's reasoning in which, in turn, Sakka's arguments echo. This observation seems incredibly accurate and important for the present considerations. Therefore, I would like to present and compare even in a more detailed form the fragments of both texts. The Pāli fragments are accompanied by some other from the *Saṃyutta Nikāya* which refer to the problem of war and fight (SN I 83, 85; IV 309). This, as it seems, will allow for a still more conspicuous picture of the mutual relations, similarities and opposites between the two ethical currents.

I Similarities

Saṃyutta Nikāya I 221-222		***Bhagavadgītā*** (the epic layer)
1. Background		
– military background (after the battle between Devas and Asuras)	=	military background (before the battle between Pāṇḍavas and Kauravas)
– dialogue between Sakka (ruler of gods) and his charioteer Mātali (*mātali-saṅgāhako*)	=	dialogue between Arjuna (the prince of Pāṇḍavas) and his charioteer Kṛṣṇa
2. Similarities in argumentation:		
A) Sakka	=	**Arjuna**
SN I 221: ... ***kathaṃ*** *hi mādiso* ***viññu*** *bālena paṭisaṃyuje* ‖[24] ...		BhG 1.35: *etān na hantum icchāmi ghnato 'pi madhusūdana* । ...
SN I 222: *tass-eva tena* ***pāpīyo*** *yo* kuddhaṃ *paṭikujjhati* । *kuddham apaṭi-kujjhanto saṅgāmam jeti dujjayaṃ* ‖		BhG 1.36: *nihatya dhārtarāṣṭrān naḥ kā prītiḥ syāj janārdana* । ***pāpam*** *evāśrayed asmān hatvaitān* ātatāyinaḥ ‖
ubhinnam atthaṃ carati attano ca parassa ca । *paraṃ* saṅkupitaṃ ***ñatvā*** *yo sato upasammati* ‖[25]		BhG 1.38: *yady apy ete na paśyanti* lobhopa-hatacetasaḥ । ...
		BhG 1.39: ***kathaṃ*** *na* ***jñeyam*** *asmābhiḥ* ***pāpād*** *asmān nivartitum* । (*kulakṣayakṛtaṃ doṣaṃ prapaśyadbhir janārdana* ‖)

[24] "... How should any man / Who lacks not understanding, such as I, / Engage himself to band with a fool?"

[25] "Worse of the two is he who, when reviled, / Reviles again. Who doth not, when reviled, / Revile again, a twofold victory wins. / Both of the other and himself he seeks / The good; for he the other's angry mood / Doth understand and groweth calm and still."

B) Mātali	=	**Kṛṣṇa**
SN I 221: ***bhayā*** *nu mathavā sakka* ***dubbalyā*** *no titikkhasi* I *suṇanto pharusaṃ vācaṃ sammukhā vepacittino ti* II[26]		BhG 2.3: *klaibyaṃ mā sma gamaḥ pārtha naitat tvayy upapadyate* I *kṣudraṃ hṛdaya****daurbalyaṃ*** *tyaktvottiṣṭha paraṃtapa* II
SN I 221: *etad eva titikkhāya vajjam passāmi vāsava* I *yadā naṃ* ***maññati*** *bālo* ***bhayā*** *myāyam titikkhati* I *ajjhārūhati dummedho go va bhiyyo palāyinan-ti* II[27]		BhG 2.35: ***bhayād*** *raṇād uparataṃ* ***maṃsyante*** *tvāṃ mahārathāḥ* I *yeṣāṃ ca tvaṃ bahumato bhūtvā yāsyasi lāghavam* II

(In both cases a similar thought construction: referring to the opponent's opinions to support one's own argumentation.)

II Opposites
(the most important for the final meaning of both texts)

Saṃyutta Nikāya	***Bhagavadgītā*** (the epic layer)

1. Different approach to the concept of *dharma* and sin:

Sakka	≠	**Kṛṣṇa**
cf. especially:		
SN I 222: *abalaṃ taṃ balam āhu yassa bālabalaṃ balaṃ* I *balassa* ***dhamma-guttassa*** *paṭivattā na vijjati* II		BhG 2.31: ***svadharmam*** *api cāvekṣya na vikampitum arhasi* I *dharmyād dhi yuddhāc chreyo 'nyat kṣatriyasya na vidyate* II
tass' eva tena ***pāpīyo*** *yo kuddhaṃ paṭikujjhati* I *kuddham apaṭikujjhanto* saṅgāmam *jeti dujjayaṃ* II		BhG 2.33: *atha cet tvam imaṃ* ***dharmyaṃ*** saṃgrāmaṃ *na kariṣyasi* I *tataḥ* ***svadharmaṃ*** *kīrtiṃ ca hitvā* ***pāpam*** *avāpsyasi* II

---

[26] "Now is it, Sakka, that thou art afraid, / Or because thou art weak that thou forbear'st, / When thou dost hear these speeches scurrilous / By Vepacitti cast into thy teeth?"

[27] "In this, that thou dost patiently forbear, / A grievous error, Vāsava, I see. / For when the fool doth fancy: ''t is from fear / He bears with me,' the dolt will press you hard, / Like cow [that charges] more when you do flee."

... ubhinnam tikicchantaṃ taṃ attano ca parassa ca | janā maññanti bālo ti ye ***dhammassa*** *akovidā ti* ||[28]

2. Opposite call in the two texts:

Sakka and Buddha (call to patience and forbearance)	≠	**Kṛṣṇa** (call to fight)
SN I 222: *kāmam maññatu vā mā vā bhayā myāyaṃ titikkhati | sadatthaparamā atthā khantyā bhiyyo na vijjati* || *yo have balavā santo dubbalassa titikkhati | tam āhu paramam khantiṃ niccaṃ* khamati dubbalo ||[29]		BhG 2.3: *klaibyaṃ mā sma gamaḥ pārtha naitat tvayy upapadyate* | *kṣudraṃ hṛdaya*daurbalyaṃ tyaktvo*ttiṣṭha paraṃtapa* || BhG 2.37: *... tasmād uttiṣṭha kaunteya yuddhāya kṛtaniścayaḥ* ||
... idha kho taṃ bhikkhave sobhetha yaṃ tumhe evaṃ svākhyāte dhamma-vinaye pabbajitā samānā khamā ca bhaveyyātha soratā cā ti ||[30]		

3. Opposite attitude to victory in a battle as well as an opposite conception of the posthumous fate of warriors killed on a battlefield:

Buddhism	≠	**Epic Layer of the BhG**
A) victory does not bring about happiness in this world		**A**) victory brings about happiness in this world

---

28 "Whoso doth think the strength of fools is strength, / Will say of the strong man: A weakling he! / For the strong man whom righteousness doth guard, / To bandy words comes not into his thought. / Worse of the two is he who, when reviled, / Reviles again. Who doth not, when reviled, / Revile again, a twofold victory wins. ... He who of both is a physician, since / Himself he healeth and the other too, / Folk deem him fool, they knowing not the Norm."

29 "O let him fancy as he will – or won't: – / That I do bear with him because I fear. / 'Mong highest matters of our spirit's growth / Nought ranks above forbearing patiently. / Yea, surely he that hath tha upper hand / And beareth patiently with him that's down; – / Ever to tolerate the weaker side: – / This the supreme forbearance hath been called."

30 "Now in this Rule, bhikkhus, ye do enhance his [= Sakka's] virtue when ye who have gone forth under a Norm and Discipline so well proclaimed become forbearing and gentle."

SN I 83 (DhP 201):
jayaṃ veram pasavati dukkaṃ seti parājito | upasanto sukhaṃ seti hitvā jayaṃ parājayan-ti ||
SN I 85:
hantā labhati hantāraṃ jetāraṃ labhati jayaṃ |[31]

B) After death on a battlefield: either hell or rebirth as an animal
SN IV 309:
... sa ce kho panassa evaṃdiṭṭhi hoti | yo so yodhājīvo saṅgāme ussahati vāyamati | taṃ enaṃ ussahantaṃ vāyamantaṃ pare hananti pariyāpādenti | so kāyassa bhedā param maraṇā sarājitānam devānaṃ sahavyatam upapajjatīti || sāssa hoti micchādiṭṭhi || micchādiṭṭhikassa kho panāham gāmaṇi purisapuggalassa dvinnaṃ gatīnam aññataraṃ gatiṃ vadāmi | nirayaṃ vā tiracchānayoniṃ vā ti ||[32]

B) after death on a battlefield: heaven
BhG 2.32:
yadṛcchayā copapannaṃ svargadvāram apāvṛtam | sukhinaḥ kṣatriyāḥ pārtha labhante yuddham īdṛśam ||

BhG 2.37:
hato vā prāpsyasi svargaṃ jitvā vā bhokṣyase mahīm | tasmād uttiṣtha kaunteya yuddhāya kṛtaniścayaḥ ||

---

[31] SN I 83: "Conquest engenders hate; the conquered lives / In misery. But whoso is at peace / And passionless, happily doth he live; / Conquest hath he abandoned and defeat." SN I 85: "The slayer gets a slayer in his turn; / The conqueror gets one who conquers him." In both fragments the Buddha expresses his attitude towards war commenting upon the war between Ajatasattu, the king of Magadha and Pasenadi, the king of Kosala. Arjuna's words from BhG 1.32, 35 correspond with the thought of SN I 83.

[32] In this fragment of the *Saṃyutta* the chief of the warriors (*yodhājīvo gāmaṇi*) tells the Buddha that he heard from his ancestral teachers of the warcraft that for a warrior, the reward for his keen fight on the battlefield is the rebirth in the worlds of gods. He asks the Enlightened One if this is the truth. The Buddha's reply is obviously quite contrary: "Now if his view was this: 'A fighting-man who exerts himself, puts forth effort in battle, thus exerting himself, thus putting forth effort, is tormented and made an end of by others. When body breaks up, after death he is reborn in the company of the Devas of Passionate Delight,' – then I say that view of his is perverted. Now, trainer, I declare that for one who is guilty of perverted view one of two paths is open, either purgatory or rebirth as an animal."

Arjuna's argumentation clearly echoes Sakka's reasoning while Kṛṣṇa (Arjuna's charioteer) uses the same arguments as Mātali (Sakka's charioteer). The echo of the Pāli fragment is more audible because the same words appear in the *Gītā*. Sakka exhorts not to respond to violence with violence because that causes still greater sin (*pāpīyo*). Similarly, in his moral dilemma Arjuna refers to sin (*pāpa*) as the consequence of war and killing (BhG 1.36, 39, 45). They are both presented as more aware of the consequences of violence than their opponents; they wish to avoid it even though their enemies use it against them. Also Sakka's and Arjuna's interlocutors, on the one hand Mātali and on the other Kṛṣṇa, use similar arguments. Fear (*bhaya*), weakness (Pāli *dubbala* – Skt. *daurbalya*) and consequently ill-fame, all these both Sakka and Arjuna can be suspected of by their opponents, and this is supposed to spur them to action.

It should be remarked that Kṛṣṇa's words in the earliest part of the *Gītā* are mostly based on arguments well known and frequently presented in the *Mahābhārata*. It is repeated many times in the epic that the basic duty of a kṣatriya is to fight in war. One who does not is exposed to sin, loss of honour, bad reputation. Those who take up their duties, however, can rely on rewards and gain, no matter if they win or lose: in case of victory they gain fame, kingdom, happiness, earthly joys, in case of death on the battlefield (and only there) they go and dwell in heaven, Indra's domain, and enjoy divine pleasures.[33] Buddhism, on the contrary, condemns any war or fight which destroys human life.[34] It is evil even if it is a king's

[33] Cf. Hara 2001a, where one can find many references to the *Mahābhārata* (cf. also Hara 2001b).

[34] Jayatilleke 1955: 144-149; Upadhyaya 1983: 528-539. A good example of the Buddhist opposition to war is a story from the *Jātaka*s (5.412-414). It is said there that the Buddha once found himself in a similar situation to that of Kṛṣṇa, namely, before the battle between people of his own tribe, Sākiyas and their blood brothers Koliyas. The direct reason for the coming battle was an argument about water from the river Rohiṇī, flowing between their territories. The Buddha

duty (*rañño ... rājakaraṇīyam kātum*, MN II 191). Even trading in arms (*satthavaṇijjā*) is regarded as an evil way for a layman to make a living (AN III 208). Monks are forbidden to get involved in talking about the army, dangers or battles (*senākatham, bhaya-katham, yuddhakatham*) as these are among the topics not conducive to the holy life and do not lead to the supreme goal (SN V 419-420). The only winner in any battle is the one who has conquered himself (DhP 103). According to the Buddha, the reason for all conflicts, fights and cruel violence is passion or desire, attachment to sense pleasures, and the inevitable consequence is suffering during life and hell after death (MN I 86-87; SN IV 309). Hell appears as a Buddhist response to the old Vedic and traditional conviction about Indra's heaven as a destination for kṣatriyas killed on the battlefield while fulfilling their dharma. The polemical meaning of the *Vepacitti Sutta* is more conspicuous when one realizes that it is Indra himself who is advocating patience and forbearance.[35]

Arjuna's attitude from the epic layer of the *Bhagavadgītā* is surprisingly close to the Buddhist ideal of *ahiṃsā*. It is neither cowardice nor selfishness that makes him throw his bow and arrows away, but a deliberate choice. He is ready to sacrifice victory, king-

---

enters at the moment when the soldiers of both armies stand opposite each other (similarly to Kauravas and Pāṇḍavas at the beginning of the *Gītā*). The Buddha asks the reason for the fight and is told it is water. He then asks how much the water is worth and is told it is not much. Then why, asks the Buddha, do you want to destroy the priceless lives of the warriors because of some water of little value?

[35] In the *Sakkapañha Sutta* of the *Dīgha Nikāya* (DN II 263-289) it is described how Sakka, the king of gods, visited the Buddha, talked to him and asked him certain questions about ethics and psychology. The Buddha answering the questions persuaded Sakka to convert to Buddhism. In the *Saṃyutta Nikāya* 1.220-240 (cf. especially SN I 233-237) Sakka is portrayed as the follower and worshipper of the Buddha. Norman (1983: 40) commenting upon the sutta of the *Dīgha Nikāya* writes: "It would seem to have been intended as a piece of propaganda to persuade non-Buddhists not to be afraid of the new religion since even the gods of their own religion accepted it."

ship, pleasures and even his life (BhG 1.32, 35, 46) to avoid causing death. Compassion (*kṛpā*, 1.28, a typical Buddhist virtue) for relatives, masters and friends (1.26-31) as well as consideration of the catastrophic consequences of war (1.38-43) constitutes the basis for his dilemma, despondency and decision *na yotsye* (2.9).[36] Kṛṣṇa's attitude, however, is decidedly contrary to the Buddhist one.

Coming back to the comparison of our *Gītā* passage with the dialogue of Sakka and Mātali, it must be noticed that the final meaning of both fragments owes much more to their differences than their similarities.[37] In the Buddhist text, Sakka's argument clearly prevails. Mātali and his "martial" arguments are silenced and defeated (just as in the next sutta Vepacitti, using the same arguments as Mātali, is defeated by the same arguments of Sakka). But in the *Gītā* it is the "martial" arguments of Kṛṣṇa that prevail and supersede the Buddhist-like arguments of Arjuna. Kṛṣṇa advocates the concept of righteous war (*dharmya saṃgrāma*, 2.33) according to which the fight with villains is justified and morally right.[38] What Buddhist ethics reject is extolled in the epic layer of the *Bhagavadgītā*.

4.

No less than in the *Gītā* passage presented above, BhG 2.11-30 contains polemics against Buddhist concepts. In these stanzas, so skilfully inserted between the stanzas of the epic layer, attention is drawn to metaphysical speculations. It is interesting to notice that this part can also be seen as a polemical discussion with the Buddhist *anattā* doctrine.

---

[36] Jayatilleke (1955: 148) writes about Arjuna that "... his general attitude is Buddhist to the core."

[37] Upadhyaya 1983: 133, 533-534.

[38] Upadhyaya 1983: 526-528.

As some scholars have shown, the Buddha's doctrine of Selflessness emerged in response to views existing in India in his day.[39] The Pāli canon seems to contain arguments with ideas found in the early Upaniṣads. Generally speaking, the Upaniṣads contain a series of speculations pointing out that in every individual being, beside changeable and mortal elements, physical and mental, there exists an unchanging and immortal element, Self or Soul, permanent and blissful "I", most frequently defined as *ātman*. The *ātman* is identified with *brahman*, the absolute, ultimate reality and the Self of the universe. The immortal Self at the microcosmic level reflects the Self at the macrocosmic level, and realization of the nature of reality, awareness of this equality, leads to liberation and immortality. The Buddha rejects this type of speculation. The idea of unchanging substance, *ātman-brahman*, is imaginary and false. Firstly, it is discordant with the Buddha's perception of the nature of reality and, secondly, any speculations on the Self generate merely egocentric attachment and lead in turn to confusion and suffering. They must be rejected.

The doctrine of *anattā* is a consequence of the Buddhist understanding of reality in terms of the perceptible, experienced world, becoming and moving (instead of being). The true nature of existence of every living being lies in undergoing manifold experiences. These consist of various elements, ever changing, both physical and mental forces and energies. The Buddha often describes an individual as composed of five groups or aggregates (*pañcakkhandha*): corporeality (*rūpa*), feelings or sensations (*vedanā*), perceptions (*saññā*), mental formations (*saṃkhārā*) and consciousness (*viññāṇa*). These five constitute the whole world for every individual being, they are changeable, but beyond them – beyond the temporary and changeable experience of the elements

---

[39] On the *anattā* doctrine see e.g. Collins 1982; Upadhyaya 1983: 301-335; Wijesekera 1994: 3-12, 43-52, 71-83, 257-265; Norman 1981; Harvey 1995; Rahula 1998: 51-66.

of existence – an individual does not experience any permanent and eternal Self, any immortal "I". The Buddha often carries out a thorough analysis of those elements of the human personality, showing that nothing permanent can be found in any or all of them. It is only due to people's clinging to the five aggregates that one speculates on the Self. Clinging is rooted in ignorance.[40] By recognition of the truth, perceiving things the way they are (*yathābhūta*), all clinging is extinguished, including clinging to the conceit of Self.

One of the most important texts illustrating the Buddha's teaching of *anattā* is an extensive passage from the *Alagaddūpama Sutta* (22) of the *Majjhima Nikāya* (MN I 135-139). We need to paraphrase this text here.

> In the *Alagaddūpama*, the Buddha teaches that there exist "six views of causal relation' (*diṭṭhiṭṭhānāni*), which are wrong. The first is when someone unskilled in the *ariyadhamma* claims about material shape (*rūpa*): "this is mine, this am I, this is my self" (*etaṃ mama, eso 'ham asmi, eso me attā*). The next ones are when he claims the same about feelings (*vedanā*), perceptions (*saññā*), habitual tendencies/mental formations (*saṃkhārā*) and about whatever is *diṭṭhaṃ sutaṃ mutaṃ viññātaṃ pattaṃ pariyesitaṃ anuvicaritaṃ manasā* ('seen, heard, sensed, cognized, reached, looked for, pondered by the mind' = *viññāṇa*, consciousness). The sixth wrong view is when one states: the world and the Self are the same (*so loko so attā*), "'after dying I will become permanent, lasting, eternal, not liable to change, I will stand fast like unto the eternal', he regards this as: 'this is mine, this am I, this is my self'." (*so pecca bhavissāmi nicco dhuvo sassato avipariṇāmadhammo, sassatisamaṃ tath'eva thassāmīti, tam-pi: etaṃ mama, eso 'ham*

[40] The Buddhist doctrine of conditioned origination (*paṭicca-samuppāda*) points out that there is no absolute and everlasting substance in man. Every existence in the world, everything in the world has no independent nature, but depends on previous causes: everything is conditioned and relative. Consequently, there is no Self with an independent nature as in fact there is no existence. *Attā*, 'self, oneself' (reflexive pronoun) is not a real thing , but only a term useful in everyday life. Ignorance makes the impermanent Self into the immortal "I" by attributing substance or essence to the term *attā*. After removing ignorance the real nature of things is seen, which means that there is nothing eternal, but everything is dependent and conditioned.

asmi, eso me attā ti samanupassati). In opposition to that the one who is skilled in the *ariyadhamma* thinks in a quite contrary way about the six views, claiming: "this is not mine, this am I not, this is not my self" (*n'etaṃ mama, n'eso 'ham asmi, na meso attā*). Seeing it like this, he is not anxious about what does not exist.

When asked by a monk, in the next part of the sutta, the Buddha points out that anxiety about something external that does not exist occurs to the one who holds the view that he once possessed what does not exist any longer. "He grieves, mourns, laments, beats his breast, and falls into disillusionment" (*so socati kilamati paridevati, urattāḍiṃ kandati, sammohaṃ āpajjati*). There is no anxiety about that for the one who assumes the opposite attitude. In a similar way the Buddha answers the question about anxiety about something internal that does not exist. He says about grieving, mourning, lamenting ... of a man who at first holds the view that the world and the Self are the same (*so loko so attā*), and "after dying he will become permanent, lasting, eternal ...", then hearing the dhamma taught in order to root out those wrong views he comes to the conclusion: "I will surely be annihilated, I will surely be destroyed, I will surely not be" (*ucchijjissāmi nāma su, vinassissāmi nāma su, na su nāma bhavissāmi*), which is the reason for his despair. On the contrary, the one who does not hold the view about the sameness of the world and the Self, as well as about the permanence of his nature, does not grieve for something which does not exist internally when he hears the dhamma.

The Buddha then goes on to persuade monks that there is no possession "which is permanent, lasting, eternal ...". There is no attachment to the theory of the Self (*attavādupādāna*) nor dependence on a view which "would not arouse grief, suffering, anguish, lamentation, despair".

Then, considering the *attā*, the Buddha asks whether, if the Self existed one could say "It belongs to my Self?" (*attani vā sati, attaniyam me ti assa*); and, on the other hand, if there existed something belonging to the Self, one could say "It is my Self?" Both questions are answered positively. Therefore – the Buddha continues – if the Self and what belongs to the Self are truly incomprehensible, is not the view that the world and the Self are the same, and after dying one becomes permanent ..., absolute and complete folly? The monks' answer is: "Lord, how could it not be absolute complete folly?"

The Buddha proceeds by asking firstly about material shape and then about the other *khandhas* whether they are permanent or impermanent (*niccaṃ vā aniccaṃ vā ti*). On the answer that they are impermanent, he further asks whether what is impermanent is to be regarded as *dukkha* or *sukha*. The answer is: *dukkha*, unsatisfactory. The concluding question is whether what is impermanent, unsatisfactory and liable to change, is rightly to be regarded as "This is mine, this am I, this is my Self". The answer is: no.

> Thus the Buddha sums up by saying that the *khandhas* should be seen according to their real nature (*yathābhūtam*) by the perfect intuitive wisdom (*sammāpaññāya*) as: "This is not mine, this am I not, this is not my Self" (*n'etaṃ mama, n'eso 'ham asmi, na meso attā*). The one seeing thus is freed and dispassionate, he is the Tathāgata.[41]

The meaning and significance of this passage have probably been shown best by K. R. Norman and, a little later, by R. Gombrich.[42] The Buddha here responds to the central teaching of the oldest Upaniṣads, *Bṛhadāraṇyaka* and *Chāndogya*, and he rejects the Upaniṣadic view of the nature of reality (the immortal essence of man, *ātman*, as being identified with the immortal essence of the world). He does so by referring to expressions very similar to those appearing in the Upaniṣads. The most spectacular remark seems to be that when the Buddha considers the following conviction wrong: *eso 'ham asmi*, 'I am this', he clearly alludes to the crucial statement from the *Chāndogya Upaniṣad* (6.8.7–6.16.3): *tat tvam asi* ('Thou are that'). This Buddhist statement, repeatedly referred to in the suttas (especially in the negative form: *n'etaṃ mama, n'eso 'ham asmi, na meso attā*), appears as a response to the statement identifying the individual Self with the Self of the universe, referred to time and again (nine times) in the *Chāndogya*. But the net of Buddhist verbal allusions in the *Alagaddūpama* is more dense. Referring above all to Norman's and Gombrich's findings[43], let me here present appropriate passages.

---

[41] At the end of the *Alagaddūpama Sutta* (MN I 141) the Buddha uses one more argument in support of the *anattā*-concept. He points at grass, sticks, branches and foliage being gathered, burned and used in some other way in the Jeta wood (where the discussion takes place) and asks the monks: "If someone does so, does it mean he does the same to them." The answer is "no" because there is no Self in them nor anything belonging to the Self. Thus the Buddha finally tells the monks, for their welfare and happiness, to put away what is not theirs, which mean the five khandhas.

[42] Norman 1981; Gombrich 1990: 14-16; 1996: 38-39.

[43] Norman 1981; Gombrich 1990: 14-16; 1996: 38-39; cf. also Jayatilleke 1963: 60-61; Upadhyaya 1983: 101.

	MN I 135: *cha-y-imāni bhikkhave diṭṭhiṭṭhā- nāni, katamāni cha: īdha bhikkhave assutavā puthujjano ariyānaṃ adassāvī ariyadhammassa akovido ... rūpaṃ:* etaṃ mama, ***eso 'ham asmi, eso me attā*** *ti samanupassati ...*
BĀU 4.5.6 (cf. 2.4.5; 3.8.11): ātmani *khalu are* ***dṛṣṭe śrute mate vijñāta*** *idaṃ sarvaṃ* viditam.	*yam-p'idaṃ* ***diṭṭhaṃ sutaṃ mutaṃ viññātaṃ*** *pattaṃ pariyesitaṃ anuvicaritaṃ manasā tam-pi:* etaṃ mama, ***eso 'ham asmi, eso me attā*** *ti samanupassati,*
BĀU 1.4.15: ***ātmānam*** *eva* ***lokam*** *upāsīta; ...* BĀU 1.4.16: *atho ayaṃ vā* ***ātmā*** *sarveṣāṃ bhūtānāṃ* ***lokaḥ****.* BĀU 4.4.22: *etad dha sma vai tat pūrve vidvāṃsaḥ prajāṃ na kāmayante. kiṃ prajayā kariṣyāmo yeṣāṃ no 'yam* ***ātmāyaṃ loka*** *iti.*[44]	*yam-p'idaṃ diṭṭhiṭṭhānaṃ: so* ***loko*** *so* ***attā***
ChU 3.14.1: *... yathā kratur asmiṃl loke puruṣo bhavati tathetaḥ* ***pretya bhavati****, sa kratuṃ kurvīta.*	*so* ***pecca bhavissāmi***
ChU 3.14.4: eṣa ma ātmā*ntar hṛdaye etad brahma, etam itaḥ* ***pretyābhisaṃ- bhavitāsmīti*** *...*	
BĀU 4.4.23: *eṣa* ***nityo*** *mahimā brāhmaṇasya ...*	***nicco***
BĀU 4.4.20: *... aja* ātmā *mahān* ***dhruvaḥ***	***dhuvo***

[44] Cf. also e.g. BĀU 4.4.13: *yasyānuvittaḥ pratibuddha* ***ātmāsmin*** *saṃdehye gahane praviṣṭaḥ* ǀ *sa viśvakṛt sa hi sarvasya kartā tasya* ***lokaḥ*** *sa u* ***loka*** *eva* ǁ 4.5.7 (= 2.4.6): *idaṃ brahma, idaṃ kṣatram, ime* lokāḥ, *ime devāḥ, ime vedāḥ, imāni bhūtāni, idaṃ sarvaṃ yad ayam* ***ātmā****.*

BĀU 4.6.14: avināśī *vā are'yam ātmā*, anucchittidharmā.	sassato avipariṇāmadhammo
BĀU 5.10.1: *yadā vai puruṣo 'smāl lokāt* ***praiti*** *sa vayum āgacchati ... tena sa ūrdhva ākramate ... sa lokam āgacchaty aśokam ahimam; tasmin vasati* ***śāśvatīḥ samāḥ***.	***sassatisamaṃ*** *tath'eva ṭhassāmīti,*
ChU 6.8-16: *sa ya eṣo 'ṇimā, etad ātmyam idaṃ sarvam, tat satyam,* sa ātmā: ***tat tvam asi***	*tam pi: etaṃ mama,* ***eso 'ham asmi,***
ChU 3.14.3-4: ***eṣa ma*** *ātmāntar hṛdaye ...*	***eso me attā*** *ti samanupassati.*
BĀU 3.4.1-2: ***eṣa ta ātmā*** *sarvāntaraḥ*.	
BĀU 3.7.3-23: *...* ***eṣa ta*** ***ātmā****ntaryāmy amṛtaḥ.*[45]	

One could probably find still more verbal references and direct polemical allusions to the earliest Upaniṣads in this fragment of the *Alagaddūpama*. It is certain that in other parts of the Pāli canon one can encounter more references, echoes or allusions revealing the Buddha's discussions and arguments with Brahmins and the Brahminical writings (which was probably best shown by Gombrich in his publications[46]). This remarks bring us much nearer to the recognition of one of the basic methods the Buddha used while teaching his dhamma. To quote Gombrich's words:

---

[45] The formula is repeated 22 times in BĀU 3.7.3-23. Cf. 3.7.23: *adṛṣṭo* draṣṭā*śruto* śrotā*mato* mantā*vijñāto* vijñātā. *nānyo 'to 'sti* draṣṭā *nānyo 'to 'sti* śrotā *nānyo 'to 'sti* mantā *nānyo 'to 'sti* vijñātā. ***eṣa ta ātmā****ntaryāmy* ***amṛtaḥ***. *ato 'nyad ārtam*.

[46] Gombrich 1990; 1992; 1996.

> ... the Buddha, like anyone else, was communicating in a social context, reacting to his social environment and hoping in turn to influence those around him. ... The *dharma* is the product of argument and debate, the debate going on in the oral culture of renounces and brahmins (*samaṇa-brāhmaṇa*), ..., in the upper Ganges plain in the fifth century B.C. (Gombrich 1996: 13.)

As far as the doctrine of *anattā* is concerned, the Buddha mainly discusses and argues with the Upaniṣadic sages propagating the concept of *ātman-brahman*. A person unskilled in the *ariya-dhamma* appears from the above Pāli passage (MN I 135-136) to be nobody other than a product of Brahminical education. The suggested alternative to his attitude is that (MN I 136) represented by the Buddha's disciple who regards "the six views with causal relation" as "this is not mine, this am I not, this is not my Self".[47]

Even a superficial reading of stanzas 2.11-30 of the *Bhagavad-gītā*, considered in this very context, makes clear that Kṛṣṇa's teaching on the immortal *dehin* contradicts what can be found in the Pāli canon on *attā*.

First of all, to start with the most general observations, the Buddha urges rejection of the Upaniṣadic-like speculations on the Self, immortal essence, as irrelevant, as well as impeding the way to salvation. On the contrary Kṛṣṇa in the *Gītā*, following the Upaniṣadic line[48], presents a series of ontological speculations and tries to induce Arjuna to achieve the cognition and realization of the immortal Self.

---

[47] It must be noticed that in other fragments of the canon the Buddha underlines that the conceit of the Self is possible only in relation with the five khandhas and not separately from them, beyond them; cf. e.g. SN III 46: "Those recluses and brahmins, brethren, who regard the Self in divers ways, regard it as the body mass of five factors based on grasping, or as some one of these." (*Ye hi keci bhikkhave samaṇā vā brāhmaṇā vā anekavihitam* attānam *samanupassamānā samanupassanti, sabbe te pañcupādānakkhandhe samanupassanti etesaṃ vā aññataram.*)

[48] On the *Gītā*'s relations with the early Upaniṣads see e.g. Haas 1922; Sarma 1929; Devasthali 1953; Zaehner 1969 (*passim*).

Further, stanzas 2.11-30 can be recognized as a polemic against the Buddhist negation of *attā* as indispensable for salvation.[49] It is worth noting that Kṛṣṇa in his polemics sometimes uses expressions close to the Buddhist ones, like the Buddha when he takes issue with the earliest Upaniṣads.

Part 2.11-30, 38, as has been assumed above, creates a textual layer inserted between stanzas of the epic layer. The formal factors of this *sāṃkhya* layer have been noticed, namely its beginning and ending markers.[50] They occur firstly in stanzas 2.11 and 2.30: *aśocān anvaśocas* tvam (2.11a); *na* tvaṃ *śocitum* arhasi (2.30d); secondly, the terms *sukhaduḥkha*(*sama*) used both in 2.14-15 and in 2.38. I would like to draw attention to the Buddhist connotations of both markers.

In the first stanza of this passage, 2.11, Kṛṣṇa refers to the attitude of *paṇḍitāḥ* as those who grieve for neither those who have gone nor those who have not gone. This attitude is like the one recommended in Buddhism, stanza 2.11 even resembles a fragment from the beginning of the *Saṃyutta Nikāya* I 5 (*Devata Saṃyutta* 1.1.10).[51]

SN I 5:	BhG 2.11:
atītaṃ ***nānusocanti***, nappajappanti ***nāgatam***, ...	*aśocyān anvaśocas tvaṃ* ...
anāgatappajappāya, atītassānusocanā, etena bālā *sussanti* ...[52]	gatāsūn ***agatāsūṃś ca nānuśocanti*** paṇḍitāḥ ‖

Both fragments emphasize that grieving is improper for wise men. The *Gītā*'s argument in 2.11, however, must be considered quite

[49] I assume that even the oldest textual layers of the *Gītā* are later than the corpus of the Pāli canon.

[50] Cf. above, footnote 17.

[51] Cf. Upadhyaya 1983: 130.

[52] "They make no lamentation over the past, / They yearn not after that which is not come, ... By yearning after that which is not come, / By making lamentation over the past, / Hence comes it that the foolish wither up ..."

contrary to the Buddhist one. In the *Alagaddūpama Sutta* (MN I 136-137) the Buddha answers a question concerning anxiety about something internal that does not exist. The one who was led astray by the Upaniṣadic-like understanding of immortality ("This the world, this the self; after dying I will become permanent ...") and then hears the truth announced by a Tathāgata, undergoes frustration and allows nihilistic thoughts to rule him ("I will surely be annihilated, I will surely be destroyed, I will surely not be") and suffers: "he grieves (*so socati*), mourns, laments (*paridevati*), beats his breast, and falls into disillusionment (*sammoham āpajjati*)". Later, the Buddha speaks about the opposite feelings and behaviour of one who is not deluded by speculations on the Self and immortality ("He does not grieve, mourn, lament ..."). A little further on, the Buddha harshly criticizes clinging to the false theory of the Self (*attavādupādāna*), described also in terms of grieving: "I do not, monks, see that theory of Self, from the grasping of which there would not arise grief, suffering, anguish, lamentation, despair" (*sokaparidevadukkhadomanassupāyāsā*).[53] The *Gītā* goes in the opposite direction. One should not complain (2.11) because none of us (neither I nor you, nor those rulers of men, says Kṛṣṇa) has stopped or will stop existing (2.12). These words anticipate the speculations on an eternal Self in man which does not die with the body's death. In 2.25, Kṛṣṇa points out the necessity of learning the truth about its existence (though it or lit. "he" is unmanifested, unthinkable, immutable) as a condition for freedom from grief. In

[53] Cf. also SN III 19, 42-44. It is worth pondering whether in the frequent Buddhist expressions of this kind one cannot find an allusion to early Upaniṣads, cf. e.g. ChU 7.1.3, where Nārada addresses Sanatkumāra: *so 'haṃ, bhagavaḥ, mantravid evāsmi nātmavid; śrutaṃ hy eva me bhagavaddṛśebhyaḥ,* tarati ***śokam*** ātmavid *iti; so 'ham, bhagavaḥ,* ***śocāmi****, taṃ mā, bhagavañ* ***śokasya*** *pāraṃ tārayatv iti*; ("But, Venerable Sir, I am only like one knowing the words and not a knower of Self. It has been heard by me from those like you that he who knows the Self crosses over sorrow. Such a sorrowing one am I, Venerable Sir. Do you, Venerable Sir, help me to cross over to the other side of sorrow." – Transl. by Radhakrishnan.)

2.28, taking for granted that there exist both manifested and unmanifested elements of the universe, Kṛṣṇa asks Arjuna: "What complaint can there be over this?"[54] Kṛṣṇa's exposition of the immortal *dehin* ends in stanza 2.30, which is a concluding recapitulation and a reminder that no being should be grieved for as the Self in every one is eternally inviolable.

MN I 136-137: *idha ... ekacassa na evaṃ diṭṭhi hoti:* *so loko so attā* ...	BhG 2.11cd: *gatāsūn agatāsūṃś ca* ***nānuśocanti*** *paṇḍitāḥ* || BhG 2.12: *na tv evāhaṃ jātu nāsaṃ na tvaṃ* *neme janādhipāḥ* |
tassa ***na*** *evaṃ* hoti: *ucchijjissāmi* *nāma su,* ***vinassissāmi*** *nāma su,* ***na*** *su nāma* ***bhavissāmīti****. So* ***na socati*** *na kilamati* na paridevati, *na* *urattāliṃ kandati, na* sammohaṃ *āpajjati.* ...	***na*** *caiva* ***na bhaviṣyāmaḥ*** *sarve* *vayam ataḥ param* || 2.17: ***avināśi*** *tu tad viddhi yena sarvam* *idaṃ tatam* | vināśam *avyayasyāsya* na kaścit kartum arhati || BhG 2.25cd: *tasmād eva viditvainaṃ* ***nānuśocitum*** *arhasi* ||
aham-pi kho taṃ bhikkhave *attavādupādānaṃ na samanu-* *passāmi yaṃ sa attavādupādānam* *upādiyato na uppajjeyyum* ***soka-*** paridev*adukkhadomanassupāyāsā.*	BhG 2.30: *dehī nityam avadhyo'yaṃ dehe* *sarvasya bhārata* | *tasmāt sarvāṇi* *bhūtāni* ***na*** *tvaṃ* ***śocitum*** *arhasi* ||
	(BhG 2.13d: *dhīras tatra* na muhyati || BhG 2.28d: *tatra kā* paridevanā ||)

[54] Moreover, while presenting in a picturesque way the concept of *saṃsāra* in 2.13, Kṛṣṇa states: "the wise man is not deluded about this" (*dhīras tatra na muhyati*).

If the problem is considered in terms of *śoka* it is obvious that the starting point of both texts is a similar conviction: one who has learned the truth about reality has no cause to grieve. The two systems, however, see that truth differently. The Buddha teaches that one should reject the thoughts: *vinassissāmi* (I will be destroyed), *na bhavissāmi* (I will not be), because that is a wrong way of reasoning about a permanent element which does not exist, whereas Kṛṣṇa teaches: *na ... na bhaviṣyāmaḥ* as there exists something *avināśi*. While for the Buddha eternal being is an illusion, for Kṛṣṇa it is the only reality. And consequently, while according to the Buddha he who rejects immortal and eternal essence does not grieve, according to Kṛṣṇa he who accepts and tries to fully recognize what is immortal and eternal in man has no cause to grieve.[55]

Equanimity in the face of the obstacles in human life is an ideal common to Buddhism and the *Gītā*.[56] A wise man should live his life between pairs of opposites, not attached to any extremes, and follow the path of sameness on his way to perfection. In both traditions it is often expressed as having the same attitude towards pleasure and pain (Pāli *sukha-dukkha*, Skt. *sukha-duḥkha*). In the Pāli canon this expression is common.[57] The Buddha repeatedly recommends that one put the extremes away, bear them, become the same towards them.[58] Similarly in the *Bhagavadgītā* the idea of

---

[55] Understanding the immortal element in man is quite strongly emphasized in our passage of the *Gītā*, cf. 2.17: *avināśi tu tad* ***viddhi*** *yena sarvam idaṃ tatam* ...; 2.21: ***vedāvināśinaṃ*** *nityaṃ ya enam ajam avyayam* ...; 2.25: ... *tasmād evaṃ* ***viditvainaṃ*** *nānuśocitum arhasi*. On the other hand, cf. manifold Buddhist assertions that the Self is something entirely imperceptible, and any considerations about it lead merely to confusion and suffering.

[56] Upadhyaya 1983: 359-363.

[57] Cf. e.g. DN III 260: *aṭṭha loka-dhammā: lābho ca alābho ca yaso ca ayaso ca nindā ca pasaṃsā ca* sukhañ ca dukkhañ ca. ("Eight matters of worldly concern, to wit, gain and loss, fame and obscurity, blame and praise, pleasure and pain.")

[58] Cf. e.g. DN I 183, III 51, 187-188; SN II 22-23, 39-41, IV 71, 123-124, 171-172, 188; AN II 158-159, III 440; Sn. 67, 737-739; Th. 93, 662-665; 986; Thī. 388; Cp. 120, 124. Th. 664-665: *na h'eva lābhe nālābhe na yase na ca*

sameness, endurance, being free from the affliction of pairs of opposites appears not only in our passage but also in the next parts (textual layers) of the poem.[59] As far as stanzas 2.14-15 are concerned, one can find several Pāli passages expressing the same idea in a very similar way, e.g.:

SN IV 71: ***phassena*** phuṭṭho *na* ***sukhena*** *majje* I ***dukkhena*** phuṭṭho *pi na sampavedhe* I ***phassadvayaṃ sukha-dukkhe*** *upekho* I *anānuruddho aviruddha kenaci* II[60]	BhG 2.14-15: *mātrā**sparśās** tu kaunteya śītoṣṇa-**sukhaduḥkhadāḥ*** I *āgamāpāyino 'nityās tāṃs titikṣasva bhārata* II
Sn. 737-739: *ye ca* ***phassaṃ*** *pariññāya* I *aññāya upasame ratā* I *te ve* ***phassābhisamayā*** *nicchātā* parinibbutā II ***sukhaṃ*** *vā yadi vā* ***dukkhaṃ*** adukkhamasukhaṃ *sadā* I *ajjhattañ ca bahiddhā ca* I *yaṃ kiñci atthi veditaṃ* II *etaṃ dukkhan ti ñatvāna* I *mosadhammaṃ palokinaṃ* I phussa phussa *vayaṃ passaṃ* I *evaṃ tattha virajjati* I *vedanānaṃ khayā bhikkhu* I *nicchāto* parinibbuto II[61]	*yaṃ hi na vyathayanty ete puruṣaṃ puruṣarṣabha* I sama***duḥkhasukhaṃ*** *dhīraṃ* so 'mṛtatvāya *kalpate* II

---

kittiyā I *na nindāyaṃ pasaṃsāya* na te dukkhe sukhamhi ca II *sabbattha te na lippanti udabindu va pakkhare* I *sabbattha sukhitā vīrā sabbattha aparājitā* II ("Not to profit or loss, not to fame or reputation, not to blame or praise, not to pain or happiness, to nothing do they cling, as a drop of water does not cling to a lotus leaf. Everywhere wise men are happy, everywhere they are unconquered.")

[59] BhG 2.45, 48, 56-57; 4.22; 5.18, 20; 6.7-9; 12.13-14, 15, 17-19; 14.22-25; 15.5.

[60] "By pleasures' impact not inebriate, / Nor yet distracted by the touch of pain, To pain and pleasure both indifferent / Let him be free from likings and dislikes."

[61] Sn. 737: "But those who, understanding (and renouncing) contact, delight in quiescence because of their knowledge, they indeed because of the full comprehension of contact are without craving, quenched." ... 738-739: "Happiness or

In these fragments *sukha* and *duḥkha* are said to have originated from contact (with objects or feelings), lit. from touching (Pāli *phassa* = Skt. *sparśa*).[62] Becoming independent of them is an indispensable condition on the way to the ultimate goal (BhG 2.15: *amṛtatva* – Sn. 737, 739: *parinibbuta*). However, despite their similarity, the two attitudes towards life often diverge. The final ethical meaning of our *Gītā* passage and Buddhism, i.e. their approaches to war and fighting, are at the two extremes.[63]

SN I 83 (DhP 201)	BhG 2.37-38:
jayaṃ veraṃ pasavati dukkhaṃ *seti parājito* I *upasanto* sukhaṃ *seti hitvā jayaṃ parājayan-ti* II	*hato vā prāpsyasi svargaṃ jitvā vā bhokṣyase mahīm* I *tasmād uttiṣṭha kaunteya yuddhāya kṛtaniścayaḥ* II sukhaduḥkhe same kṛtvā *lābhālābhau* jayājayau I *tato yuddhāya yujyasva nainaṃ pāpam avāpsyasi* II

At SN I 83, cited above, the Buddha decidedly condemns all action connected with war and violence. Generally speaking, the Buddhist *sukhadukkha-sama* (or *samāna*) merely confirms the ideal of *ahiṃsā* and patience in the face of violence.[64] But *Gītā* 2.38, also referring to *sukhaduḥkha-sama*, shows that equanimity, indifference and detachment are the recommended virtues of the warrior. Arjuna is to be such a one and thus join the fight.

Stanza 2.37 ends the epic layer supporting the concept of righteous war (2.33: *dharmya saṃgrāma*). It is reinterpreted by 2.38,

misery, (or) neither happiness nor misery together, whatever is sensed, both inside and outside, knowing this to be misery, false by nature, destined to break up, realising it again and again, seeing it passing away, thus one is freed from passion for it. Because of the destruction of sensations a bhikkhu is without craving, quenched." (Transl. by Norman.)

[62] On *phassa* as fundamental in attachment see e.g. Sn. 736-737, 778, 870-872.

[63] Cf. Upadhyaya 1983: 528-529.

[64] Cf. e.g. MN III 136-137.

which equips it with a new message: the concept of disinterested war. This is based on the ethic of *samatva*. 2.38 is also a conclusion of the layer in which Kṛṣṇa refers to certain metaphysical assumptions. The concept of disinterested war in the *Gītā* is based on metaphysics. In great part, this metaphysics continues and develops the line of the early Upaniṣads, and in so doing enters upon a dialogue with early Buddhist ideas.

In the first part of BhG 2.16, it is stated that there is no being or essence (*bhāva*) of what does not really exist (*asat*) just as there is no non-being (*abhāva*) of what does really exist (*sat*). Thus it may be concluded by implication that there is being/essence (*bhāva*) of what really exists (*sat*). In the second part of this stanza Kṛṣṇa says that the boundary (*anta*) between these two (or: the right conclusion about them) is seen by seers of the truth. This stanza seems worth comparing particularly with the *Kaccāyanagotto Sutta* of the *Saṃyutta Nikāya* (SN II 17), where the Buddha teaches Kaccāyana about the right view on existence and non-existence.[65] The Buddha says that the world bases itself on two opposite views, either existence (*atthitam*) or non-existence (*natthitam*). But the one who perceives the world as it really is (*yathābhūtam*) with perfect insight (*sammāpaññāya*) does not follow either of these views. Perceiving the arising of the world he does not hold the view of the non-existence of the world, while beholding the ceasing of the world he does not hold the view of its existence. Instead of being attached to the dogmatic view: "this is my self", he thinks about the arising and passing away of *dukkha*. The Tathāgata follows neither the extreme (*anta*) that everything exists (*sabbam atthi*), nor that nothing exists (*sabbaṃ natthi*). Instead, he notices the conditioned origination of everything and that the ceasing of it results in the ceasing of suffering (*dukkha*).

[65] This sutta is retold by Ānanda in SN III 134-135. Cf. also SN II 77.

The Buddha emphasizes becoming (in some other passages of the canon sometimes defined as *bhava*), the dependent origination of everything, continuous flux as the only reality.[66] Meanwhile, he opposes the two opposite views (and in other places in the canon he does so as often as possible), that of so-called eternalists (everything exists) and that of annihilationists (nothing exists). On the other hand, Kṛṣṇa referring to the established Brahminic tradition[67] in BhG 2.16 also speaks about existence and non-existence, but stresses the former as the only reality.

SN II 17:
sabbaṃ atthī*ti kho kaccāyana ayam* eko anto. sabbaṃ natthī*ti ayam* dutiyo anto. *ete te kaccāyana* ***ubho ante*** *anupagamma majjhena tathāgato dhammam deseti.*[68]

BhG 2.16:
nāsato *vidyate bhāvo nābhāvo vidyate* sataḥ | ***ubhayor*** *api dṛṣṭo* ***'ntas*** *tu* anayos *tattvadarśibhiḥ* ||

According to the Buddha, rejection of being as well as non-being is the basic step leading to the ultimate; then the cessation of dependent origination is the cessation from *dukkha* (SN II 17), the cessation of becoming is *nibbāna* (*bhava-nirodho nibbānaṃ*, SN II 117). But according to Kṛṣṇa, it is the realization of true being among changeable and transient – one could say "becoming" – elements of reality that leads to the goal.

Stanza 2.17 allows for another reflection. The expression *sarvaṃ idam,* standing for the whole world, recalls the early Upa-

---

[66] Cf. Wijesekera 1994: 10: "Then how we understand the negative description of personality as *anattā*? The answer to the question is found in the Buddha's pregnant conception of *bhava* or 'becoming', a continuous flux. It is not change, for to change there must be a substance, which Buddha denied. It is the individual himself who is the 'becoming', there is no immanent 'becom-er'. There is *bhava* but no *satta* or eternal being behind the process."

[67] See Zaehner 1969: 127-129 (commentary to BhG 2.16).

[68] "Everything exists: – this is the one extreme. Nothing exists: – this is the other extreme. Not approaching either extreme the Tathāgata teaches you a doctrine by the middle [way]."

niṣads. In the Upaniṣads the expression is a frequent designation for the whole universe. The *ātman-brahman* concept is characterized by claims that *ātman* and/or *brahman* as the essence of man and the universe pervades "this all", that *he/it* is the lord of "this all", that the whole universe is contained in or springs from the *ātman/brahman*.[69] *Ātman/brahman* is often identified with *idaṃ sarvam*[70], and it is said that he who learns the essence of everything learns everything.[71] About this too Buddhist polemics can be traced.[72] Towards the end of the *Alagaddūpama Sutta* (MN I 141), one can find exposed the fallacy that everything derives from the Self (*na hi no etam ... attā vā attaniyaṃ va ti*). In some other places the Buddha's teaching speaks of the world as void of Self and what belongs to Self (*suññam idam attena vā attaniyena vā*, MN I 397-398, II 263; SN IV 54). This sounds like rejection of the Upaniṣadic *ātmata eva, idaṃ sarvam* (ChU 7.26.1). The concept of the world as *suñña* (and consequently the expression *suññam idam*) is probably also a Buddhist response to the Upaniṣadic teaching that

---

[69] Cf. BĀU 3.4.1-2: *eṣa ta ātmā* sarvāntaraḥ; 4.4.22: *sa vā eṣa mahān aja ātma yo 'yaṃ vijñānamayaḥ praneṣu. ya eṣo 'ntar hṛdaya ākāśas tasmiñ chete* sarvasya *vaśī* sarvasyeśānaḥ sarvasyādhipatiḥ *sa na sadhunā karmaṇā bhuyān no evāsadhunā kanīyān. eṣa* sarveśvaraḥ; 5.6.1: *manmayo 'yaṃ puruṣo bhāḥ satyas tasmin antarhṛdaye yathā vrīhir vā yavo vā. sa eṣa* sarvasyeśānaḥ sarvasyādhipatiḥ sarvam idaṃ *praśāsti yad idaṃ kiṃca*. ChU 7.26.1: *ātmata eva*, idaṃ sarvam; 8.1.4: ... *asmiṃś* cedaṃ *brahmapure* sarvaṃ *samāhitam* ...

[70] Cf. BĀU 2.5.1-14 (repeated 14 times): ... *so yo 'yam ātmā, idaṃ amṛtam idam brahma*, idaṃ sarvam; 4.5.7 (= 2.4.6): *idaṃ brahma, idaṃ kṣatram, ime lokāḥ, ime devā, ime vedā, imāni bhūtāni*, idaṃ sarvaṃ *yad ayam ātmā*; 5.3.1: *eṣa prajāpati yaddhṛdayam etad brahma, etad* sarvam. ChU 3.214.1: sarvaṃ *khalu* idaṃ *brahma* ...; 6.8.7-16 (repeated 9 times): *sa ya eṣo 'ṇimaitad ātmyam* idaṃ sarvaṃ *tat satyam sa ātmā tat tvam asi*; 7.25.1: *sa eva*, idaṃ sarvam, *aham eva*, idaṃ sarvam; 7.25.2: *ātmā, eva*, idaṃ sarvam; (7.26.1: *ātmata eva*, idaṃ sarvam).

[71] Cf. e.g. BĀU 4.5.6 (= 2.4.5): *ātmani khalv are dṛṣṭe śrute mate vijñāta* idaṃ sarvaṃ *viditvā*; 4.4.23: *eṣa nityo mahimā brāhmaṇasya ..., tasmād evaṃ vicchanto dānta uparatasthitikṣuḥ samāhito bhūtvātmany evātmānaṃ paśyati*, sarvam *ātmānaṃ paśyati*.

[72] Wijesekera 1994: 43-47, 257-265.

the world is *pūrṇa* (*pūrṇam idam*).[73] The Buddha also seems to refer directly to the Upaniṣadic pantheistic view of *idaṃ sarvam* when he condemns the concept of "allness", *sabbam*, as pervaded or identified with essential Being.[74]

The *Gītā* returns in 2.17 to Upaniṣadic terminology supporting and continuing the Upaniṣadic point of view.[75] In the concise expression *avināśi tu tad viddhi yena sarvam idaṃ tatam* (2.17ab) Kṛṣṇa refers to identification of the imperishable Self in man with the Self of the universe, the Self which pervades everything.

---

[73] On the one hand, see BĀU 5.1: *pūrṇam adaḥ pūrṇam idaṃ pūrṇāt pūrṇam udacyate | pūrṇasya pūrṇam ādāya pūrṇam evāva śiṣyate ||* On the other hand, see SN IV 54: *suñño loko suñño loko ti bhante vuccati. kittāvatā nu kho bhante suñño loko ti vuccati. yasmā ca kho ānanda suññam attena vā attaniyena vā, tasmā suñño loko ti vuccati.* (Ānanda asks the Buddha: "'Void is the world! Void is the world!' is the saying, Lord. Pray, Lord, how far does this saying go?" The Buddha replies: "Because the world is void of the Self, Ānanda, or of what belongs to the Self, therefore is it said 'Void is the world.'")

In the *Sutta Nipāta* 1119, the Buddha says to the young brāhmaṇa named Mogharājā: "Look upon the world as void, O Mogharājan, being always thoughtful; having destroyed the view of oneself (as really existing), so one may overcome death; the king of death will not see him again." (Transl. by Fausbøll.) (*suññato lokaṃ avekkhassu mogharājā sadā sato attānudiṭṭhim ūhacca, evaṃ maccutaro siyā: evaṃ lokaṃ avekkhantaṃ maccurājā na passati ti.*)

[74] In the *Brahmanimantaṇika Sutta* of the *Majjhima Nikāya* (MN I 329) the Buddha discusses with a Brahmā named Baka. During the discussion, the Buddha rejects the Upaniṣadic-like concepts (cf. below, p. 211) and states among others: "I, Brahmā, knowing the all to be the all, to that extent knowing that, which is not reached by the allness of all, do not think: 'It is all, (of Self) in (regard to) all, (of Self) as all, all is mine' – I do not salute the all." (sabbaṃ *kho brahme* sabbato *abhiññāya yavatā* sabbassa sabbatena *ananubhūtaṃ tad – abhiññāya* sabbaṃ *nāhosi,* sabbasmiṃ *nāhosi,* sabbato *nāhosi,* sabbam-*me ti nāhosi,* sabbaṃ *nābhivadim.*) Cf. also SN IV 65: "He should have no conceit of being the all or in the all or by the way of the all. He should not think 'the all is mine.'" (sabbaṃ *na maññeyya,* sabbasmiṃ *na maññeyya,* sabbato *na maññeyya,* sabbaṃ *me ti na maññeyya.*) See also SN II 77 (and Jayatilleke 1963: 49-57).

[75] Zaehner (1969: 130) draws attention to the common idea of "spreading out" or "spinning" the whole universe by brahman in both the Upaniṣads (BĀU 2.1.20; MuṇḍU 1.1.7) and the *Gītā*. Expression *yena sarvam idaṃ tatam*, cf. BhG 8.22; 18.46; in later textual layers the idea is referred to Kṛṣṇa himself, 9.4; 11.38.

The Buddhist *anattā* doctrine is comprised in a well-known *ti-lakkhaṇa* formula: *sabbe saṃkhārā aniccā, sabbe saṃkhārā dukkhā, sabbe dhammā anattā* ("all conditioned things are impermanent, all conditioned things are painful [or: unsatisfactory], all *dhammas* are without Self"), DhP 277-279 (= Th. 676-678). It is significant that when impermanence and unsatisfactoriness are in question, the word *saṃkhārā* is used, but it is replaced by *dhammā* in the case of selflessness.[76] The term *saṃkhārā* in this context refers to all conditioned, compounded, originated things both physical and mental, in other words it refers to the five aggregates. But *dhammā* is much broader as the term means not only all conditioned things but also the non-conditioned. Thus *dhammā* also includes *nibbāna*. The differentiation is used here to highlight the unquestionable: there is no Self even beyond all conditioned things. *Nibbāna*, the *summum bonum*, which is neither *anicca* nor *dukkha*, is definitely *anatta*.[77]

Norman (1981: 207) mentions that the *ti-lakkhaṇa* formula "in its truncated form" occurs as: *sabbe saṃkhārā aniccā, sabbe dhammā anattā* (MN I 228; SN III 132, 133). The main burden of the polemics in *Gītā* 2.11-30 seems to be directed against a Buddhist statement of this sort. The Buddhist terms *aniccā* and *anattā* mark the strategy of Kṛṣṇa's metaphysical argument.

In BhG 2.14 the term *anitya* is used to characterize material contacts (*mātrāsparśāḥ*). Among the early Upaniṣads only the *Kaṭha* uses the term in one place (2.2.10), where it is said that the world is impermanent (*anitya*), but by impermanent things one may obtain the permanent (*nitya*). A similar line is assumed in the *Bhagavadgītā*. In 2.14 Kṛṣṇa encourages Arjuna to endure and not

[76] Cf. Norman 1981: 207; Rahula 1998: 57-58.

[77] This differentiation is also present in Vin. V 86: *aniccā sabbe saṃkhārā dukkhānattā ca saṃkhatā, nibbānañ c'eva paññatti anattā iti nicchayā* ("Impermanent are all constructs, painful, non self, and constructed, and certainly *nibbāna* is a description meaning non-self." – Norman 1981: 207.)

be troubled by changeable and impermanent elements of matter, but to assume the attitude of the wise or steady (*dhīra*), which is the basis of the way to immortality (*amṛtatva*). (Again, it should be remarked that this stanza corresponds perfectly to the Buddhist attitude: *amṛtatva* in the *Gītā* is an escape from what is *anitya*, as *nibbāna* is an escape from what is *anicca*, DhP 277.) It is here, however, that the basic metaphysical split occurs. While in the Buddha's teaching what is escape from *anicca* is *anatta*, according to Kṛṣṇa what is *nitya* is *ātman*. In the *Gītā* the permanent essence as opposed to the impermanence of the world is repeatedly defined *expressis verbis* as *nitya* (2.18, 20, 21, 24). Apart from that, the response to the Buddhist *sabbe dhammā anattā* is the whole range of epithets used to characterize the immortal Self. This, again, appears as a continuation of the discussion earlier undertaken by the Buddha.

Among manifold descriptions of *ātman-brahman* in the *Bṛhadāraṇyaka* and *Chāndogya Upaniṣad* one finds epithets to which the Buddha's teachings sometimes seem to allude directly: *nitya*, *dhruva*, *anucchittidharma*, *aja*, *ajara* (or *vijara*), *amṛta* (*vimṛtyu*). Some of these Buddhist allusions have been pointed out above. In the *Alagaddūpama Sutta* (MN I 135-136) the Buddha speaks against perceiving either the individual or the world in categories of *nicca*, *dhuva*, *sassata*, *avipariṇāmadhamma* (*sassatisamam ... ṭhassāmi*). This passage is frequently repeated in other suttas.[78]

An important polemic against the early Upaniṣads seems to be the *Brahmanimantaṇika Sutta* (Discourse on a challenge to a

[78] Cf. DN I 21; MN III 273-274, 277; SN III 98, 138, 143-144, 147. The *tilakkhaṇa* formula happens to be changed to *anicca*, *dukkha* (contrast: *ānanda*, BĀU 3.9.28, 4.3.33) and *vipariṇāmadhamma* (MN III 217-218, 270-277, 278), when the changeable character of the world is focused on (but then the last epithet does not refer to *nibbāna*). Such an expression also stands in opposition to the Upaniṣadic vision of the Self as constant (*dhruva*, *avināśī*).

Brahmā) of the *Majjhima Nikāya* (MN I 326-331).[79] There the Buddha challenges a god Brahmā named Baka. The Brahmā, who represents brahminic lore, in the presence of the Buddha presents his view of the nature of reality (MN I 326):

> This is permanent (*niccam*), this is stable (*dhuvam*), this is eternal (*sassatam*), this is entire (*kevalam*), this is not liable to passing away (*acavanadhammam*), this is not born (*na jāyati*), does not age (*na jīyati*), does not die (*na mīyati*), does not pass away (*na cavati*), does not arise (*na upapajjati*), and there is no another further escape from this.[80]

In the discourse, the Buddha condemns this view as "steeped in ignorance" (*avijjāgata*).[81] This is certainly an example of the Buddha's discussions with followers of the Upaniṣadic type of speculation.[82]

---

[79] Two other recensions of this story have been preserved: SN I 142-144 and Jāt. No. 405.

[80] Cf. e.g. BĀU 4.4.20: *ekadhaivānudraṣṭavyam etad aprameyam* dhruvam | *virajaḥ para ākāśād* aja *ātmā mahān* dhruvaḥ || 4.4.23: *eṣa* nityo *mahimā brāhmaṇasya* ...; 4.4.24-25: *sa vā eṣa mahān* aja *ātmānnādo vasudānaḥ, vindate vasu ya evaṃ veda. sa vā eṣa mahān* aja *ātm*ājaro *'maro* 'mṛto *'bhayo brahma*; 4.5.14: avināśi *vā are 'yam ātm*ānucchittidharmā; ChU 8.1.5: nā*sya jarayaitaj* jīryati *na vadhenasyāsya hanyate* | *etad satyaṃ brahmapuram asmin kāmāḥ samāhitāḥ* || *eṣa ātmāpahatapāpmā* vijaro vimṛtyur *viśoko vijighat so 'pipāsaḥ satyakāmaḥ satyasaṅkalpaḥ*. 8.10.1 (11.1): *etad* amṛtam *abhayam etad brahma*.

[81] MN I 326: "Indeed, Baka the Brahmā is steeped in ignorance, ..., inasmuch as he says "permanent" although it is indeed impermanent (*aniccam*), "stable" although it is indeed instable (*adhuvam*), "eternal" although it is indeed not eternal (*asassatam*), "entire" although it is indeed not entire (*akevalam*), "not liable to passing away" although it is indeed liable to passing away (*cavanadhammam*), and because in regard to what is born (*jāyati*), and ages (*jīyati*), and dies (*mīyati*), and passes away (*cavati*), and uprises (*upapajjati*), he says: "This is not born, nor does it age or die or pass away or uprise", and although there is another further escape, he says: "There is not another further escape".

[82] The *Brahmanimantaṇika Sutta* is based on allusions, also satirical, to the brahmins' ideas and concepts. The Brahmā is defeated during the debate with the Buddha and, moreover, the Buddha proves in this sutta that the supernormal powers of the Brahmā are inferior to his own. The name of the Brahmā, Baka, means "heron", which is probably a jocular allusion (see Gombrich 1996: 91, who also notes that in Indian fable a heron is associated with hypocrisy).

But if some stanzas of the second canto of the *Bhagavadgītā* are looked at in this context, it can be noticed that the discussion is continued. It is undertaken by Kṛṣṇa, who to a great extent bases his teachings on those Upaniṣadic speculations. In stanza 2.20 (which is mostly a quotation from the *Kaṭha Upaniṣad* 1.2.18), verbal similarities with the quoted Pāli fragment seem to be remarkable.

MN I 326:	BhG 2.20:
idaṃ ***niccaṃ*** *idaṃ dhuvam idaṃ* ***sassataṃ*** *idam kevalam idam acavanadhammaṃ, idaṃ hi* ***na jāyati*** *na jīyati* ***na mīyati*** *na cavati* na upapajjati, ...	***na jāyate mriyate*** *vā kadācin* nāyaṃ bhūtvā bhavitā vā na bhūyaḥ I ajo ***nityaḥ śāśvato*** *'yaṃ purāṇo na hanyate hanyamāne śarīre* II

What the Buddha condemns and advises us to reject constitutes the substance of Kṛṣṇa's teaching to Arjuna.

In several stanzas between 2.11 and 30 occur a great many epithets for the Self. Some of them are of Upaniṣadic origin. What is immortal in man is characterized as: *avināśin* (2.17, 21) and *anāśin* (18), *avyaya* (17, 21), *nitya* (18, 20, 21, 24), *aprameya* (18), *aja* (20, 21), *śāśvata* (20), *purāṇa* (20), *sarvagata* (24), *sthāṇu* (24), *acala* (24), *sanātana* (24), *avyakta* (25), *avikārya* (25), *nityam avadhya* (30), and as *acchedya, adāhya, akledya, aśoṣya* (23-24).[83]

It is hard to resist the impression that amassing so many epithets for the Self in such a short piece of text was intended to create a voice to argue with the religion which denied the existence of the Self and rejected all speculations about it.[84]

---

[83] The Self is named: *dehin* (2.13, 22, 30) or *śarīrin* (18), *sat* (16), *tat* (17), *ayam* (19, 20, 24, 25), [*enam* – acc. sg. (19, 21, 23, 25)].

[84] Stanzas 2.26-27 seem quite unlike this cluster of epithets and the univocal meaning of the majority of stanzas in this part. Kṛṣṇa tells Arjuna: "Even if you think that it [the Self] is born eternally and eternally dies, even then you should not grieve for it. For there is certain death of what has been born and there is certain birth of what has died; thus you should not grieve about the inevitable

Seeing this passage of the *Gītā* from the Buddhist angle, its opinions about a permanent essence appear as a continuation of the views which, according to Buddhist terminology, are presented by eternalists. The most detailed classification of all views at the time of the Buddha is presented in the *Brahmajāla Sutta* of the *Dīgha Nikāya* (DN I 1-46). Among the 62 views presented about the Self (or soul, which is another translation of *attā*) which were assumed wrong and requiring rejection, one can find the views of eternalists (*sassatavādā*)[85]. Among the four kinds of *sassatavādā*, there are opinions strikingly similar to those of the early parts of the *Bhagavadgītā* (in 2.20 Kṛṣṇa describes the Self as *śāśvata*). In particular, the argument that the eternal element exists independently of living beings, their transmigration and passing away.

> Eternal is the soul; and the world, giving birth to nothing new, is steadfast as a mountain peak, as a pillar firmly fixed; and though these living creatures transmigrate and pass away, fall from one state of existence and spring up in another, yet they are for ever and ever.[86]

---

order of things." This sounds like annihilationism, criticized as much as eternalism in the canon. Kṛṣṇa thus assumes that there is a point of view which denies the existence of an immortal Self. The epic context must be remembered: Kṛṣṇa is trying to make Arjuna fight. He does so by mentioning opposite arguments. What is interesting is that he does not mention the middle way; maybe he omits it deliberately. The two opposite metaphysical attitudes convey ethical determinism (an attitude quite contrary to the Buddhist one, cf. Jayatilleke 1955: 138-141), intended to defeat the Buddhist-like ethics presented by Arjuna. (It is not unlikely that stanzas 2.26-27 are a later interpolation. In both the stanzas pāda d would be a duplication of the original 2.25d and 30d.)

[85] DN I 13: "There are, brethren, some recluses and Brahmans who are Eternalists, and who, on four grounds, proclaim, that both the soul and the world are eternal." (*santi bhikkhave eke samaṇa-brāhmaṇā sassatavādā sassatam attānañ ca lokañ ca paññāpenti catūhi vatthūhi.*)

[86] DN I 14: *sassato attā ca loko ca vañjho kuṭaṭṭho esikaṭṭhāyiṭṭhito, te ca sattā sandhāvanti saṃsaranti cavanti upapajjanti, athi tv eva sassatisamam*. The epithet *kūṭastha,* which does not appear in the principal Upaniṣads, occurs three times in later textual layers of the BhG: in 6.18 as a designation of a perfect yogin or *yukta*, in 12.3 and 15.16 as a designation of the Self (in 15.16 *kūṭastha* is the imperishable *puruṣa*, in 12.3-4, in the bhakti layer, the Self is identified with, or subordinated to, Kṛṣṇa as the highest personified god).

This view is apparently continued in Kṛṣṇa's argument (cf. BhG 2.12, 13, 16-18, 22). But while the Buddha urges escaping from such views (DN I 17), for Kṛṣṇa they are the basic arguments encouraging Arjuna to fight.

> *antavanta ime dehā nityasyoktāḥ śarīriṇaḥ* I
> *anāśino 'prameyasya tasmād yudhyasva bhārata* II (BhG 2.18)

A further remark has been triggered by an interesting observation by R. Gombrich (1996: 62-64). He noticed that the *Mallikā Sutta* of the *Saṃyutta Nikāya* (SN I 75), which is concerned with a conversation between King Pasenadi and his Queen Mallikā is a reminiscence of the famous conversation in the *Bṛhadāraṇyaka Upaniṣad* (2.4 and 4.5) between the sage Yājñavalkya and his favourite wife Maitreyī. The Buddhist discourse appears as a subtle polemic against the Upaniṣadic one. In the *Bṛhadāraṇyaka* Maitreyī asks Yājñavalkya to teach her about immortality. The sage begins by saying that it is not through love for a husband that the husband is dear, but it is through love (*kāma*) for *ātman* that a husband is dear (*priya*). Similarly, it is not through love for wife, children, wealth etc. that a wife, children, wealth etc. are dear, but it is through love for *ātman* that they are dear. A series of parallel statements then lead to the conclusion that to know *ātman* means to know everything. In these fragments *ātman* is the essence of the individual and the universe, the Self. In the passage of the *Saṃyutta Nikāya*, Pasenadi asks Mallikā if there is anyone dearer (*piyatara*) to her than *attā*. The queen replies that there is no one dearer to her than *attā*. The king replies the same when asked, in turn, by Mallikā if there is anyone dearer to him than *attā*. Having met the Buddha, Pasenadi reports this conversation to him. The Buddha, understanding the matter, responds in verse: "Having traversed all directions in thought, he nowhere found one dearer than *attā* (*piyataram attanā*). In this way, for others too the separate *attā* is dear (*piya*). Therefore one who loves *attā* (*attākāma*) should not harm others."[87]

According to Gombrich, the Buddha refers here to Yājñavalkya's teaching in a way "half playful and half serious" and yet draws quite contrary conclusions. Making use of the ambiguity of the word *ātman*/*attā*, he equips the echoed Upaniṣadic term for the Self with quite a humdrum meaning; *attā* in the Pāli text is the reflexive pronoun (hence, in this fragment of the *Saṃyutta*, *attā* should be understood as 'herself' or 'himself' respectively). Recognition of this allusion yet again shows how the Buddha teaches the problem of the Self to be illusory. What is the true essence in both individual and universal dimensions in the Upaniṣad, is reduced by the Buddha to mere egoism in human terms (everyone loves first of all himself). But the Buddha makes an ethical use of that: "who loves himself should not harm others". "Ethics in place of metaphysics", to quote the author of this observation.[88]

The whole *Mallikā Sutta* is repeated in the *Udāna* 5.1 (Ud. 47).[89] The same teaching, by which the "*attā*-argument" is transformed into ethics, is conveyed by some other texts, for example, two stanzas from the *Dhammapada*, 129-130 (10.1-2). They are placed among other stanzas recommending a suitable and peaceful life. But if the two stanzas are considered from the point of view of the *Gītā*, one may come to the conclusion that the Sanskrit poem continues the discussion and that stanza 2.21, in turn, alludes to the stanzas of the *Dhammapada*.

---

[87] Transl. by Gombrich (1996: 62-63). I leave the term *attā* untranslated.

[88] Gombrich 1996: 63. (Cf. p. 64: "So here too we see the Buddha reacting to Upaniṣadic teachings by shifting attention away from what the world is, ontology, to how we should behave: morally, and in particular kindly.")

[89] Moreover, the final verse uttered by the Buddha is repeated later in *Visuddhimagga* 9 (p. 297).

DhP 129-30:
sabbe tassanti dandassa sabbe bhāyanti maccuno | attānam *upamaṃ katvā* ***na haneyya na ghātaye*** ||
sabbe tassanti dandassa sabbesaṃ jīvitaṃ piyam | attānam *upamaṃ katvā* ***na haneyya na ghātaye*** ||[90]

BhG 2.21:
*vedā*vināśinaṃ nityaṃ *ya* enam ajam avyayam | *kathaṃ sa puruṣaḥ pārtha* ***kaṃ ghātayati hanti kam*** ||

– For all beings life is dear – claims, among others, the *Dhammapada* – and so it is for me. Considering myself (*attānam*) equal to others (just as I do not want to experience any harm) I should neither kill nor contribute to it.
– Who speaks of killing or contributing to it – the *Gītā* seems to reply – if the imperishable Self is as inherent in you as in all other beings? Considering yourself equal to others, you should realize that in fact neither you nor others are able to destroy what is imperishable, permanent, unborn, unchanging. (So stand up to fight!)

While the Buddhist thought points to indisputable *ahiṃsā*, in its ethics bypassing any metaphysical (ontological) speculations, the *Bhagavadgītā* returns to metaphysical speculations and bases the ethics of the *kṣatriya* on them.

5.

Most of what is contained in the early parts of the *Bhagavadgītā* stands in contradiction to the views of early Buddhism. Referring to the same or similar words and expressions may corroborate the hypothesis that what we face here is polemics. To complete the picture, let us return to stanza 2.11, as it seems to be in agreement

[90] "All are frightened of the rod. / Of death all are afraid. / Having made oneself the example, / One should neither slay nor cause to slay. / All are frightened of the rod. / For all, life is dear. / Having made oneself the example, / One should neither slay nor cause to slay." (Carter & Palihawadana 1987: 202-203.)

with the anti-Buddhist context of Kṛṣṇa's statement as presented above. Using the compound *prajñāvādāḥ* in this very place seems to be meaningful.

The word *prajñā* and its cognates appear occasionally in the *Brāhmaṇas* to define common human knowledge or intelligence useful for practical purposes.[91] In the earliest Upaniṣads *prajñā* or *prajñāna* is used several times to designate knowledge, besides such terms as *jñāna*, *buddhi* and *vidyā*.[92] In a few places *prajñā* (and *prajñāna*) is associated with the concept of *ātman* and *brahman* (BĀU 4.1.2, 4.3.21, 4.3.35, 4.5.13). It is difficult to claim, though, that the term was equipped with any special meaning.[93] The *Kauṣītaki Upaniṣad* and, less conspicuously, the *Aitareya Upaniṣad* are exceptions (both said to be composed around the 5th century BC, which means around the time when Buddhism was arising).[94] The term *prajñā* (and *prajñāna*) used there represents fundamental knowledge, is identified with *prāṇa* (vital breath) as well as equated with *ātman* and *brahman*. But outside the *Kauṣītaki*, *prajñā* does not often appear in the Upaniṣads. Nor does it seem to be of special significance, particularly when compared to other synonymous expressions.

On the other hand, the word and the concept of *prajñā* or Pāli *paññā* shines bright in Buddhist thought. *Paññā* frequently appears in the Pāli canon and is one of the most important terms in the suttas. It is also one of the most important aims of all schools of early Buddhism. It refers to true intuitive wisdom, is considered the supreme virtue, and is synonymous with achieving the truth in the full sense of the word. *Paññā* allows man to reject the delusive

---

[91] Cf. Barnett 1931: 287.

[92] Barnett 1931: 187-188; Watanabe 1997-98: 259-260.

[93] In BĀU 4.5.1 it is said that of Yājñavalkya's two wives Maitreyī had some knowledge of the Brahmanic lore (being *brahmavādinī*), but Kātyāyanī was *strīprajñā*, "having only a woman's knowledge".

[94] Watanabe 1997-98: 261-264; Barnett 1931: 288, fn. 1.

appearance of things and understand their true nature. Thus it does not mean the common knowledge of phenomenal things, but an insight into the real nature of the world and human condition. Throughout the different parts of canon several aspects of *paññā* are presented, but almost everywhere the term is connected with liberating wisdom.

It is said that owing to *paññā* the Four Noble Truths are known and seen, which leads to the cessation of pain (DhP 190-192; DN I 83-84).[95] By means of understanding the nature of the *dhamma*, *paññā* releases from any clinging, including clinging to different theories or views (MN I 133-134, III 72; DhP 40). Thanks to intuitive wisdom the highest truth is directly realized and seen (MN I 480, II 173; AN II 115). *Paññā* is said to be the great power leading to enlightenment, immortality and *nibbāna*, the ultimate salvation.[96] What seems to be especially important for the purpose of this paper is the early Buddhist conviction that thanks to *paññā* the doctrine of *anattā* is fully understood. The Buddha teaches that when one sees reality objectively as it is, one rejects the extreme views of eternalism and annihilationism. The Tathāgata paces the

---

[95] In the Buddha's teaching the concept of *paññā* is connected with the Fourth Noble Truth, i.e. with the way leading to cessation of *dukkha*, which is the Noble Eightfold Path. The eight parts of this way aim to master the three crucial elements of Buddhist training: moral conduct (*sīla*), mental discipline or meditation (*samādhi*) and – at the highest level – intuitive wisdom (*paññā*). (Cf. DN I 62-85, 206-209, II 81, 84; MN I 301; AN I 125; It. 51.) It is also emphasised that moral preparation and meditation are essential for obtaining the true intuitive wisdom just as *paññā* is necessary for moral conduct and meditation (DN I 124; AN I 102; DhP 372).

[96] Sn. 174-175; Th. 1.1.3. The Buddha says (SN V 249) that there are five powers: the power of faith (*saddhābalam*), of energy (*viriyabalam*), of mindfulness (*satibalam*), of concentration (*samādhibalam*) and, finally, of insight or intuitive wisdom (*paññābalam*). Cultivation and making the right use of these powers leads to attaining *nibbāna*. The five powers are also called the five faculties (*pañcindriyāni*) that lead to immortality (SN V 200, 232). The most important of these faculties for attaining enlightenment (*bodhi*) is said to be *paññā* (SN V 200, 231).

middle way and thanks to *paññā* he holds with neither the existence nor the non-existence of the world (SN II 17, III 134-135). *Paññā* is a direct understanding of the impermanence (*anicca*) and unsatisfactoriness (*dukkha*) of all conditioned things, as well as of the selflessness (*anatta*) of everything including *nibbāna*. This is stated in the *tilakkhaṇa* formula:

sabbe saṃkhārā aniccā'ti yadā ***paññāya*** *passati* I ...
sabbe samkhārā dukkā'ti yadā ***paññāya*** *passati* I ...
sabbe dhammā anattā'ti yadā ***paññāya*** *passati* I
atha nibbindatī dukkhe, esa maggo visuddhiyā II[97]

Towards the end of the *Alagaddūpama Sutta* (MN I 139) passage cited above the Buddha says that through perfect insight (*sammāpaññāya*) one learns reality objectively as it is (*yathābhūtam*) and frees oneself from the false views: "This is mine, this am I, this is my Self". The established formula: *etaṃ yathābhūtaṃ sammāpaññāya*, is very frequently repeated in the suttas, ending and summing up passages on *anattā*.[98] The Buddhist idea of wisdom, the attainment of *paññā*, liberates from speculations on the Self.[99]

---

[97] DhP 277-279: When through wisdom one perceives: "All *sankhāras* are transient" ... When through wisdom one perceives: "All *sankhāras* are suffering" ... When through wisdom one perceives: "All *dhammas* are without self", then one is detached as to misery. This is the path of purity. (Carter & Palihawadana 1987: 310-312.)

[98] Cf. SN III 49-50, 68, 84, 89, 103, 136-137, 165-166, 169, 170; MN I 185, 188, 235, 421. It seems worth asking the question if, when one compares some passages of the *Kauṣītaki* and *Aitareya Upaniṣads* with passages on *anattā* from the Suttas, one can find any other traces of discussions due to the emergence of the Buddhism. The discussion pertaining to the concept of the Self might also concern the question what the true wisdom was, *paññā* versus Upaniṣadic *prajñā*. In the Buddha's teaching, owing to *paññā* one is able to abandon any speculations regarding the concept of *attā*; in *Kauṣītaki* and *Aitareya prajñā* is closely connected with *ātman-brahman*. Cf. especially KauṣU 3.8: sa eṣa prāṇa *eva* ***prajñā***tmānando *'jaro 'mṛto na sādhunā karmaṇā bhūyān bhavati no evāsādhunā kanīyān ... eṣa lokapālaḥ, eṣa lokādhipatiḥ, eṣa lokeśaḥ.* ***sa ma ātmā****, iti vidyāt* ***sa ma ātmā****, iti vidyāt.* Again compare the *Alagaddūpama Sutta*, MN I 139: *n'etaṃ mama, n'eso 'ham asmi,* ***na meso attā*** *ti evam-etaṃ yathābhūtaṃ* ***sam-***

On the basis of what has been said, it seems that the *Gitā*'s expression *prajñāvādāṃś ca bhāṣase* may be considered against the background of Buddhist thought, like the immediately following stanzas.[100] In 2.11 Kṛṣṇa starts a teaching which takes issue

---

māppaññāya daṭṭhabbaṃ. See also Watanabe 1997-98: 263-265 on *prajñā* in the AitU 3.1-4 as contrasted with Buddhist thought.

[99] Upadhyaya (1983: 187): "... according to Buddhism, the attainment of wisdom (*paññā*) and consequent salvation (*vimutti*) by means of concentration (*samādhi*) is conceived as naturalistic, causally accountable and capable of clear and systematic analysis. There is nothing mysterious or supernatural about it." Gombrich (1996: 96-134), using some passages in the Pāli canon, retraces a very probable ancient debate on the role of *paññā* in the process of enlightenment. The debate took place at least several decades after the Buddha's death (at least two-three generations after the Buddha's *parinibbāna*, according to Gombrich). The scholar shows that in the texts considered to be the oldest and referring to the doctrine as preached by the Buddha himself the achievement of enlightenment (*bodhi* = *nibbāna*) was not possible without meditation; *paññā-vimutti* was not a separate salvific way, meditation and insight supplemented each other (and consequently, for example, the standard formula: *ceto-vimutti paññā-vimutti* does not imply two separate ways but is to be considered as synonymous, "release of the mind, release by insight"). In some suttas, which must be recognized as later, one can notice a tendency to extol the meaning of *paññā* as salvific even at the cost of meditation (which, in turn, might have evoked reactions among some monks and redactors who wished to remain true to the doctrine of the Buddha himself, SN II 119-128, *Susīma Sutta*, versus SN II 115-118, *Kosambi Sutta*).

For the purpose of this paper it is significant that the term *paññā* is a key-word of early Buddhism and using it in BhG 2.11, in the layer which may have been composed around the time of great Buddhist expansion, could have had an unambiguous association for even the non-Buddhist hearer or reader.

[100] Barnett (1931), while attempting to identify a Greek term *pramnai*, which Strabo (Geogr. XV, C. 719 = 15,1.70) uses to define the opponents of *brahmanai*, suggests that in the word (*prámnas* – acc. pl.) "is concealed some form of *prājña*, 'the clever man'". He refers the Sanskrit term to sectarians like Jains or Buddhists. Having analysed the term *prajñā* in the Upaniṣads Barnett comes up with the suggestion that it is BhG 2.11 that reflects the general Upaniṣadic feeling about the word as the "common-place wisdom". He supposes that Kṛṣṇa refers *prajñāvādāḥ* to "shortsighted conventional moralists like Jains and Buddhists, who preach on the text 'thou shalt not slay' without understanding the higher law" (Barnett 1931: 288). In Barnett's interpretation Kṛṣṇa's words therefore refer directly to the concept of *ahiṃsā* of both Jains and Buddhists. (Barnett also supposes that the term *prajñā* in BhG 17.14 is connected with "sectarian teachers" as differentiated from Brahmins (*dvija*) and "elders" (*guru*), i.e.

with the early Buddhist attitude towards both metaphysics (2.11-30) and ethics (2.31-37, 38). In this context, the allusion of the expression *prajñāvādāḥ* to one of the crucial terms of Buddhism becomes much more conspicuous. Therefore I assume that the first part of 2.11 (pādas a-b) is contrasted with its second part, which means that Arjuna's attitude as well as his "words of wisdom" are contrasted with the attitude of (Brahminic) paṇḍits. Thus the suggested interpretation of this stanza is based not on the understanding: "you act in an unwise way although [otherwise/generally or partly] you speak wise words", but on the understanding: "you both act and speak in an unwise way".

Hence, the implied meaning emerges: "you speak words of *prajñā* which is apparent or even false wisdom" (especially in reference to both your tradition and your social position); in other words: "you speak words considered wise by those who preach heresy". Arjuna, therefore, is in a sense claiming or pretending to words of wisdom (as some suppose, see above, p. 177), but the allusion builds on the assumption that he refers to the contrary thought system and thus negates his own tradition. Behaving like a heretic, he in fact speaks unwise words.[101]

But we can go even further and look for an allusion in the whole compound *prajñāvādā*. As mentioned above, in the *Brahmajāla Sutta* of the *Dīgha Nikāya* (DN I 1-46), in a detailed classification, there were presented 62 wrong views about the Self,

orthodox teachers.) The hypothesis of Barnett was rejected by Belvalkar (1947: lxxxii, fn. 1), the editor of the *Bhīṣmaparvan*, as "not particularly convincing". I have not noticed any other researcher mention it (his attempt to reconstruct the word *pramnai* was subject to severe criticism from the point of view of Greek phonetics, see Karttunen 1997: 59-60). Barnett's attempt to interpret BhG 2.11 is the closest so far to that proposed in this paper.

[101] It is not unlikely that the polemical meaning of the term *prajñā* could also refer more generally to "heretics" (or Jains and Buddhists as advocates of *ahiṃsā*, according to Barnett's suggestion), but – as this paper has been trying to show – the polemic against Buddhism (as well as the "Buddhist" attitude of Arjuna) is the most significant and meaningful as well as the most perceptible.

starting with the four kinds of "eternalists", *sassatavādā*. Among the terms for the followers of other different views, compounds with the last word *-vādā* prevail (i.e.: *ekaccasassatavādā*, *antānantavādā*, *amarāvikkhepavādā*, *adhiccasamuppannavādā*, *saññivādā*, *asaññivādā*, *nevasaññi-nāsaññivādā*, *ucchedavādā*, *diṭṭhadhammanibbānavādā*). Sometimes, as in the well known parable about the wanderer Vacchagotta (SN IV 400-401), the Buddha more generally calls us to follow the middle way beyond the two extreme views, the one of the *sassatavādā*, and the other of the *ucchedavādā* (annihilationists). In the quoted passage of the *Ālagaddūpama Sutta* (MN I 136-137), the Buddha encourages us to abandon "attachment to the theory of the Self", *atta-vād[a]-upādāna*, as causing grief etc. to arise, by means of perfect intuitive wisdom (*sammāpaññāya*). One may then ask whether Kṛṣṇa in BhG 2.11, on his part, is not making an allusion to those Buddhist terms.[102] In the context of Kṛṣṇa's utterance, *prajñāvādā* may be as specific as "Buddhist views", "doctrines" or "theories", being almost "a technical term" created in response to such terms as *atta-vādā* or *sassatavādā*.[103]

It has been remarked that in some Pāli texts one may notice that the Buddha, while discussing with brahmins and trying to defeat Brahminic concepts, from time to time used satire as well as irony.[104] It is difficult to resist an impression that likewise in

---

[102] Ch. Lindtner (1995: 207-209) interestingly suggests that the term *prajñāvādā* in the *Gitā* refers to Mahāyāṇa Buddhism. However, assuming that the discussed parts of the poem are older than the earliest parts of the Mahāyāna texts (i.e. of the *Prajñāpāramitā Sutra*), I do not follow this hypothesis. Moreover, Lindtner does not take into consideration the discussion about the Self which is basic for the argument of this paper.

[103] MN II 147-148 witnesses that the Buddha himself was known to the brahmins as *dhammavādi* ("a teacher of the *dharma*"). In a passage of the *Maitrayāṇīya Upaniṣad* (7.8-10), which most probably bears a polemic tone against the early Buddhists (cf. Jayatilleke 1963:66-68), the Buddhist doctrine, among others, is characterized as *nairātmyavāda* (7.8, "the doctrine that denies the Self").

[104] Cf. Gombrich 1990: 12-14; 1996: 80-83, 90-92.

Kṛṣṇa's response one can find a similar weapon, a sort of subtle irony. Arjuna refuses to take part in the battle, and in his moral dilemma he refers to Buddhist-like arguments (as shown above, pp. 184-191).[105] Having listened to Arjuna's words and observing his attitude, Kṛṣṇa smiles gently (2.10: *prahasann iva*), which must be the ironic smile of a sage superior to his ignorant interlocutor.[106] He then speaks, at the beginning ironically, then seriously: "You act wrongly and moreover you speak like some *prajñāvādin* (read: Buddhist) heretic, a follower of a pseudo-wisdom; but what you attempt to call pity and compassion is to be regarded as weakness and faintheartedness; the true wisdom is manifested by the attitude of the wise men of your own tradition, for it makes you notice the basic difference between the mortal body and the immortal, eternal Self, it lets you observe the immortality in every living being, and allows you to assume an inflexible attitude towards the manifested world; the true wisdom is conveyed by your *dharma*." Much indicates that this could have been the primary intention in using the term *prajñāvāda* at this juncture.

One can obviously not forget the epic context and meaning of this part of the text. The early layers of the *Gītā* are well embedded in the main, military plot of the *Mahābhārata*. At times Kṛṣṇa enriches his argumentation with elements of early Sāṃkhya, early Vedānta, makes references, sometimes direct, to the Upaniṣads. (Then he goes much further beyond the epic context and portrays himself as the one and only supreme goal.) Yet no matter how these parts are understood, the echo of polemics with early

---

105 I realize how easy it is, in this type of textual interpretation, to be charged with exaggeration and creating problems that do not exist. I would nevertheless remark that in 2.9, towards the end of the description of Arjuna's dilemma when he refuses to fight, it is said that "he became silent" – *tūṣṇīṃ babhūva*, which might also contain some allusion. The Buddha himself is sometimes said to "become silent" as a refusal to continue some irrelevant discussion (*bhagavā tuṇhī ahosi*, e.g. SN IV 400).

106 Cf. Lindtner 1995: 209.

Buddhism in the chapter 2 seems to be quite conspicuous. It must have been conspicuous for the ancient hearer (or reader) in the first centuries BC, at the time of the *Bhagavadgītā*'s rise and development, when Buddhism in India was a great religion, supported by kings (and rich merchants), becoming the most serious rival of Brahmanism, and when philosophical and religious discussions between supporters of the so-called orthodox tradition and those of the heterodox currents must have taken place. The poem emerges as a voice in this discussion.

6.

With the appearance of new textual layers, the *Gītā* moves away from the main epic plot. The epic itself changes its character over time, growing from inside. The *Mahābhārata* became a perfect medium for propagating the doctrines of the more and more broadly understood Brahminism, which must also have reflected discussions and polemics with followers of heterodoxy. In the subsequent textual layers of the *Bhagavadgītā* one can trace some more elements of, so to say, an anti-Buddhist campaign.

To sketch the way in which polemics with Buddhism is supposedly continued in our poem, let me make some additional remarks. Stanzas 2.39–4.42 of the *Gītā* (apart from the later interpolations) constitute the next textual layer, the so-called first *yoga* layer.[107] At the beginning of this layer, 2.42-46, one faces the criticism of, generally speaking, the post-Vedic way of thinking and behaving.[108] The criticism concerns attachment to the "flowery" words of the Vedas (what is meant is probably Vedic mantras recited extremely carefully during sacrificial ceremonies), to Vedic ritualism – its excessively developed and exaggeratedly specialized

[107] Cf. Ježić 1979.

[108] In 2.42 *vedavāda-* seem to make (similarly to *prajñavādā*) a sort of "technical term".

forms, as well as short-sighted and egoistic purposes (fulfilment of desires, heaven, rebirth as a fruit of action and religious rituals, enjoyment, power). The whole passage might be compared to the Buddhist criticism, found repeatedly in the Pāli suttas, of the Vedic tradition and brahmin ritual activity. However, what is significant is that the criticism does not come from a religious opponent but, as it were, from an "enlightened" follower of an old tradition. Kṛṣṇa himself suggests going beyond Vedic and old Brahminic ritualism (the metaphorical meaning of the term *yajña* also serves the purpose) by means of true insight, *buddhi*, based on *samādhi* (2.44-46; cf. Buddhist *paññā* based on *samādhi*). The one who is to realize the higher truth is said in 2.46 to be *brāhmaṇa vijānant* – the knowing or wise brahmin (although Arjuna, to whom the teaching is directed, is a *kṣatriya*). This kind of criticism from within looks like taking a weapon from the opponent's hand. The evolving orthodox tradition shows that referring to the Buddha's teachings and joining a heterodoxy is not necessary in order to find the true way to the ultimate goal. The true salvific way in the first *yoga* layer of the *Bhagavadgītā* is *karmayoga*, non-egoistic activity in everyday life based on insight (*buddhi*) into the nature of reality. It may be recognized as a neo-Brahminical alternative to the early Buddhist way of salvation reserved for the Tathāgata, a monk living in detachment from the activity of the world and secular life. In this context, Kṛṣṇa's words in 2.49 *buddhau śaraṇam anviccha* may be understood as a further ironical allusion (based on word play) to the formula which constitutes the Buddhist expression of faith, viz. to the first of the Three Refuges (*tisaraṇa*): *Buddhaṃ saraṇaṃ gacchāmi* (followed by: *dhammaṃ saraṇaṃ gacchāmi, saṃghaṃ saraṇaṃ gacchāmi*).[109] Kṛṣṇa appeals to Arjuna: "Seek

---

[109] It was Prof. M. K. Byrski who drew my attention to this association. Cf. also Malinar 1996: 147-148, fn. 55. In the Pāli canon the formula often appears as *bhagavantaṃ/gotamaṃ saraṇaṃ gacchāmi dhammañ ca bhikkhusaṃghañ ca* (e.g. DN I 85; MN I 24, 489, 512; SN II 21; AN IV 179), but that commonly

refuge in [your own] *buddhi*" (which will allow you to walk the true way of life, the way of action with non-attachment to the fruits of action), *buddhi* in the implied meaning replacing *buddha*. This seems to suggest: "By seeking refuge in your *buddhi* you do not need to seek refuge in the Buddha".[110]

There are many references, echoes, allusions to Buddhist thought in the next two textual layers of the *Gītā*, the so-called second and third *yoga* layer, i.e. in the fifth and sixth chapter of the poem. But they too serve mostly to make another polemical discussion possible. In chapters 5 and 6, the polemics concerns mainly the ultimate goal, *summum bonum*, as well as the way leading to it (again the *Gītā*'s view of *ātman-brahman* versus the Buddhist *anattā*). The Buddhist concept of *nibbāna* is confronted in the *Gītā* with the concept of *brahma-nirvāṇa* (5.24-26), the *Gītā* again using the terminology of its opponent.[111] The essence of meditation presented in chapter 6 is realization of *ātman*, which is (meaningfully) described as the liberation from *duḥkha* (6.17, 22, 23) and leading to the highest bliss, *sukha* (6.21, 27, 28).[112]

Kṛṣṇa's argument with Buddhist thought is by no means an open fight. It is rather a subtle polemical discussion in which both great Bhagavats (the Buddha arguing with older Brahminic tradi-

---

known and quoted by the followers of Buddhism has been the one containing the word "Buddha" (cf. DhP 190-192).

[110] Stanzas 2.54-60 and 67-68, where *prajñā* replaces *buddhi* of the original layer, are contained in the so-called *prajñā* interpolation (cf. Ježić 1979: 549-550), which is a later fragment inserted into the original text of the first *yoga* layer. It is important here to notice that *prajñā* of BhG 2.11 and *prajñā* of 2.54-60, 67-68 belong to two different textual layers of the poem, the latter being a later interpolation. Any possible allusions of the latter fragment to Buddhism should be analysed separately (as in the case of *Kauṣītaki* and *Aitareya Upaniṣad*, see above, footnote 98).

[111] Cf. Szczurek 2003.

[112] Moreover, at the beginning of both chapters (5.1-6; 6.1-4) the concept of *karmayoga*, the discipline of action, is referred to. Here one encounters a brahminic redefinition of the concept of freedom from activity and renunciation (*saṃnyāsa*).

tion, Kṛṣṇa arguing with the Buddha) also do not hesitate to emphasize the similarities between their doctrines or refer to the common tradition. The polemics is straightforward and literal at times, but sometimes indirect and allusive; mostly serious, but sometimes containing elements of satire or irony. Elements of the polemics can be found in parts referring directly to one's own ideas and concepts, emphasizing them, using words and expressions characteristic of a particular thought system. From time to time, however, the discussion refers to the concepts and terminology of the opponent, sometimes takes them over or adapts them to its own purpose, sometimes equips them with a fairly new or even contrary meaning. These can be seen as attempts to win over followers of the opposite religion.

The polemics with early Buddhism could not obscure the main plot and meaning of the *Gītā*. The poem has been understood in many ways by interpreters and commentators, mainly without any reference to Buddhism. It seems, however, that Buddhism must have played a significant role in inspiring the poem's rise and development. The *Bhagavadgītā* must also be seen as a collection of suggestions alternative to the powerful heterodox ideology. This ideology must have influenced representatives of the *kṣatriya varṇa*, the more so as it contrasted the hardship of ruling and the discomfort of war campaigns to the abandonment of violence, taking refuge in a monastery and listening to the teachings of the Enlightened One about how to end *dukkha* and reach *nibbāna*. Therefore, while arguing with such an ideology, Kṛṣṇa directs his polemics to Arjuna, the ideal embodiment of a warrior's virtues, who stands at the crossroads before the most important choice in his life, the choice which way of life to follow.

REFERENCES

BAHM, A. J. (transl.) 1970. *The Bhagavad Gita or The Wisdom of Krishna.* Bombay: Somaya Publications Pvt. Ltd.

BARNETT, L. D. 1931. Pramnai. In: *A Volume of Indian Studies Presented by His Friends and Pupils to Edward James Rapson* (BSOS): 285-290. London.

BELVALKAR, S. K. 1939. The so-called Kashmir recension of the Bhagavad-Gītā. *New Indian Antiquary* 2.4: 211-251.

—— (transl.) 1943. *The Bhagavadgītā.* Poona: The Bilvakunja Publishing House.

—— (ed.) 1947. *The Bhīṣmaparvan. Being the Sixth Book of the Mahābhārata, the Great Epic of India.* (Mahābhārata ... for the first time critically edited, 7.) Poona: The Bhandarkar Oriental Research Institute.

BUITENEN, J. A. B. van (ed. & transl.) 1981. *The Bhagavadgītā in the Mahābhārata.* Text and translation. Chicago: The University of Chicago Press.

CARTER, J. R. & M. PALIHAWADANA 1987. *The Dhammapada.* A new English translation with the Pali text and the first English translation of the commentary's explanation of the verses with notes translated from Sinhala sources and critical textual comments. New York: Oxford University Press.

COLLINS, S. 1982. *Selfless Persons. Imagery and Thought in Theravada Buddhism.* Cambridge: Cambridge University Press.

DEUTSCH, E. (transl.) 1968. *The Bhagavad Gītā.* Lanham, N.Y.: University Press of America.

DEVASTHALI, G. V. 1953. *Bhagavad-gītā and Upaniṣads.* In: J. N. Agrawal & B. D. Shastri (eds.), *Sarūpa-Bhāratī or the Homage of Indology being the L. Sarup Memorial Volume*: 132-142. Hoshiarpur: Vishveshvanand Institute.

EDGERTON, F. 1932. [Review of F. Otto Schrader, *The Kashmir Recension of the Bhagavadgītā.*] *Journal of the American Oriental Society* 52: 68-75.

—— (ed. & transl.) 1939. *The Bhagavad Gītā*, I-II. (Harvard Oriental Series, 39.) London: Oxford University Press. (Reprint: Delhi: Motilal Banarsidass, 1994.)

GARBE, R. 1905. *Die Bhagavadgītā.* Leipzig: H. Haessel Verlag.

GETHIN, R. 1998. *The Foundations of Buddhism.* Oxford: Oxford University Press.

GHOSE, Aurobindo 1938. *The Message of the Gita, as Interpreted by Sri Aurobindo.* Ed. by A. Roy. London: George Allen & Unwin Ltd.

GOMBRICH, R. 1990. Recovering the Buddha's message. In: D. S. Ruegg & L. Schmithausen (eds.), *Earliest Buddhism and Madhyamaka* (Panels of the VIIth World Sanskrit Conference, Leiden: August 23-29, 1987): 5-23. Leiden: Brill.

—— 1992. The Buddha's Book of Genesis? *Indo-Iranian Journal* 35: 159-178.

—— 1996. *How Buddhism Began. The Conditioned Genesis of the Early Teachings*. London: The Athlone Press.

GOTSHALK, R. (transl.) 1993. *Bhagavad Gītā*. Delhi: Motilal Banarsidass.

HAAS, G. C. O. 1922. Recurrent and parallel passages in the principal Upanishads and the Bhagavad-Gītā. *Journal of the American Oriental Society* 42: 1-43.

HARA, M. 2001a. Apsaras and hero. *Journal of Indian Philosophy* 29.1-2: 135-153.

—— 2001b. The death of the hero. *Journal of the International College for Advanced Buddhist Studies* 4: 340-315.

HARVEY, P. 1995. *The Selfless Mind. Personality, Consciousness and Nirvana in Early Buddhism*. Richmond: Curzon Press.

HERMAN, A. L. (transl.) 1973. *The Bhagavad Gītā. A Translation and Critical Commentary*. Springfield, Ill.: Charles Thomas Publisher.

JAYATILLEKE, K. N. 1955. Some aspects of Gita and Buddhist ethics. *University of Ceylon Review* 13.2-3: 135-151.

—— 1963. *Early Buddhist Theory of Knowledge*. London: Georg Allen & Unwin Ltd.

JACOB, G. A. 1891. *A Concordance to the Principal Upanisads and Bhagavadgītā*. (Bombay Sanskrit Series, 39.) Bombay. (Reprint: Delhi: Motilal Banarsidass, 1971.)

JEŽIĆ, M. 1979. The first Yoga layer in the Bhagavadgītā. In: *Ludwik Sternbach Felicitation Volume*, I: 545-557. Lucknow: Akhila Bharatiya Sanskrit Parishad.

—— 1986. Textual layers of the Bhagavadgītā as traces of Indian cultural history. In: *Sanskrit and World Culture. Proceedings of the Fourth World Sanskrit Conference* (Schriften zur Geschichte und Kultur des Alten Orients, 18): 628-638. Berlin: Akademie Verlag.

—— 2002. The Bhāṣkalamantra-Upaniṣad and the Bhagavadgītā. In: M. Brockington (ed.), *Stages and Transitions. Temporal and Historical Frameworks in Epic and Purāṇic Literature*: 35-54. Zagreb: Croatian Academy of Sciences and Arts.

KARTTUNEN, K. 1997. *India and the Hellenistic World*. (Studia Orientalia, 83.) Helsinki: The Finnish Oriental Society.

LINDTNER, Ch. 1995. Lokasaṃgraha, Buddhism and buddhiyoga in the Gītā. In: S. P. Narang (ed.), *Modern Evaluation of the Mahābhārata. Prof. R. K. Sharma Felicitation Volume*: 199-220. Delhi: Nag Publishers.

MALINAR, A. 1996. *Rājavidyā: Das königliche Wissen um Herrschaft und Verzicht. Studien zur Bhagavadgītā.* (Purāṇa Research Publications Tübingen, 5.) Wiesbaden: Harassowitz Verlag.

MINOR, R. N. 1982. *Bhagavad-Gītā. An Exegetical Commentary.* New Delhi: Heritage Publishers.

NORMAN, K. R. 1981. A note on attā in the Alagaddūpamasutta. In: *Collected Papers*, II: 200-209. Oxford: The Pali Text Society.

—— 1983. *Pāli Literature. Including the Canonical Literature in Prakrit and Sanskrit of All the Hinayāna Schools of Buddhism.* Wiesbaden: Otto Harrassowitz.

PREBISH, C. 1995. *Historical Dictionary of Buddhism.* Delhi: Sri Satguru Publications

RADHAKRISHNAN, S. (ed. & transl.) 1953. *The Principal Upanishads.* London: George Allen & Unwin Ltd. (Reprint: New Delhi: Harper Collins Publishers India, 1995.)

RAHULA, W. 1959. *What the Buddha Taught.* New York: Grove Press. (Reprint: Oxford: Oneworld Publications, 1998.)

RAMACHANDRA AIYAR, C. V. (transl.) 1988. *Sri Sankara's Gita Bhashya. Sri Sankaracharya's Commentary on the Gita.* Bombay: Bharatiya Vidya Bhavan.

RIVIERE, J. 1979. *La Sainte Upanisad de la Bhagavad Gītā.* Milano: Arche.

SADDHATISSA, H. 1970. *Buddhist Ethics. Essence of Buddhism.* London: George Allen & Unwin Ltd.

SAMPATKUMARAN, M. R. (transl.) 1985. *The Gītābhaṣya of Rāmānuja.* Bombay: Ananthacharya Indological Research Institute.

SARMA, D. S. 1929. One of the sources of the Bhagavad Gitā. *The Journal of Oriental Research* 3: 6-22.

SCHRADER, F. O. 1930. *The Kashmir Recension of the Bhagavadgītā.* Stuttgart: W. Kohlhammer.

SENART, É. (transl.) 1922. *La Bhagavadgītā.* Paris: Éditions Bossard.

SINHA, D. M. 1995. *Bhagavad Gita for Changing Times.* Bombay: Bharatiya Vidya Bhavan.

SPEYER, J. S. 1902. Ein alter Fehler in der Überlieferung der Bhagavadgītā. *Zeitschrift der Deutschen Morgenländischen Gesellschaft* 56: 123-125.

SZCZUREK, P. 2002. Some remarks on the so-called Epic Layer of the Bhagavadgītā. In: M. Brockington (ed.), *Stages and Transition. Temporal and*

Historical Frameworks in Epic and Purāṇic Literature: 55-72. Zagreb: Croatian Academy of Sciences and Arts.

—— 2003. Brahmanirvāṇa versus nirvāṇa (nibbāna). Some remarks on the polemics with Buddhism in the Bhagavadgītā. In: R. Czekalska, H. Marlewicz (eds.), *Cracow Indological Studies* 4-5 (*2nd International Conference on Indian Studies, Proceedings*): 547-575. Cracow: Księgarmia Akademicka.

TELANG, K. N. 1882. *The Bhagavadgītā with the Sanatsugātīya and the Anugītā.* (Sacred Books of the East, 8.) Oxford: The Clarendon Press.

UPADHYAYA, K. N. 1971. *Early Buddhism and the Bhagavadgita.* Delhi: Motilal Banarsidass.

YOGANANDA, P. 1995. *God Talks with Arjuna. The Bhagavad Gītā, Royal Science of God-Realization*, I. Los Angeles: Self-Realization Fellowship.

WATANABE, S. 1997-98. A reconsideration of *prajñā:* From the Upaniṣads to Buddhism. *Indologica Taurinensia* 23-24: 257-270.

WIJESEKERA, O. H. De A. 1994. *Buddhist and Vedic Studies. A Miscellany.* Delhi: Motilal Banarsidass.

ZAEHNER, R. C. 1969. *The Bhagavad-Gītā. With the Commentary Based on the Original Sources.* London: Oxford University Press.

Studies in Indo-Tibetan Buddhist Hermeneutics (6): Validity and Valid Interpretation of Scripture according to Vasubandhu's *Vyākhyāyukti*

P. C. VERHAGEN

In the vast wealth of Buddhist literature, with its enormous quantity of texts and its variety of types of text to match, we find that commentaries constitute a significant portion of the Buddhist scriptures. Either commenting on a basic text proper, or, as is often the case, commenting on another commentary, or supplying some form of survey or synopsis of the contents of a basic text and/or its commentaries, a considerable part of the Buddhist scholastic literature is commentarial in nature.[1] This being the case, one might also expect Buddhist scholastics to have devoted considerable attention to exposés on the theoretical principles or practical methods of the composition of commentaries, in other words, of the act of interpretation or exegesis. In fact, relatively few treatises are devoted specifically to these matters.

In the open-ended *Khuddaka-nikāya* section of the Pāli canon, we find among the later accretions in the Burmese redaction, two works that were intended as manuals for the exegesis of the *Buddhavacana*, namely *Netti-pakaraṇa*[2] and *Peṭakopadesa*.[3] The

[1] Cf. e.g. Schoening 1996; Wilson 1996.

[2] Cf. von Hinüber 1996: 77-80.

two are closely related works – that much is clear – yet the exact relationship between the two – whether one precedes the other chronologically, or if both derive from a common source – has not been definitively established as yet.[4] In a number of recent articles, Stefano Zacchetti has added significantly to the data pertinent to these texts in his investigations of what he calls *Peṭaka* passages in early Chinese translations.[5] Since the publication of the two texts, and since translations of both by Bhikkhu Ñāṇamoli became available to the academic world in the early sixties, very little serious attention has been given to these works. They may certainly be characterized as opaque in certain aspects, they are nonetheless of tremendous intrinsic significance. Compare in this connection the observation by Bond in 1979 that "Of all the works [...] in early Pāli literature, the Netti-Pakaraṇa is probably one of the least read and least understood".[6]

As for the Indian Mahāyāna literature, the only early *śāstra* dealing exclusively with the art and craft of commenting, in so far as I am aware, is the text discussed in this paper: *Vyākhyāyukti* by Vasubandhu.

1. THE *VYĀKHYĀYUKTI* BY VASUBANDHU

The *Vyākhyāyukti* (henceforth VY), i.e. 'Proper Application of Exegesis', is a manual for the interpretation of the *Buddhavacana* i.e. the 'words of the Buddha' and the methods of expounding the doctrine within the conceptual framework of the *Yogācāra* school of Mahāyāna Buddhism.[7] The traditional attribution of VY to the

---

[3] Cf. von Hinüber 1996: 80-82.

[4] Von Hinüber (1996: 81) agrees with and argues for the position taken by Hardy and Alsdorf, who regard *Netti-pakaraṇa* as the older of the two, whereas Ñāṇamoli regards *Peṭakopadesa* as the older.

[5] Zacchetti 2002a; 2002b.

[6] Cf. von Hinüber 1996: 77.

famous author Vasubandhu[8] (4th-5th century CE) appears to be reliable.[9] The text is in prose[10] interspersed by verses, often so-called "verse summaries" (Skt. *saṃgraha-śloka*), a format which seems to be characteristic of the work of Vasubandhu.[11]

The Sanskrit original of VY appears not to have come down to us. A small number of passages have been preserved in the original language, specifically in quotations in later treatises, for instance in the *Mahāyānasūtrālaṃkāra* and Haribhadra's *Ālokā* commentary on *Abhisamayālaṃkāra*.[12] For the entire text we have only a Tibetan translation which is extant in the *Bstan-'gyur* canon under the title *Rnam-par-bśad-pa'i-rigs-pa*[13] and which was produced by the Indian scholars Viśuddhasiṃha and Śākyasiṃha, and the Tibetan translator Rtsaṅs Devendrarakṣita.[14] Approximately the same team of translators was also responsible for the Tibetan translations of two ancillary works to VY.[15]

---

[7] The most important secondary source for this work is Skilling 2000, which offers a fine general investigation of VY.

[8] The colophon of the Indian manuscript, as reflected in the Tibetan translation, states: "The *Vyākhyāyukti*, written by master Vasubandhu, has [now] been completed", *rnam-par-bśad-pa'i-rigs-pa* | *slob-dpon-dbyig-gñen-gyis-mdzad-pa-rdzogs-so* ||, 156r5-156r6.

[9] Cf. e.g. Schmithausen 1987: 262-263, n. 101; Skilling (2000: 297-303, 309-313, 336) supplies arguments for Vasubandhu's authorship of VY and for the identity of "this" Vasubandhu with the Kośakāra.

[10] "*Śāstra* prose", as Skilling (2000: 316) styles it.

[11] Cf. Prapod & Skilling 1999: 14, 20-22; Skilling (2000: 317, 337-338). On the *Saṃgraha-śloka* in general, cf. Mimaki 1980.

[12] Cf. below; also Prapod & Skilling 1999: 16, 20-22; Skilling 2000: 331, 332-333.

[13] Peking *Bstan-'gyur, Mdo-'grel* (*Sems-tsam*) vol. *si*, f. 31v8-156r5, Otani repr. title no. 5562; Sde-dge *Bstan-'gyur, Mdo-'grel* (*Sems-tsam*) vol. *śi*, f. 29r2-134v2, Tohoku catalogue title no. 4061. All references in the present article are to the Peking edition.

[14] *rgya-gar-gyi-mkhan-po-bi-śuddha-siṅha-daṅ-* | *śākya-siṅha-daṅ-* | *zhu-chen-gyi-lo-tsa-ba-bande-rtsaṅs-de-bendra-rakṣi-tas-bsgyur-ciṅ-zhus-te-gtan-la-phab-pa'o*, 156r5.

[15] Cf. Skilling 2000: 329-330.

The first of these is the **Vyākhyāyukti-sūtra-khaṇḍa-śata*, a work consisting of the quotation *in extenso* of the slightly more than one hundred passages from the *Buddhavacana* which VY introduces as examples for various forms and techniques of exegesis.[16] The second is the elaborate *Ṭīkā* commentary by Guṇamati,[17] probably 5th century, who was, one might say, the spiritual grandson of Vasubandhu, being the pupil of Vasubandhu's pupil Guṇaprabha.[18] These works too have been preserved in a Tibetan translation only, the latter occupying no less than an entire volume of the Peking xylograph edition of the *Bstan-'gyur* canon. Moreover, both works are tremendously important for our understanding of VY.

2. FIVE CATEGORIES

The importance of VY in the Indo-Tibetan Mahāyāna scholastic traditions is evident from the numerous citations from and references to it in major Sanskrit as well as Tibetan treatises.[19] One specific verse seems to have been the most frequent quotation from VY in the Sanskrit as well as the Tibetan scholastical literature. It is, for example, often repeated in the extensive commentary literature on *Abhisamayālaṃkāra.*

The verse introduces five categories, or perhaps better characteristic aspects, of scriptural interpretation. The five elements are here set forth as indispensable features of a proper commentary on the Words of the Buddha. It is probably the paradigmatic nature of

---

16 *Rnam-par-bśad-pa'i-rigs-pa'i-mdo-sde'i-dum-bu-brgya*, Peking *Bstan-'gyur*, *Mdo-'grel* (*Sems-tsam*) vol. *si* f. 19r2-31v7, Otani repr. title no. 5561; Derge *Bstan-'gyur*, *Mdo-'grel* (*Sems-tsam*), vol. *śi* f. 17v1-29r2, Tohoku catalogue title no. 4060.

17 *Rnam-par-bśad-pa'i-rigs-pa'i-bśad-pa*, Peking *Bstan-'gyur*, *Mdo-'grel* (*Sems-tsam*) vol. *i* f. 1r1-194r6, Otani repr. title no. 5570; Derge *Bstan-'gyur*, *Mdo-'grel* (*Sems-tsam*) vol. *si* f. 139v1-301r7, Tohoku catalogue title no. 4069.

18 Skilling 2000: 313-314.

19 For more details, cf. Skilling 2000: 330-334 and Verhagen 2005.

this verse which explains its frequent citation throughout Mahāyāna Buddhist literature. As it is cited by Haribhadra in his *Abhisamayālaṃkārālokā* the original Sanskrit of the verse is preserved there:

> *prayojanaṃ sapiṇḍārthaṃ padārthaḥ sānusaṃdhikaḥ* |
> *sacodyaparihāraś ca vācyaḥ sūtrārthavādibhiḥ* ||[20]
>
> | *mdo-don-smra-ba-dag-gis-ni* |
> | *dgos-pa-bsdus-pa'i-don-bcas-daṅ-* |
> | *tshig-don-bcas-daṅ-mtshams-sbyor-bcas* |
> | *brgal-lan-bcas-par-bsñad-par-bya* ||[21]
>
> Those who expound the meaning of a *sūtra* must state [its] intention along with [its] summarized meaning, and the meaning of [its] words along with [its] structure and [possible] objections [to its contents] and [their] rebuttals.

The five basic categories which are introduced here are:

(1) Skt. *prayojana*, Tib. *dgos-pa*
'intention', 'purpose'
(2) Skt. *piṇḍārtha*, Tib. *bsdus-(pa'i-)don*
'summarized meaning [of the *sūtra*]'
(3) Skt. *padārtha*, Tib. *tshig-(gi-)don*
'meaning of the words [of the *sūtra*]'
(4) Skt. *anusaṃdhi*, Tib. *mtshams-sbyor* or *mtshams-sbyar*
'connection [of the various parts of the *sūtra*]'[22]
(5) Skt. *codya-parihāra*, Tib. *brgal-lan*
'objections and [their] rebuttals'

---

[20] *Abhisamayālaṃkārālokā*, ed. Wogihara, p. 15.

[21] VY f. 33v5-33v6; cf. e.g. Cabezón 1992: 237-238, n. 16; Skilling 2000: 318-319; this well-known verse is also quoted in Bu-ston's *Chos-'byuṅ*, transl. Obermiller, vol. I, p. 71. Slightly variant forms can be found also, e.g. in Dharmamitra's *Prasphuṭapadā* commentary on *Abhisamayālaṃkāra*, Peking *Bstan-'gyur Mdo-'grel*, title no. 5194, vol. *ña* f. 4r (cf. Schoening 1992: 224-225 note 34) and Atiśa's *Pañjikā* commentary on his *Bodhipathapradīpa*, Peking *Bstan-'gyur Mdo-'grel* vol. *ki* 278r7-8.

[22] Or 'structure [of the *sūtra*]'.

These five aspects should be represented in a proper commentary:

- The commentator should explicitly indicate the *intention* of the basic text (and, secondarily, occasionally also his own intention in writing the commentary on that scripture).
- He should present his reader with a *summary* or outline of the major points in the basic text.
- He should of course where necessary explain the *meaning of the words* of the text he is providing a commentary on.
- He should make explicit the *connection* between the various sections and topics of the basic text, in other words its *structure*.
- And, finally, the commentator should formulate possible *objections* that could be set forth by opponents and, naturally, provide *rebuttals* to or refutations of these objections. The *pūrvapakṣin* – *siddhāntin* type of discussion is of course a prominent feature of scholastic commentaries in classical Indian culture in general.

It should be mentioned at this point that obviously this set of five categories is at some points reminiscent of the set of so-called *anubandha*s, 'requisites' for the composition of a *śāstra*, which were quite common in contemporaneous Brahmanical as well as Buddhist scholastics. Another possible parallel (or antecedent?) could be seen in the set of so-called *tantrayukti*s, an unsystematized group of didactical categories, also found in a Brahmanical context as early as Caraka and Suśruta. These are also discussed in the paper by Ilona Manevskaia, who was part of the considerable Leiden delegation at the Helsinki conference, so I will not expatiate on them here.

The basic structure of the entire text (or at least by far the major part of the text)[23] follows the fivefold schema of categories introduced in the *śloka* quoted above. The "body" of VY in fact consists of a successive treatment of these five aspects of the composition of a commentary in a Buddhist context.

The first two, "intention" and "summary", are dealt with quite briefly. One might have expected a somewhat more elaborate discussion of "purpose" or "intention", Skt. *prayojana*, as this might be linked to the notion of *abhiprāya* which plays a central role in Buddhist hermeneutics, in particular in connection with the *nītārtha* vs. *neyārtha* opposition. This is not the case, however: Vasubandhu merely introduces four types of "purpose", namely: "proper instruction to the deluded", "bringing the careless properly to accept [the practice]", "proper uplifting of the despondent" and "bringing proper delight to those who are well established [in the practice]".[24] His discussion of the second subject, "summary", is extremely brief as well. In another article on VY, I point out a correspondence between VY's fivefold classification of the rubric "summary" and a fivefold schema for the *artha-pratisaṃvid*s in *Saṃdhinirmocana-sūtra* (Verhagen 2005: 581).

The third section, on "the meaning of the words", is in fact the lengthiest of the five. After an introductory discussion on semantics, distinguishing polysemy and synonymy, it consists for the most part of commentaries on 108 excerpts from the *Buddhavacana* by way of example of the various techniques and devices which are at the commentator's disposal. Skilling has argued that the phraseology (and other indications) in the more than one

[23] Skilling (2000: 318) is of the opinion that the final, fifth *le'u*, "chapter", of the text (i.e. f. 133r4-156r5) does not fall under the fifth category, but is a kind of "appendix".

[24] Tib. *kun-tu-rmoṅs-pa-rnams-la-yaṅ-dag-par-bstan-pa*, *bag-med-pa-rnams-la-yaṅ-dag-par-len-du-gzhug-pa*, *kun-tu-zhum-pa-rnams-la-yaṅ-dag-par-gzeṅ-bstod-pa* and *yaṅ-dag-par-zhugs-pa-rnams-la-yaṅ-dag-par-dga'-bar-bya*.

hundred citations point to an origin in a *Sarvāstivādin* or *Mūla-sarvāstivādin āgama*.[25]

The fourth topic is, again, summarily dealt with. Central to Vasubandhu's discussion here is the distinction between the relationship in general between the various topics in a *sūtra*, and the order in which the successive topics are expounded in the *sūtra*.

The fifth and final section of the work consists primarily of an elaborate treatment of a wide range of specific objections that can be (and quite likely, during the lifetime of the author, actually were) raised by doctrinal opponents, and the various forms of reply that can serve as response to these objections, in this case focusing on objections with regard to the claim of authenticity for the Mahāyāna canon. Arguably the major issue in this section is the question of the validity and authenticity of the Buddha-Word (*Buddha-vacana*). A lengthy discussion is devoted to this topic, in particular the problem of establishing the authenticity of the Mahāyāna canon, here specifically the *vaipulya* class of *sūtras*.[26] A selection of passages from this authenticity debate in the fifth section of VY has been studied by Cabezón (1992).

3. FOUR "MODES" OF EXPLANATION

At the very end of the long section on topic no. 3, Vasubandhu introduces a schema of four "aspects" or perhaps here rather "types" or "modes" (*rnam-pa*) of exegetical procedures:[27]

---

[25] Cf. Skilling 2000: 315-316, 327-328.

[26] A first formulation of the question already at 103v2-104r4. It is repeated at 113r8-113v1, which is followed by the main discussion: 113v2-133r3, i.e. up to the end of chapter (*le'ur-bcad-pa*) four; cf. Cabezón 1992: 239, n. 2.

[27] Lit. 'by means of [the following] four aspects (*rnam-pa*) the meaning of words can be known', *rnam-pa-bzhi-dag-gis-tshig-gi-don-rig-par-bya*, 98r7. Note that this subsection constitutes the beginning of chapter (*le'ur-byas-pa*) no. 3.

(1) Supplying 'synonyms' (Tib. *rnam-grańs*, Skt. **paryāya*; 98r8, 98v2-98v4)
(2) Supplying 'definitions' (Tib. *mtshan-ñid*, Skt. **lakṣaṇa*; 98r8; 98v4-98v6)
(3) Supplying 'etymologies' (Tib. *ńes-pa'i-tshig*, Skt. **niruktivacana*; 98r8; 98v6-98v7)
(4) Supplying classifications or subdivisions (Tib. *rab-tu-dbye-ba*, Skt. **prabheda*?; 98r8-98v1; 98v7-98v8).[28]

In his comments, he briefly characterizes these four as follows:

> Of these [áspects] the synonym is [the supplying of] another term [with the same meaning].
> The definition is [the statement] concerning [the question] with what meaning a specific term occurs.
> The etymology is the statement of the basis (lit. cause) of a term.
> The classification amounts to statements based on subdivisions, such as between [elements] that have form and [elements] that are formless, and between [notions] that can be expounded and [notions] that cannot be expounded.[29]

Vasubandhu then quotes four canonical passages as examples of these four "modes":

> Sometimes the Bhagavat [Buddha] explained merely by [supplying] a synonym, as, for instance, in the *Pratītyasamutpāda-sūtra* [i.e. *Pratītya-samutpādādi-vibhańga-nirdeśa-sūtra*]
>
> "Ignorance with regard to the true nature of this and that, not-seeing, not-realizing, darkness, confusion, not-knowing and blindness; this is what is called *avidyā*."[30]

---

[28] Cf. Bu-ston's *Chos-'byuń* transl. Obermiller, vol. I, p. 72; also Cabezón 1992: 238, n. 16.

[29] *de-la-rnam-grańs-ni-miń-gzhan-yin-no* || *mtshan-ñid-ni-don-gań-la-miń-de-yod-pa'i'o* || *ńes-pa'i-tshig-ni-miń-gi-rgyu-mtshan-brjod-pa'o* || *rab-tu-dbye-ba-ni-brjod-par-bya-ba-de-gzugs-can-dań-* | *gzugs-can-ma-yin-pa-dań-* | *bstan-du-yod-pa-dań-* | *bstan-du-med-pa-la-sogs-pa'i-rnam-par-rab-tu-dbye-bas-so* |, 98r8-98v1; cf. also Bu-ston's *Chos-'byuń* transl. Obermiller, vol. I, p. 72.

Sometimes [the Bhagavat Buddha explained] merely [by supplying] a definition, as, for instance, in that same [*sūtra*]:

> "Name-and-form has perception as its cause. What is name? The four form-less *skandhas*, viz. from *vedanā-skandha* up to and including *vijñāna-skandha*. What is form? Each and every thing which is matter, viz. the four great elements and that which is derived from the four great elements".[31]

Sometimes [the Bhagavat Buddha explained] merely [by supplying] an etymology, as, for instance, in:

> "Because form [arises] from that which is like food and is therefore suited for [the generation of (?)] form, therefore it is called *rūpopādāna-skandha*".[32]

---

[30] *bcom-ldan-'das-kyis-kyaṅ-lan-'ga'-ni-rnam-graṅs-tsam-zhig-bśad-de* | *dper-na-rten-ciṅ-'brel-bar-'byuṅ-ba'i-mdo-las* | *de-daṅ-de-las-yaṅ-dag-pa-ji-lta-ba-bzhin-du-mi-śes-pa-daṅ-* | *mi-mthoṅ-ba-daṅ-* | *mṅon-par-ma-rtogs-pa-daṅ-* | *mun-khuṅ-daṅ-* | *kun-tu-rmoṅs-pa-daṅ-* | *ma-rig-pa-daṅ-* | *mun-pa-gaṅ-yin-pa-'di-ni-ma-rig-pa-zhes-bya'o-zhes-'byuṅ-ba-lta-bu'o*, 98v2-98v4. The Sanskrit original of the quotation, as found in *Pratītyasamutpādādi-vibhaṅga-nirdeśa-sūtra* (ed. Vaidya 117.18-19): *yad atra tatra yathābhūtasyājñānam adarśanam anabhisamayaḥ tamaḥ saṃmohaḥ avidyāndhakāram iyam ucyate 'vidyā* |, cf. Frauwallner 1969: 40; cf. also *Saṃyutta-nikāya* 33.1-55 and the lists of synonyms of *avijjā* in *Dhammasaṅganī* 79,5, 190,19, etc.; Vetter 2000: 283.

[31] *kha-cig-las-ni-mtshan-ñid-tsam-zhig-ste* | *dper-na-de-ñid-las-rnam-par-śes-pa'i-rkyen-gyis-miṅ-daṅ-gzugs-zhes-bya-ba-la* | *miṅ-gaṅ-zhe-na* | *gzugs-can- ma-yin-pa'i-phuṅ-po-bzhi-dag-ste* | *tshor-ba'i-phuṅ-po-nas-rnam-par-śes-pa'i-phuṅ-po'i-bar-du'o* || *gzugs-gaṅ-zhe-na* | *gzugs-gaṅ-ci-yaṅ-ruṅ-ste* | *de-thams-cad-'byuṅ-ba-chen-po-bzhi-dag-daṅ-* | *'byuṅ-ba-chen-po-bzhi-dag-rgyur-byas-pa-ste-zhes-'byuṅ-ba-lta-bu'o*, 98v4-98v6; cf. *Pratītyasamutpādādi-vibhaṅga-nirdeśa-sūtra* (ed. Vaidya, 117.24-26): *vijñāna-pratyayaṃ nāma-rūpam iti nāma katamat ? catvāra arūpiṇaḥ skandhāḥ* | *katame catvāraḥ ? vedanā-skandhaḥ saṃjñā-skandhaḥ saṃskāra-skandhaḥ vijñāna-skandhaḥ* | *rūpaṃ katamat ? yat kiṃcid rūpam, sarvaṃ tac catvāri mahābhūtāni* | *catvāri ca mahābhūtāny upādāya itīdaṃ ca nāma* [...]; cf. Frauwallner 1969: 41; Vetter 2000: 21-22.

[32] *kha-cig-las-ni-ṅes-pa'i-tshig-tsam-zhig-ste* | *dper-na-bza'-ba-lta-bu-las-gzugs-śiṅ-gzugs-su-ruṅ-bas-na-de'i-phyir-gzugs-ñe-bar-len-pa'i-phuṅ-po-zhes-bya'o-zhes-'byuṅ-ba-lta-bu'o*, 98v6-98v7. This can evidently not be identified as the well-known *nirukti* we find in *Abhidharmakośa-bhāṣya* sub 1.13 (ed. Pradhan, p. 6, 11): *uktaṃ bhagavatā* | *rūpyate rūpyata iti bhikṣavas tasmād rūpopādāna-skandha ity ucyate*? Cf. also *Abhidharmakośa-bhāṣya* sub 7.40 (ed. Pradhan, p. 419, 19-20): *nirvacanaṃ niruktiḥ* | *yathā rūpyate tasmād rūpam ity evamādi*, cf. Ruegg 1998: 137, n. 48. For the term *rūpa*, cf. Vetter 2000: 20-22; for the term *upādānakkhandha/upādānaskandha*, cf. Vetter 2000: 73-83.

> Sometimes [the Bhagavat Buddha explained] merely [by supplying] a classification, as, for instance, in:
>
> > "The impulses have ignorance as their cause. What are the impulses? The impulses are threefold: body-impulses, speech-impulses and mind-impulses. Perception has the impulses as its cause. What is perception? The six groups of perception, viz. [...]".[33]

The examples which Vasubandhu adduces for these four modes of exegesis are quite straightforward *per se*. The phenomenon of explaining a concept by supplying synonymous terms (as in 1), or by giving a definition (as in 2) or an etymology (as in 3), or, finally, by stating classifications applying to that concept (as in 4), can be found throughout Indian Buddhist literature. What *is* striking about these examples, however, is the fact that at least three – and most probably all four – stem from a *sūtra* (the *Pratītyasamutpādādi-vibhaṅga-nirdeśa-sūtra* to be precise), in other words from the Buddha-Word proper, *not* from a commentary. At this point it becomes clear that Vasubandhu is not only speaking about exegetical or hermeneutical techniques and devices, but also about more general didactical and expository principles. So the scope of his work (at least here) extends beyond the commentarial literature to include the *Buddhavacana* proper as well.

[33] *kha-cig-las-ni-rab-tu-dbye-ba-tsam-zhig-ste* | *dper-na-ma-rig-pa'i-rkyen-gyis-'du-byed-rnams-zhes-bya-ba-la* | *'du-byed-rnams-gaṅ-zhe-na* | *'du-byed-rnams-ni-gsum-ste* | *lus-kyi-'du-byed-daṅ-* | *ṅag-gi-'du-byed-daṅ-* | *yid-kyi-'du-byed-rnams-so* || *'du-byed-kyi-rkyen-gyis-rnam-pa* [emend: *par*] *-śes-pa-zhes-bya-ba-la* | *rnam-par-śes-pa-gaṅ-zhe-na* | *rnam-par-śes-pa'i-tshogs-drug-rnams-te-zhes-'byuṅ-ba-lta-bu'o*, 98v7-98v8; Sanskrit original in *Pratītyasamutpādādi-vibhaṅga-nirdeśa-sūtra* (ed. Vaidya, 117.20-22): *avidyā-pratyayāḥ* [add: *saṃskārā iti* |] *saṃskārāḥ katame ? trayaḥ saṃskārāḥ – kāya-saṃskārāḥ, vāk-saṃskārāḥ, manaḥ-saṃskārā iti* | *saṃskāra-pratyayaṃ vijñānam iti vijñānaṃ katamat ? ṣaḍ vijñāna-kāyāḥ* [...].

4. THREE *PRAMĀṆAS*

In the course of the fifth, final chapter of VY, Vasubandhu *inter alia* discusses a method for establishing the validity of scripture, namely by means of testing its compatibility with three 'valid means of cognition' (Skt. *pramāṇa*, Tib. *tshad-ma*; 102v6-104r4).

Vasubandhu identifies these three types of *pramāṇa* at the beginning of this passage as 'sensory perception' (Skt. *pratyakṣa*), 'inference' (Skt. *anumāna*) and 'authoritative statement' (probably Skt. *āptavāda*, Tib. *yid-ches-pa'i-gsuṅ*).[34] Subsequently he briefly discusses, on the basis of examples, the criteria of compatibility with *pratyakṣa* (102v7-102v8), with *anumāna* (102v8-103r7) and with *āptavāda* (103r8-104r4). The full Tibetan text of this passage is added in an appendix to this article.

This passage would seem to be of some significance for the history of Buddhist epistemology, in so far as it offers an attestation of the application of three *pramāṇas* in pre-Dignāga Buddhist epistemology. In the few Buddhist treatises addressing epistemological issues which antedate Dignāga (ca. 480-540 CE) we have the treatment of four *pramāṇas* in the *Upāya-hṛdaya*.[35] They are *de facto* identical to those prevalent in the *Nyāya* tradition, namely "sensory perception", "inference", "analogy" and "scripture". The *Upāya-hṛdaya* only being available in a Chinese translation, the last term has been reconstructed as **āpta-śruti*, but in fact literally reads "in accordance with the *sūtra*-book" and could – as Professors Vetter and Katsura have suggested in personal communications – probably better be regarded as reflecting *āptāgama*, or just *āgama*.

The equally early *Bodhisattvabhūmi*, in its fourth chapter (*Tattvārthapaṭala*), also speaks of a set of three *pramāṇas* in its

---

[34] *mdor-na-rigs-pa-ni-'dir-tshad-ma-rnam-pa-gsum-po-mṅon-sum-daṅ-rjes-su-dpag-pa-daṅ-yid-ches-pa'i-gsuṅ-ṅo*, 102v6-102v7.

[35] Viz. *pratyakṣa*, *anumāna*, *upamāna* and *āptaśruti*, cf. Nagasaki 1991: 221; cf. also Hattori 1968: 78, n. 1.12.

discussion of *tattvārtha* which is 'established by logical reasoning' (*yuktiprasiddha*), *scil. pratyakṣa*, *anumāna* and *āptāgama*.[36] And, most significantly, in the *Saṃdhinirmocana-sūtra* also we find the precise same set of three *pramāṇas*,[37] as we have learnt from the paper by Prof. Chizuko Yoshimizu presented during the Helsinki conference.

The present passage in VY may therefore constitute another, intermediate, stage in the transition from the system of four *pramāṇas* of the *Nyāya* logicians (which were of such tremendous formative influence on early Buddhist epistemology)[38] to the classical Buddhist schema of two *pramāṇas* only, i.e. *pratyakṣa* and *anumāna*, which was prevalent from Dignāga onwards.[39] It is of course no surprise to find elements of logic and epistemology in VY, as Vasubandhu is known to have been an active scholar in the budding field of Buddhist epistemology, although only fragments of his works in this field remain.[40]

Already in the late 1920s, Tucci suggested that the application of a threefold set of *pramāṇas* may have been a peculiarity of the *Yogācāra* tradition.[41] The present attestation as well as the above mentioned attestations in *Saṃdhinirmocana-sūtra* and *Yogācāra-bhūmi* would fit in with this view as well.

---

[36] Ed. Dutt, 25.17-21: *yuktiprasiddhatattvaṃ katamam | satāṃ yuktārtha-paṇḍitānāṃ vicakṣaṇānāṃ tārkikāṇāṃ mīmāṃsakānāṃ tarkaparyāpannāyāṃ bhūmau sthitānāṃ svayaṃ prātibhānikyāṃ pārthagjanikyāṃ mīmāṃsānu-caritāyāṃ pratyakṣam anumānam āptāgamaṃ pramāṇaṃ niścitya suvidita-suviniścitajñānagocarajñeyaṃ vastūpapattisādhanayuktyā prasādhitaṃ vyava-sthāpitam | idam ucyate yuktiprasiddhaṃ tattvam*; transl. Frauwallner (1969: 271-272).

[37] Ed. Lamotte, p. 157: *de-ltar-'thad-pa'i-sgrub-pa'i-rigs-pa-de-ni-mṅon-sum-gyi-tshad-ma-daṅ- | rjes-su-dpag-pa'i-tshad-ma-daṅ- | yid-ches-pa'i-luṅ-gi-tshad-mas-mtshan-ñid-lṅa-po-dag-gis-yoṅs-su-dag-pa-yin-no.*

[38] Cf. e.g. van Bijlert 1989: 1-44.

[39] Cf. e.g. Hattori 1968: 78-79, n. 1.12.

[40] Cf. e.g. Stcherbatsky 1930: 29-31; van Bijlert 1989: 45-54.

[41] Cf. Tucci 1929: xvii, n. 1.

It is tempting also to speculate whether this threefold schema of *pramāṇas* in VY may be in some way an antecedent to the 'threefold analysis' (*dpyad-pa-gsum*) which became current in later Tibetan scholastics. The *dpyad-pa-gsum* is a set of three criteria for establishing the validity of a particular scripture or scriptural passage.[42]

This *dpyad-pa-gsum* analysis is founded on the distinction between three epistemological domains, namely (1) that which is 'perceptible' (Skt. *pratyakṣa*, Tib. *mthoṅ-ba-mṅon-'gyur*), (2) that which is 'imperceptible' (Skt. *parokṣa*, Tib. *lkog-'gyur*) and (3) that which is 'completely imperceptible' (Skt. *atyanta-parokṣa*, Tib. *śin-tu-lkog-'gyur*). The first domain pertains to things such as material form, which are immediately accessible to perception by means of the senses. The second consists of items that can be perceived only on the basis of inference, specifically the type of inference which is technically termed *vastu-bala-pravṛtta*, 'functioning by the force of reality', for instance notions such as the four Noble Truths and the non-substantiality of the self. The third domain, however, contains the type of things that cannot be perceived by the senses or by inference which proceeds on the basis of such direct perception, for instance the various supramundane heavens, or the precise workings of the law of karmic retribution, which are, one might say, "beyond the limits of ordinary rationality".[43]

These three domains are then identified as the objects of cognition for three types of 'means of valid cognition' (*pramāṇa*) respectively: the first is the object of 'sensory perception' (*pratyakṣa*), the second the object of 'inference' (*anumāna*), and the third is the object of 'authoritative statement' (*āptavāda*, also termed 'inference [based on] authoritative [statement], *yid-ches-rjes-dpag*, or 'the transmitted scripture as valid means of cognition' *luṅ-(gi-)*

[42] Cf. e.g. Ruegg 1969: 229, n. 2; Tillemans 1986; 1990: 27-29; 1999: 30.

[43] Tillemans 1990: 26 (= 1999: 29); on these matters, cf. also Cabezón 1994: 56, 97-108; Dreyfus 1997: 293-296.

tshad-ma). Within their respective domains these means of cognition are invoked as the standard to test the validity of a scriptural statement, and therefore the *dpyad-pa-gsum* amount to criteria of compatibility with perception, inference and authoritative statement.

The purpose for which the *dpyad-pa-gsum* are applied is very similar to that of the present application in VY. Although the Tibetan – particularly *Dge-lugs-pa* – scholastics themselves usually traced the schema of the *dpyad-pa-gsum* to Dharmakīrti, specifically *Pramāṇavārttika* I.215-217,[44] it seems conceivable that the present passage in VY may have played a role in the development of the *dpyad-pa-gsum* schema as well. A second argument for hypothesizing this connection – in addition to the functional similarity mentioned above – would be the fact that in the *dpyad-pa-gsum* the three criteria appear to function on a par, precisely as in the three *pramāṇa* schema of VY, whereas Dharmakīrti's (and Dignāga's) analysis regards the third criterion (scriptural authority) not as a *pramāṇa* proper, but as another form of inference, the second *pramāṇa*.[45] Note in this connection also the observations by Dharmakīrti on the reason for specifying 'authoritative statement' separately from 'inference', namely primarily 'difference of scope' (Skt. *viṣayabheda*).[46]

I shall leave it to others better qualified in the field of Buddhist logic to further evaluate the intricacies of this particular passage and its historical implications.

5. CONCLUDING OBSERVATIONS

In his recent study on this text, Peter Skilling characterized Vasubandhu's VY as "one of the most important Buddhist works re-

---

[44] Cf. Tillemans 1986 (= 1990: 24-29 = 1999: 27-30); 1999: 37-51.

[45] Cf. e.g. Vetter 1984: 16-17; Tillemans 1990: 28-29 (= 1999: 30).

[46] *Pramāṇavārttika* IV.102-104; cf. Tillemans 2000: 143-147.

maining to be studied", concluding that, therefore, it "can no longer be safely ignored".[47] A pressing desideratum in this case is the preparation of critical editions of VY proper, of the *Sūtra-khaṇḍa-śata* appendix and of Guṇamati's *Ṭīkā* commentary. Fortunately, Skilling is acquitting himself of this onerous yet noble task.[48]

The present paper has offered a mere few glimpses of the wealth of information awaiting exploration in the VY literature. As I am investigating the linguistic principles underlying the hermeneutics of Indo-Tibetan Buddhism, VY has been one of the focal points of my research for some time now. The intrinsic importance of VY is enormous on several counts. Let me just highlight two factors here. From the point of view of my own research its prime importance lies in the fact that it informs us about the methodology of didactics and scriptural interpretation prevalent in 4th- to 5th-century Buddhist scholasticism. Secondly, from the standpoint of Buddhist studies in general, VY is unique in the sense that it documents an extensive debate on the authenticity of the *Mahāyāna* canon between anonymous *Śrāvaka* opponents and our author, who assumes the doctrinal position of the *Yogācāra Vijñānavāda*. This allows us insight into the actual argumentation set forth in the exchanges between the adherents of *Nikāya* Buddhism and the early exponents of the *Yogācāra* tradition.

We have, in the above, firstly encountered specifications and classifications of hermeneutical and expository techniques and devices, primarily in the five hermeneutical "categories" which form the backbone of the entire treatise of VY, but also in the distinction of a range of commentarial and explanatory techniques. Secondly, we have found an attestation of a schema of three means of valid

---

[47] Skilling 2000: 336.

[48] Cf. Skilling 2000: 336, n. 120. The edition by Lee Jong-cheol, *The Tibetan Text of the Vyākhyāyukti* (Tokyo 2001), appears not to be a critical edition, although I have not been able to consult the publication myself; nor have I yet seen the same author's study (in Japanese) entitled *A study of Vasubandhu – with Special Reference to the Vyākhyāyukti*, Tokyo 2001.

cognition, which might either point to a transitory phase in the proto-history of Buddhist epistemology, later leading to the classical set of two, or might be a trait characteristic of *Yogācāra* scholasticism.

Summing up, we can affirm that a preliminary exploration of the veritable gold-mine which is Vasubandhu's *Vyākhyāyukti* already supplies ample proof of considerable sophistication in the handling of, and the theoretical infrastructure for, scriptural interpretation and manipulation, precisely as one would expect in the highly developed scholastic traditions of early *Mahāyāna* Buddhism and – taking a wider perspective – equally as one would expect in the rich literary and scholastic traditions of classical India.[49]

REFERENCES

BIJLERT, V. A. van 1989. *Epistemology and Spiritual Authority. The Development of Epistemology and Logic in the Old Nyāya and the Buddhist School of Epistemology with an Annotated Translation of Dharmakīrti's Pramāṇavārttika II (Pramāṇasiddhi) vv. 1-7.* (Wiener Studien zur Tibetologie und Buddhismuskunde, 20.) Wien: Arbeitskreis für Tibetische und Buddhistische Studien.

CABEZÓN, J. I. 1992. Vasubandhu's *Vyākhyāyukti* on the Authenticity of the Mahāyāna Scriptures. In: J. Timm (ed.), *Texts and Contexts: Traditional Hermeneutics in South Asia*: 221-243. Albany: State University of New York Press.

—— 1994. *Buddhism and Language. A Study of Indo-Tibetan Scholasticism.* (SUNY Series, Toward a Comparative Philosophy of Religions.) Albany: State University of New York Press.

DREYFUS, G. B. J. 1997. *Recognizing Reality. Dharmakīrti's Philosophy and Its Tibetan Interpretations.* (SUNY Series in Buddhist Studies.) Albany: State University of New York Press.

[49] This research was made possible by a subsidy of the Netherlands Organisation for Scientific Research (Nederlandse Organisatie voor Wetenschappelijk Onderzoek, NWO). Cordial thanks are due to Professor T. Vetter (Leiden University, emeritus) for carefully reading draft versions of this article and providing a number of valuable suggestions for improvement.

DUTT, N. (ed.) 1966. *Bodhisattvabhūmi.* (Tibetan Sanskrit Works Series, 7.) Patna: K.P. Jayaswal Research Institute.

FRAUWALLNER, E. 1969. *Die Philosophie des Buddhismus.* 3. durchgesehene Auflage. (Philosophische Studientexte, Texte der indischen Philosophie, 2.) Berlin: Akademie-Verlag.

HATTORI, M. 1968. *Dignāga, On Perception.* Being the Pratyakṣapariccheda of Dignāga's Pramāṇasamuccaya from the Sanskrit fragments and the Tibetan versions translated and annotated. (Harvard Oriental Series, 47.) Cambridge, Mass: Harvard University Press.

HINÜBER, O. von 1996. *A Handbook of Pāli Literature.* (Indian Philology and South Asian Studies, 2.) Berlin: De Gruyter.

LAMOTTE, E. 1935. *Saṃdhinirmocanasūtra, L'explication des mystères.* Texte tibétain édité et traduit. Louvain: Université de Louvain, Bureau du Recueil.

MIMAKI, K. 1980. Sur le rôle de l'*antaraśloka* ou du *saṃgrahaśloka*. In: *Indianisme et bouddhisme. Mélanges offerts à Mgr. Étienne Lamotte* (Publications de L'Institut Orientaliste de Louvain): 233-244. Louvain-la-Neuve: L'Institut Orientaliste.

NAGASAKI, H. 1991. Perception in pre-Dignāga Buddhist texts. In: E. Steinkellner (ed.), *Studies in the Buddhist Epistemological Tradition. Proceedings of the Second International Dharmakīrti Conference, Vienna, June 11-16, 1989* (Österreichische Akademie der Wissenschaften, Philosophisch-historische Klasse, Denkschriften, 222; Beiträge zur Kultur- und Geistesgeschichte Asiens, 8): 221-225. Wien: Verlag der Österreichische Akademie der Wissenschaften.

OBERMILLER, E. (transl.) 1931-32. *History of Buddhism (Chos ḥbyung) by Buston*, I-II. Heidelberg: Institut für Buddhismus-Kunde.

PRADHAN, P. (ed.) 1975. *Abhidharmakośabhāṣyam of Vasubandhu.* Rev. 2nd edition. (Tibetan Sanskrit Works Series, 8.) Patna: K.P. Jaysaswal Research Institute. [First edition: Patna 1967.]

PRAPOD, A. & P. SKILLING 1999. Vasubandhu on travel and seclusion. *Manusya. Journal of Humanities* (Chulalongorn University) 2.1: 13-24.

RUEGG, D. S. (1998). Sanskrit-Tibetan and Tibetan-Sanskrit dictionaries and some problems in Indo-Tibetan philosophical lexicography. In: B. Oguibénine (ed.), *Lexicography in the Indian and Buddhist Cultural Field. Proceedings of the Conference at the University of Strasbourg 25 to 27 April 1996*: 115-142. München: Kommission für Zentralasiatische Studien, Bayerische Akademie der Wissenschaften.

SCHMITHAUSEN, L. 1987. *Ālayavijñāna. On the Origin and the Early Development of a Central Concept in the Yogācāra Philosophy*, I: *Text*; II: *Notes, Bibliography and Indices.* (Studia Philologica Buddhica,

Monograph Series 4a-b.) Tokyo: The International Institute for Buddhist Studies.

SCHOENING, J. D. 1996. *Sūtra* commentaries in Tibetan translation. In: J. I. Cabezón & R. R. Jackson (eds.), *Tibetan Literature: Studies in Genre*: 111-124. Ithaca: Snow Lion.

SKILLING, P. 2000. Vasubandhu and the *Vyākhyāyukti*. *Journal of the International Association of Buddhist Studies* 23.2: 297-350.

STCHERBATSKY, F. I. 1930. *Buddhist Logic*, I-II. Leningrad: Izdatel'stvo Akademii Nauk SSSR. (Reprint: New York: Dover Publications, 1962.)

TILLEMANS, T. J. F. 1986. Dharmakīrti, Āryadeva and Dharmapāla on scriptural authority. *Tetsugaku* (Hiroshima) 38: 31-47.

—— 1990. *Materials for the Study of Āryadeva, Dharmapāla and Candrakīrti. The Catuḥśataka of Āryadeva, Chapters XII and XIII, with the Commentaries of Dharmapāla and Candrakīrti.* Introduction, Translation, Sanskrit, Tibetan and Chinese texts, Notes, I. (Wiener Studien zur Tibetologie und Buddhismuskunde, 24.1.) Wien: Arbeitskreis für Tibetische und Buddhistische Studien.

—— 1999. *Scripture, Logic, Language. Essays on Dharmakīrti and his Tibetan Successors.* (Studies in Indian and Tibetan Buddhism.) Boston: Wisdom Publications.

TUCCI, G. 1929. *Pre-Diṅnāga Buddhist Texts on Logic from Chinese Sources.* (Gaekwad Oriental Series, 49.) Baroda: M.S. University of Baroda.

VAIDYA, P. L. 1961. *Mahāyāna-sūtra-samgraha*, I. (Buddhist Sanskrit Texts, 17.) Darbhanga: Mithila Institute of Post-Graduate Studies in Sanskrit Learning.

VERHAGEN, P. 2005. Studies in Indo-Tibetan Buddhist Hermeneutics (4): The *Vyākhyāyukti* by Vasubandhu. *Journal Asiatique* 293.2: 559-602.

VETTER, T. E. 1984. *Der Buddha und seine Lehre in Dharmakīrti's Pramāṇavārttika – Der Abschnitt über den Buddha und die vier edlen Wahrheiten im Pramāṇasiddhi-Kapitel.* (Studien zur Tibetologie und Buddhismuskunde, 12.) Wien: Arbeitskreis für Tibetische und Buddhistische Studien.

—— 2000. *The "Khandha Passages" in the Vinayapiṭaka and the Four Main Nikāyas.* (Österreichische Akademie der Wissenschaften, Philosophisch-Historische Klasse, Sitzungsberichte, Bd. 682; Veröffentlichungen zu den Sprachen und Kulturen Südasiens, H. 33.) Wien: Österreichische Akademie der Wissenschaften.

WILSON, J. B. 1996. Tibetan commentaries on Indian *Śāstras*. In: J. I. Cabezón & R. R. Jackson (eds.), *Tibetan Literature: Studies in Genre*: 125-137. Ithaca: Snow Lion.

WOGIHARA, U. (ed.) 1934. *Abhisamayālaṃkārāloka Prajñāpāramitāvyākhyā,* Tokyo: Toyo Bunko.

ZACCHETTI, S. 2002a. Some remarks on the "*Peṭaka* passages" in the *Da zhidu lun* and their relation to the Pāli *Peṭakopadesa. Annual Report of the International Research Institute for Advanced Buddhology at Soka University* 2001: 67-85. Tokyo: International Research Institute for Advanced Buddhology at Soka University.

—— 2002b. An early Chinese translation corresponding to Chapter 6 of the *Peṭakopadesa* – An Shigao's *Yin chi ru jing* T 603 and its Indian original: A preliminary survey. *Bulletin of the School of Oriental and African Studies* 65.1: 74-98.

APPENDIX:

Vyākhyāyukti* on testing scriptural validity by means of three *pramāṇas

(text according to Peking *Bstan-'gyur* xylograph)

5. Sub main topic no. 5 'objections and rebuttals' (*brgal-lan*; 100v3-156r5)

5.2. Sub second type of objection, scil. 'objections regarding content' (*don-la-brgal-ba*; 101r5-104r4)

5.2.2. Second subtype of *don-la-brgal-ba*, scil. 'objections involving incompatibilities with logical reasoning' (*rigs-pa-daṅ-'gal-bar-brgal-ba*; 101v5-104r4):

| *rigs-pa-daṅ-'gal-bar-brgal-pa-ni-dper-na-gzugs-gaṅ-yin-pa-ci-yaṅ-ruṅ-ba-thams-cad-'byuṅ-ba-chen-* [101v6:] *po* [?] *-bzhi-dag-daṅ-'byuṅ-ba-chen-po-bzhi-dag-rgyur-byas-pa'o-zhes-bya-ba-la-ci-'di-rdzas-kyi-dbaṅ-du-mdzad-de-gsuṅs-sam-'on-te-goṅ-bu-'am-'on-te-rigs-las-śe-na* |

de-las-cir-'gyur |

gal-te-rdzas-las-yin- [101v7:] *na-ni-'byuṅ-ba-daṅ-'byuṅ-ba-las-gyur-pa-rnams-kyi-so-so'i-mtshan-ñid-med-par-thal-bar-'gyur-te* | *thams-cad-kyaṅ-mtshan-ñid-thams-cad-du-gyur-ba'i-phyir-daṅ-* | *dbaṅ-po-thams-cad-kyis-'dzin-par-* [101v8:] *thal-bar-'gyur-ro* |

'on-te-goṅ-bu-las-yin-na-gzugs-'dus-pa-thams-cad-la-'byuṅ-ba-bzi-char [?] *-dmigs-par-thal-bar-'gyur-na-'od-dag-la-yaṅ-sra-ba-mi-dmigs-la* [?] *-chu-la-yaṅ-ma-yin-no* |

[102r1:] | *ñi-ma'i-'od-la-yaṅ-gśer-ba-med-la-zla-ba'i-'od-la-yaṅ-tsha-ba-med-do* |

| *nor-bu'i-'od-la-gñis-ka-med-ciṅ-rdo-ba-la-sogs-pa-dag-la-yaṅ-med-do* |

| *brtan-pa-dag-la-zhiṅ-g'yo-ba-med-do* |

| [102r2:] *de-rnams-dmigs-pa-la-bgegs-byed-pa-ni-'ga'-yaṅ-med-do* |

| *ji-ltar-med-de* | *'byuṅ-ba-gzhan-śas-che-bas-'byuṅ-ba-gzhan-zil-gyis-gnon-na-mi-dmigs-te* |
dper-na-skyur-ba'i-ros-chu-lta-bu-daṅ- |
ñi-ma'i-'od-kyis- [102r3:] *zla-ba'i-'od-lta-bu'o-zhe-na* |
yod-par-rab-tu-grub-na-ni-'di-śes-par-yaṅ-nus-na-yod-par-rab-tu-grub-pa-ma-yin-te |
thams-cad-la-kha-dog-la-sogs-pa'i-bye-brag-thams-cad-yod-par-thal-bar-gyur-na-mi-ruṅ-bas-so |

| [102r4:] *'od-la-sogs-pa-gaṅ-la-yaṅ-sra-ba-la-sogs-pa-ñid-yod-par-rab-tu-grub-pa-ma-yin-na* |
de-dag-mi-dmigs-pa-ni-med-pa'i-phyir-ma-yin-gyi-zil-gyis-non-pa'i-phyir-ro-zhes-bya-ba-'di-ji-ltar-śes-par-bya |
chu-skyur-ba- [102r5:] *btab* [?] *-kyaṅ-de'i-ro-ni-dmigs-pa-kho-na-yin-te* | *'dzin-pa-tha-dad-pa'i-phyir-ro* |

| *'o-na* [or: *'on*?] *-ni-chu-daṅ-rdo-la-sogs-pa-rnams-la-yaṅ-rkyen-gyis-khyad-par-daṅ-phrad-pas-mtshan-ñid-ltas-pa'i-phyir-sra-ba-ñid-daṅ-* | *gśer-ba-ñid-* [102r6:] *daṅ-* | *tsha-ba-ñid-dag-dmigs-pa-yin-te* | *sa'i-dri-dag-bzhin-no-zhe-na* |
mtshan-ñid-ltas-pa'i-phyir-yin-gyi-skyes-pa'i-phyir-ma-yin-pa-'di-ji-ltar-śes-par-bya |
de-lta-na-ni-ha-caṅ-thal-ches-par-'gyur-te |
reg-bya- [102r7:] *gzhan-bzhin-du-gzugs-daṅ-dri-daṅ-ro-gzhan-rnams-daṅ-* |
sgra-yaṅ-rkyen-rñed-pas-dmigs-pa'i-sña-rol-nas-yod-pa-ñid-du-thal-ba'i-phyir-ro |

| *mdo-sde-gzhan-las-kyaṅ-dge-sloṅ-bsam-gtan-byed-pa-yin-zhiṅ-rdzu-* [102r8:] *'phrul-daṅ-ldan-pa-yin-la* | *sems-la-dbaṅ-thob-pa-yin-na-śiṅ-gi-sdoṅ-po-'di-la-khams-gaṅ-daṅ-gaṅ-du-mos-pa-de-yaṅ-de-la-de-bzhin-du-'gyur-te-gzhan-du-ni-ma-yin-no* |

| *de-ci'i-phyir-zhe-na* | *śiṅ-gi-sdoṅ-po-'di-la-* [102v1:] *khams-sna-tshogs-yod-pas-so-zhes-gsuṅs-pa'o* |

| *de-ltar-na-rkyen-gyi-khyad-par-daṅ-phrad-na-sra-ba-ñid-la-sogs-pa-dag-raṅ-raṅ-gi-khams-las-'byuṅ-bar-'gyur-ro* |

| *khams-dag-dum-bu-daġ-kyaṅ-ma-yin-te* | *cha-śas-* [102v2:] *gcig-la-yaṅ-ji-ltar-mos-pa-bzhin-du-yoṅs-su-'gyur-ba'i-phyir – daṅ-* | *de-la-yaṅ-dum-bu-mtha'-yas-pa-mi-srid-pa'i-phyir-ro* |

| *sa'i-dri-ni-sṅa-nas-kyaṅ-dmigs-pa-ñid-yin-na-chus-gtor-na-rtas* [?] *-par-'gyur-par-śes-* [102v3:] *par-nus-so* |

| *gaṅ-zhig-rkyen-daṅ-phrad-pas-rtas-par-gyur-par-śes-par-ruṅ-ba-sra-ba-la-sogs-pa-rnams-ni-rkyen-med-na-chu-la-sogs-pa-rnams-la-de-ltar-yod-par-mi-dmigs-so* |

| *de-bas-na-goṅ-bur-bśad-pa-la-* [102v4:] *skyon-gyi-gnas-skabs-de-ñid-yin-no* |

| *'on-te-rigs-las-so-zhe-na* |
rgyur-byas-pa'i-gzugs-thams-cad-'byuṅ-ba-chen-po-bzhi-dag-rgyur-byas-pa-ma-yin-par-'gyur-te |
'dus-pa-kha-cig-las-'byuṅ-ba-chen-po-kha- [102v5:] *cig-yod-par-khas-ma-blaṅs-pa'i-phyir-ro* |

| *de-ltar-na-ni-mdo-sde-daṅ-'gal-te-skye-mched-so-so-ba'i-mdo-sde-las-skye-mched-dgu-po-rnams-ni-re-re-yaṅ-'byuṅ-ba-chen-po-bzhi-dag-rgyur-byas-pa'o-zhes-bśad-pa'i-phyir-daṅ-* |
[102v6:] *lag-pa-rdo-ba-pa-lta-bu-las-kyaṅ-mig-gi-śa'i-goṅ-bu-la-'byuṅ-ba-chen-po-bzhi-dag-yod-par-bśad-pa'i-phyir-ro* |

| *mdor-na-rigs-pa-ni-'dir-tshad-ma-rnam-pa-gsum-po-mṅon-sum-daṅ-rjes-su-dpag-pa-daṅ-yid-ches-pa'i-* [102v7:] *gsuṅ-ṅo-* |

| *de-dag-las-gaṅ-yaṅ-ruṅ-ba-zhig-daṅ-'gal-bar-brgal-ba-yaṅ-rig* [sic; em.: *rigs*] *-pa-daṅ-'gal-bar-brgal-ba-yin-par-rig-par-bya'o* |

| *dper-na-dge-sloṅ-dag-gzugs-'das-pa-yod-do* [or: *yoṅ-ṅo*] |
| *gzugs-ma-'oṅs-* [102v8:] *pa-yod-do* |
| *'das-pa-daṅ-* | *zad-pa-daṅ-* | *'gags-pa-daṅ-* | *bral-ba-daṅ-* | *yoṅs-su-gyur-ba-gaṅ-yin-pa-de-yod-do* [or: *yoṅ-ṅo*] *-zhes-bya-ba-ni-mṅon-sum-daṅ-'gal-ba-yin-no* |

| *'di-ltar-'das-pa-daṅ-ma-'oṅs-pa-ni-med-pa-* [103r1:] *ñid-yin-par-mṅon-sum-yin-te* | *dper-na-ru-sbal-gyi-spu-bzhin-no* |

| *'das-pa'aṅ-yin-la-yod-pa'aṅ-yin-zhes-bya-ba-'di-sṅa-phyi-'gal-ba-yaṅ-yin-te* |

gal-te-yod-na-ji-ltar-'das- [103r2:] *pa-yin* | *ma-'oṅs-pa-yaṅ-de-daṅ-'dra'o* |

| *mdo-sde-gzhan-las-*

mig-skye-ba-na-gaṅ-nas-kyaṅ-mi-'oṅ-la | *'gag-pa-na-gaṅ-du-yaṅ-sogs-par-mi-'gro'o* |

| *dge-sloṅ-dag-de-ltar-na-mig-gi-ma-skyes-pa-las-skye-zhiṅ-skyes-* [103r3:] *nas-kyaṅ-'jig-go-*

zhes-gsuṅs-pas-de-daṅ-'dir-'gal-ba-yin-no |

| *gzugs-rnams-kyi-ṅes-par-'byuṅ-ba-ni-gzugs-med-pa'o-zhes-bya-ba-ni-rjes-su-dpag-pa-daṅ-'gal-ba-yin-te* |

tshor-ba-la-sogs-pa- [103r4:] *rnams-ni-gzugs-la-rag-las-te-skye-bar-mthoṅ-ba'i-phyir-ro* |

| *de-bzhin-du-sbyin-pa-las-byuṅ-ba'i-bsod-nams-bya-ba'i-gzhi-kun-tu-bsten-ciṅ-bsgoms-te-lan-maṅ-du-byas-na-loṅs-spyod-chen-po-ñid-'grub-par-* [103r5:] *'gyur-ro-zhes-bya-ba-yaṅ-rjes-su-dpag-pa-daṅ-'gal-ba-yin-te* | *ser-sna-can-la-phyug-pa-daṅ-* | *gtoṅ-ba-la-dbul-po-yaṅ-snaṅ-ste* | *ser-sna-can-yaṅ-phyug-po-ñid-yin-pa'i-phyir-daṅ-* | *gtoṅ-ba-yaṅ-dbul-po-* [103r6:] *ñid-yin-pa'i-phyir-ro* |

| *sbyin-pa-la-goms-na-yaṅ-ser-sna-can-du-'gyur-bar-mi-'os-la-sbyin-pa-la-ma-goms-na-yaṅ-gtoṅ-ba-daṅ-ldan-pa-ma-yin-no* |

| *de-bzhin-du-gaṅ-zhig-skye-ba'i-kun-tu-sbyor-ba-ni-spaṅs-la-mṅon-* [103r7:] *par-'grub-pa'i-kun-tu-sbyor-ba-ni-ma-spaṅs-pa'i-gaṅ-zag-yod-do-zhes-bya-ba-yaṅ-rjes-su-dpag-pa-daṅ-'gal-ba-yin-te* | *gaṅ-zhig-sa-gaṅ-du-skye-ba'i-srid-pa-las-'dod-chags-daṅ-bral-ba-yin-no* |

| [103r8:] *dge-bsñen-gyi-bslab-pa'i-gzhi-lṅa-zhes-bya-ba-so-so'i-tshig-gi-don-rab-tu-dbye-ba-bśad-pa-de-las-chaṅ-'thuṅ-ba-bcad-*

pa'i-kha-na-ma-tho-ba-dan-bcas-pa-yin-no-zhes-bya-ba-ni-luṅ-daṅ-'gal-ba-yin-te | [103v1:] *lus-kyi-ñes-par-spyad-pa-rnam-pa-bzhi-ste* |

srog-gcod-pa-nas-myos-par-'gyur-ba'i-khu-ba-chaṅ-'thuṅ-ba-yin-no-zhes-bya-ba'i-bar-du-'byuṅ-bas-bcad-pa'i-kha-na-ma-tho-ba-daṅ-bcas-pa-la-ni-ñes-par-spyod-pa-yin-no |

| [103v2:] *zhes-mi-brjod-do* |

| *de-bzhin-du-śin-tu-rgyas-pa'i-sde-ni-theg-pa-chen-po-yin-no-zhes-gaṅ-bśad-pa-yaṅ-ruṅ-daṅ-'gal-ba-yin-te* |
kha-cig-na-re-mdo-sde'i-le'u'i-graṅs-rgyas-pa-rnams-ni-śin-tu-rgyas-pa'i-sde-yin-gyi- [103v3:] *theg-pa-chen-po-ni-ma-yin-no-zhes-zer-te* |
ci'i-phyir-zhe-na |
de-ni-saṅs-rgyas-kyi-gsuṅ-ma-yin-no |

| *ji-ltar-saṅs-rgyas-kyi-gsuṅ-ma-yin-zhe-na* |
'gal-ba'i-phyir-te |
de-ni-sde-pa-thams-cad-la-grags-pa'i-saṅs-rgyas- [103v4:] *kyi-gsuṅ-daṅ-'gal-ba-yin-no* |

| *'di-ltar-de-las-ni-chos-thams-cad-ni-raṅ-bzhin-med-pa* | *ma-skyes-pa* | *ma-'gags-pa* | *chos-thams-cad-ni-gzod-ma-nas-zhi-ba* | *raṅ-bzhin-gyi-yoṅs-su-mya-ṅan-las-'das-pa-* [103v5:] *zhes-bya-ba-daṅ-* |

de-bzhin-du-rab-'byor-gzugs-ni-dṅos-po-med-do |
| *rab-'byor-byaṅ-chub-kyi-bar-du-yaṅ-dṅos-po-med-do-zhes-'byuṅ-la* |

sde-pa-thams-cad-la-grags-pa'i-saṅs-rgyas-kyi-gsuṅ-las-ni-bcom- [103v6:] *ldan-'das-kyi-ma-rig-pa-gaṅ-zhe-na* |
gaṅ-de-daṅ-sṅon-gyi-mtha'-mi-śes-pa-zhes-bya-ba-rgyas-par-'byuṅ-ba-nas |
rga-śi'i-bar-du-chos-rnams-kyi-raṅ-bzhin-yaṅ-bstan |
'di-yod-pas-'di-'byuṅ- |
'di-skyes-pa'i- [103v7:] *phyir-'di-skye* |

mig-daṅ-gzugs-la-brten-nas-mig-gi-rnam-par-śes-pa-skye |
'du-byed-'di-dag-thams-cad-ni-'das-pa-zad-pa-'gags-pa-bral-ba-yoṅs-su-gyur-pa'o |

| *kye-ma-'du-byed-rnams-mi-rtag* (|)
| *skye-zhiṅ-* [103v8:] *'jig-pa'i-chos-can-yin* |
| *skyes-nas-'jig-par-'gyur-bas-na* |
| *de-dag-ñe-bar-zhi-ba-bde* |
| *dge-sloṅ-dag-'di-lta-ste* |
'du-byed-rnams-ni-sdug-bsṅal-ba'o |

| *mya-ṅan-las-'das-pa-ni-zhi-ba'o-zhes-bya-ba-daṅ-* [104r1:] *rgyu-kun-'byuṅ-ba-las-sdug-bsṅal-kun-'byuṅ-ba-yin-la* |
rgyu-'gags-pa-las-sdug-bsṅal-'gog-pa-yin-no |

| *rgyu-daṅ-bcas-pas-bde-'gror-'gro* (|)
| *rgyur-bcas-ñid-kyis-ṅan-'gror-te* |
| [104r2:] *rgyu-daṅ-bcas-pas-mya-ṅan-'da'* |
| *'di-kun-rgyu-daṅ-bcas-las-'byuṅ-*
zhes-bya-ba-daṅ- |
de-bzhin-du-gzugs-ni-mi-rtag-pa-sdug-bsṅal-ba-'gyur-ba'i-chos-can-no-
zhes-bya-ba-daṅ- |
'jig-rten-na-mkhas-pa-rnams-kyi- [104r3:] *yod-par-'dod-pa-gaṅ-yin-pa-de-ni-ṅa-yaṅ-yod-par-smra'o-*
zhes-bya-ba-de-lta-bu-la-sogs-pa-'byuṅ-bas-skye-ba-la-sogs-pa-yaṅ-bstan-to |

| *de'i-phyir-rab-tu-grags-pa'i-saṅs-rgyas-kyi-gsuṅ-daṅ-'gal-bas-theg-pa-* [104r4:] *chen-po-ni-saṅs-rgyas-kyi-gsuṅ-ma-yin-no* |
| *de-bas-na-śin-tu-rgyas-pa'i-theg-pa-chen-po-yin-no* |

| *zhes-bya-ba-ni-luṅ-daṅ-'gal-ba-yin-no* |

| *brgal-ba'i-tshul-ni-de-yin-no* |

INDEX

(Italicized page numbers refer to the footnote section)